C

The New
CAMBRIDGE
English Course

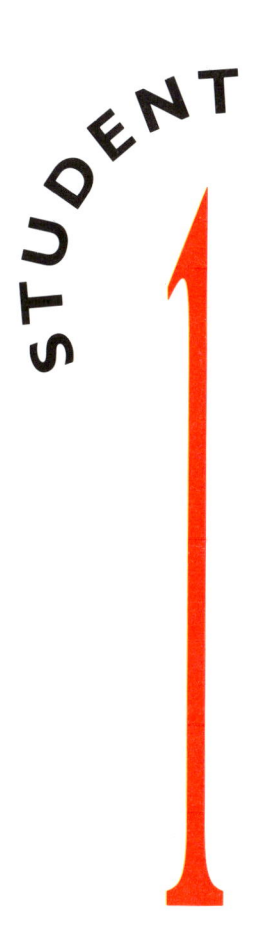

STUDENT

1

■ *mit englisch-deutschem Glossar*

MICHAEL SWAN
CATHERINE WALTER

CAMBRIDGE
UNIVERSITY PRESS

Ernst Klett Verlag für Wissen und Bildung
Stuttgart · Dresden

Published by the Press Syndicate of the University of Cambridge
The Pitt Building, Trumpington Street, Cambridge CB2 1RP
40 West 20th Street, New York, NY 10011-4211, USA
10 Stamford Road, Oakleigh, Melbourne 3166, Australia
First Published 1990
Third Printing 1993
Designed by Banks and Miles, London
Cover design by Michael Peters & Partners Limited, London
Typeset by Wyvern Typesetting, Bristol
Origination by Eric Linsell / Progress Colour Limited

Bearbeitung dieser Ausgabe:
Peter Bereza, Axel Ruland, Inge Spaughton
Margit Duda (Verlagsredakteurin)

Beratung: Christiane Wimmer

Weitere Bestandteile des *New Cambridge English Course 1* sind:

Practice Book 1	Klett-Nr. 539016 (dt. Ausgabe)
Teacher's Book 1	Klett-Nr. 539030
Test Book 1	Klett-Nr. 539040
Class Cassette Set 1	Klett-Nr. 539080
Student's Cassette Set 1	Klett-Nr. 539070
Video 1 (VHS PAL)	Klett-Nr. 539090
Video 1 Teacher's Guide	Klett-Nr. 539091
Video 1 Teacher's Guide without photocopiable tasks	Klett-Nr. 539092
Video 1 Student Activity Book	Klett-Nr. 539093

Authors' acknowledgements

We are grateful to all the people who have helped us with this book. Our thanks to:

- The many people whose ideas have influenced our work, including all the colleagues and students from whom we have learnt.
- Those institutions and teachers who were kind enough to comment on their use of *The Cambridge English Course*, and whose suggestions have done so much to shape this new version.
- The Cambridge University Press representatives and agents, for their valuable work in transmitting feedback from users of the original course.
- The people who agreed to talk within range of our microphones: Alwyn Anchors, Dai Colven, Steve Dixon, Lorna Higgs, Marilyn Norvell, Ruth Swan, Mark Walter Swan, Sue Ward, Adrian Webber and Celia Wilson.
- Steve Hall of Bell Voice Recordings, for doing a wonderful job on the songs.
- Peter Taylor of Taylor Riley Productions Ltd; Peter and Diana Thompson and Andy Tayler of Studio AVP; and all the actors and actresses; they made recording sessions seem easy and created an excellent end product.
- Susan Sheppard, Sally Palmer-Smith, Marjorie Pereira, and Denise Quinton of Banks and Miles, for their creativity, skill and hard work in the design of the printed components of the course.
- Val Mercer and Lindsey Cunningham of Michael Peters & Partners Limited for their excellent cover design.
- Eric Linsell and his colleagues at Progress Colour Limited, and all the staff at Wyvern Typesetting, for their care and attention to detail.
- Gill Clack, Cathy Hall, Avril Price-Budgen, David Seabourne and Clare Walshe for their careful and professional help with production.
- Mark Walter Swan, Helen Walter Swan and Inge Bullock, for keeping us in touch with what really matters.
- Adrian du Plessis, Colin Hayes and Peter Donovan of Cambridge University Press, whose confidence and support have made the author-publisher relationship so unproblematic.
- Desmond Nicholson of Cambridge University Press, whose encouragement and suggestions helped to get *The New Cambridge Course* underway.
- And finally Desmond O'Sullivan of ELT Publishing Services: his skills in dealing with people and with print, his devotion, patience, stamina and unfailing good humour have made this course possible.

1. Auflage   1 4 | 1994 93

Alle Drucke dieser Auflage können im Unterricht nebeneinander benutzt werden, sie sind untereinander unverändert.
Die letzte Zahl bezeichnet das Jahr dieses Druckes.
© Michael Swan and Catherine Walter 1990
© für diese Ausgabe: Ernst Klett Verlag für Wissen und Bildung GmbH, Stuttgart 1991. Alle Rechte vorbehalten.
Druck: Chase Web, Plymouth,
a St. Ives plc company.
Printed in Great Britain.
ISBN 3-12-539015-X

Vorwort

Der *New Cambridge English Course* ist ein vierbändiges Lehrwerk für den Englischunterricht in der Erwachsenen- und Weiterbildung.

Die vier Bände des Lehrwerks führen Sie zum Niveau des international anerkannten *Cambridge First Certificate*.

Während normalerweise ein oder zwei Aspekte der Sprache (z. B. Grammatik, Sprechabsichten usw.) als „Rückgrat" für die Gestaltung eines Sprachkurses dienen, bietet Ihnen das vorliegende Lehrwerk eine systematische Bearbeitung von insgesamt acht unterschiedlichen Schwerpunkten: Grammatik, Wortschatz, Aussprache, Themen, Situationen, Sprechabsichten (z. B. Einladungen aussprechen), Konzepte (z. B. Alter, Entfernung) sowie aktive und passive Sprachfertigkeiten. Der *New Cambridge English Course* gibt Ihnen darüber hinaus von Anfang an die Möglichkeit, Ihre Interessen, Erfahrungen, Gefühle und Vorlieben sowie Ihre Kreativität in zahlreiche realistische und unterhaltsame Sprachübungen einfließen zu lassen.

Eine breite Palette von Präsentationsmaterial, zeitgemäßen Themen und Lese- und Hörmaterial kommt den unterschiedlichsten Interessen, Erwartungen und Lernstilen entgegen, die erfahrungsgemäß im Englischunterricht mit Erwachsenen auftreten.

Nicht zuletzt sorgen die Kursübersicht *(Map of Book)*, die deutliche Kennzeichnung von Präsentations- und Übungsteilen, regelmäßige Wiederholungs- und Festigungslektionen *(Consolidation Units)* sowie ein englisch–deutsches Wörterverzeichnis dafür, daß Sie sich jederzeit ein klares Bild über den Aufbau, die Zielsetzung und Ihren individuellen Lernfortschritt innerhalb des Kurses verschaffen können.

Das *Practice Book* (Klett-Nr. 539016, deutsche Ausgabe) mit einer umfassenden Kurzgrammatik und einem Schlüssel zur Selbstkorrektur bietet Ihnen die Möglichkeit zur eigenständigen Festigung, Vertiefung und Erweiterung des im *Student's Book* behandelten Lernstoffes.

Wir wünschen Ihnen viel Spaß bei der Arbeit mit dem *New Cambridge English Course*.

Autoren und Redaktion

Inhalt

Authors' acknowledgements		2
Map of Book		4
Unit 1	Hello	6
Unit 2	You	10
Unit 3	People	14
Unit 4	Consolidation	18
Unit 5	Where?	24
Unit 6	Habits	28
Unit 7	Counting and measuring	32
Unit 8	Consolidation	36
Unit 9	Appearances	44
Unit 10	Wanting things	48
Unit 11	People's pasts	52
Unit 12	Consolidation	56
Unit 13	Differences	64
Unit 14	Personal information	68
Unit 15	Present and future	72
Unit 16	Consolidation	76
Unit 17	Ordering and asking	84
Unit 18	More about the past	88
Unit 19	Getting to know you	92
Unit 20	Consolidation	96
Unit 21	Knowing about the future	104
Unit 22	Telling people to do things	108
Unit 23	Predictions	112
Unit 24	Consolidation	116
Vocabulary index		124
Additional material		140
Acknowledgements		143
Phonetic symbols; Irregular verbs		144

Map of Book (Kursübersicht)

Was in den Units behandelt wird:

	Grammatik	**Aussprache**
1–4	Die Gegenwartsform von *be*; *have got*; *a* und *an*; die Mehrzahl von Hauptwörtern; das Fürwort als Satzgegenstand; das besitzanzeigende Fürwort; besitzanzeigendes *'s* und *s'*; der prädikative Gebrauch des Eigenschaftsworts; Fragen (Fragewörter und *yes/no*); *be* bei Altersangaben; räumliche Verhältniswörter; *this*; *any* in Fragen.	Wort- und Satzbetonung; Rhythmus; Binden von Wörtern; Satzmelodie; Häufung von Mitlauten; /θ/ und /ð/; /ə/; die Aussprache von *'s*; unbetonte Form von *from*.
5–8	Einfache Gegenwart; *there is/are*; die Befehlsform; *was* und *were* (Einführung); zählbare und nichtzählbare Hauptwörter; *some/any, much/many* und andere Mengenangaben; *the*; das Auslassen des Artikels bei Verallgemeinerungen; das Fürwort als Ergänzung; das Eigenschaftswort als Beifügung; Umstandswörter der Häufigkeit; Umstandswörter des Grades; Verhältniswörter zum Ausdruck von Zeit, Raum und Entfernung; das Auslassen des Artikels bei *at home* usw.; die *-ing*-Form zum Ausdruck von Tätigkeiten; *be* bei Preisangaben.	Wort- und Satzbetonung; Rhythmus; Binden von Wörtern; Satzmelodie, einschließlich höflicher Satzmelodie; unbetonte Formen; /ɪ/; /θ/ bei Ordnungszahlen; die Aussprache von *the*.
9–12	*Have got*; Verlaufsform der Gegenwart (Einführung); Einfache Gegenwart (Vertiefung); Einfache Vergangenheit; die Vergangenheitsform von *be*; *I'd like* in Verbindung mit Nominalteil / Grundform des Zeitworts; *when*-Sätze; das hinweisende Fürwort; *be* und *have*; *both* und *all*; *a…one*; räumliche Verhältniswörter; *say* und *tell*; *ago*; *What (a)…!*	Binden von Wörtern; Satzbetonung; unbetonte Formen; das Hören unbetonter Silben; Rhythmus und Satzmelodie bei Fragen; steigende Satzmelodie bei Fragen; hohe Tonlage zur Hervorhebung; Betonung in verneinten Sätzen; Betonung zur Kontrastierung; Probleme zwischen Rechtschreibung und Aussprache; /h/; stimmhaftes *s* am Ende von Zeitwörtern; Endungen der einfachen Vergangenheit; betonte Form von *have*.
13–16	*Can*; Verlaufsform der Gegenwart (zum Ausdruck von Gegenwärtigem bzw. Zukünftigem); *be* bei Alters- und Maßangaben; komplexe Fragestrukturen; Steigerungsformen des Eigenschaftsworts; Strukturen zum Ausdruck von Vergleichen; *a bit/much* vor 1. Steigerungsform; *good at* + Hauptwort/*-ing*-Form; *look like* + Nominalteil; *look* + Eigenschaftswort; *What is…like?*; Verhältniswörter bei Beschreibungen; zeitliche Verhältniswörter.	Das Erkennen und Produzieren von Betonung und Rhythmus; die Entschlüsselung von schnell gesprochener Sprache; das Hören unbetonter Silben; die Aussprache des Buchstaben *a*; die Aussprache des Buchstaben *e*; die Aussprache des Buchstaben *i*; die Rolle des /ə/ bei der Betonung; betonte und unbetonte Formen von *can* und *can't*; unbetonte Formen von *as, than* und *from*; /θ/ bei Ordnungszahlen.
17–20	*Present Perfect*; Einfache Vergangenheit (Vertiefung); Zeitwörter mit zwei Ergänzungen; *Could you, Why don't we, Let's* und *Shall we* + Grundform des Zeitworts ohne *to*; das Fragewort als Satzgegenstand; einfache indirekte Rede; verkürzte Fragesätze; *So…I*; *say* und *tell*; *for* und *since*; *How long…?*; *no = not any*; *some* und *something* bei Angeboten und Bitten; der Gebrauch des Artikels und des Verhältniswortes; Begriffe zum Ausdruck von Reihenfolge und logischer Beziehung; *both…and*; *neither…nor*; *Do you mind if…?*	Die Entschlüsselung von schnell gesprochener Sprache; Binden bei Selbstlauten am Anfang von Wörtern; Betonung zur Kontrastierung; die Aussprache des Buchstaben *u*; /iː/ und /ɪ/; höfliche Satzmelodie bei Bitten; steigende Satzmelodie bei verkürzten Fragesätzen; unbetonte Formen von *was* und *were*.
21–24	*Going to*; Zukunft mit *will*; die Grundform des Zeitworts zum Ausdruck von Absichten; die Befehlsform; Bedingungssätze; Strukturen mit *get*; das Eigenschaftswort und das Umstandswort; Umstandswörter der Art und Weise; Begriffe zum Ausdruck logischer Beziehungen zwischen Sätzen; die Stellung von *always* und *never* bei Befehlsformen.	Die Rechtschreibung bei /ɜː/; die „lange" Aussprache von *a, i, o, u* vor (Mitlaut +) *e*; die Aussprache des Buchstaben *o*; /w/; /iː/ und /ɪ/; die Aussprache des „dark l" bei verkürzten Zukunftsformen; das Erkennen und die Aussprache von *going to*; die Aussprache von *won't*.

Sprechabsichten und Situationen

Begrüßung; jemanden vorstellen; Gespräche mit Fremden einleiten; längere Gespräche führen; sich verabschieden; Informationen erfragen und geben; sich selbst und andere vorstellen; Personen beschreiben; um Wiederholung bitten; nach dem Befinden fragen; sich entschuldigen; Bedauern ausdrücken; Ebenen der Förmlichkeit unterscheiden; buchstabieren und zählen.

Informationen, Wegbeschreibungen, Angaben zur Person und Meinungen erfragen und geben; Wohnung/Wohnlage beschreiben; sagen, wo sich Dinge befinden; Zuneigung/Abneigung ausdrücken; Uhrzeit angeben; sich beschweren; längere Gespräche führen; sich höflich ausdrücken.

Informationen erfragen und geben; Beschreibungen von Personen und Dingen erfragen und geben; über Ähnlichkeiten sprechen; Begrüßungen; Verabredungen treffen; Informationen zur Zielsprache erfragen; Angebote/Bitten aussprechen und darauf reagieren; erzählen; Einkäufe tätigen; sich nach dem Fahrplan erkundigen und Hotelzimmer reservieren; Geld wechseln.

Vergleichen; Informationen und Meinungen erfragen und geben; Personen beschreiben und vergleichen; Vermutungen ausdrücken; Bitten aussprechen und darauf reagieren; Einladungen aussprechen/annehmen/ablehnen; Handlungen beschreiben bzw. darüber spekulieren; etwas planen; zählen (Ordnungszahlen); telefonieren.

Bitten aussprechen und darauf reagieren; etwas ausleihen; etwas vorschlagen; zustimmen, ablehnen und verhandeln; Einladungen aussprechen/annehmen/ablehnen; erzählen; berichten, was jemand gesagt hat; Erlaubnis erfragen/erteilen/ablehnen; Interesse bekunden; vergleichen; Informationen und Meinungen erfragen und geben; Ebenen der Förmlichkeit unterscheiden; Informationen zur Zielsprache erfragen; Gespräche einleiten; Verabredungen treffen; in einem Restaurant etwas bestellen usw.

Vorhaben ausdrücken; etwas vorhersagen; etwas erraten; etwas vorschlagen; Mitleid/Bedauern ausdrücken; Anweisungen geben; Ratschläge erteilen; zur Vorsicht mahnen; Absichten ankündigen; jemandem widersprechen, auf Widersprüche reagieren; erzählen.

Konzepte und Themenbereiche

Eigennamen; Alter; Familienstand; Staatsangehörigkeit; Adressen; Berufsbezeichnungen; Gesundheit; Familie; Aussehen; verwandtschaftliche Beziehungen; Zahlen und Buchstaben; Annäherung; Ort.

Adressen; Telefonnummern; Mobiliar; Häuser u. Wohnungen; Arbeit; Freizeitbeschäftigung u. Interessen; Essen u. Trinken; Preise; Zuneigungen u. Abneigungen; Vorlieben; Gemeinsamkeiten u. Unterschiede; Wochentage; Ordnungszahlen; Dasein; Zeit; Ort; räumliche Verhältnisse; Verallgemeinerung; Zählbarkeit; Menge; Grad; Häufigkeit; Gewohnheit.

Persönliches Erscheinungsbild; Kleidung; Familie; Farben; Körperteile; Beziehungen; physisches und emotionales Befinden; Kleidungsstücke; Orte; Preise; Größe; persönliche Vergangenheit; Geschichte; Armut; Glücklichsein; Rassismus; Kindheit; Erwachsenwerden; Ähnlichkeit.

Fähigkeiten; physische Eigenschaften und Qualitäten; Maße und Gewichte; Grund- und Ordnungszahlen; Alter; Persönlichkeit; Beruf; Monatsnamen; Zukunftspläne; Wetter; Urlaub; Orte; Reisen; Zeit; Ähnlichkeiten und Unterschiede; vorübergehende Handlungen und Zustände in Gegenwart und Zukunft.

Urlaub; Ausgehen; Essen und Trinken; alltägliche Gewohnheiten; historische Persönlichkeiten; berufliche Laufbahn; Interessen und Gewohnheiten; Zuneigungen und Abneigungen; Gegenüberstellung; Reihenfolge; Vergangenheit; Häufigkeit; Andauern bis zur Gegenwart; Ähnlichkeit.

Häuser; Jahreszeiten; Urlaub; Orte; Pläne; Gesundheit und Krankheit; Sport; Maschinen; Horoskope; Gefahr; Zweck; Absicht; Art und Weise; Zukunft.

Fertigkeiten

Das *Student's Book* und das *Practice Book* zusammen bieten regelmäßige Übung in den grundlegenden „vier Fertigkeiten". Die speziellen Fertigkeiten, die in Band 1 vorgestellt bzw. geübt werden, umfassen das Entschlüsseln schnell gesprochener Umgangssprache, Lese- und Hörverständnisübungen zur Informationssuche, das Schreiben längerer Sätze, das Verfassen von Textabschnitten, förmlichen Briefen, persönlichen Briefen und Mitteilungen, das Ausfüllen von Formularen.

Wortschatz

Der verbindliche Lernwortschatz von Band 1 umfaßt 900 Wörter und Ausdrücke der englischen Alltagssprache.

Unit 1 Hello

1A What's your name?

> Greeting and introducing; questions and answers; *it*; *is*; *my* and *your*; *not*.

1 🔊 Listen to the conversations. Then put the sentences into the pictures.

- 6 What's your name?
- 1 Hello. My name's Mary Lake.
- 9 No, it isn't.
- 5 Catherine.
- 2 Hello. Yes, room three one two, Mrs Lake.
- 4 What's *your* name?
- 8 Is your name Mark Perkins?
- 7 John.
- 3 Thank you.
- 10 It's Harry Brown.

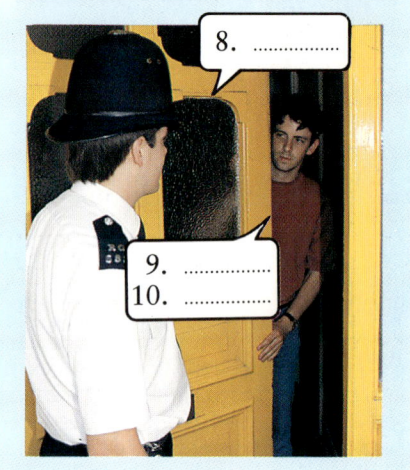

2 Pronunciation. Say these words and expressions after the recording.

what   what's   your   my   name
it   it's   isn't
Yes, it is.   No, it isn't.

3 Say your name.

'Hello. My name's ....'

4 Ask other students' names.

'What's your name?'

5 Ask and answer.

'Is your name Anne?'   'Yes, it is.'
'Is your name Alex?'   'No, it isn't. It's Peter.'

Learn: Hello; my; your; it; is; what; not (n't); Thank you; yes; no; name; one; two; three.

🔊 *This symbol means that all or part of the recording for this exercise is on one of the Student's Cassettes.*

1B His name's James Wharton

People's names; spelling; *his*, *her*.

1 Match the people and the names.

'1. Her name's Denise Quinton.'

1 one *checkcard* 2 two *driving licence* 3 three *Passport*

4 four *cheque* 5 five *letter* 6 six *Bestellung - Order*

2 Copy and complete the table.

FIRST NAME	SURNAME
1. Denise	Quinton
2. 4. Lewis	Dorrington
3. Jean	Sheppard
4. 2. Gavin Nicholas	Dexter Jowitt
5. James	Wharton
6. Gillian	Sharpe

3 Write sentences and read to other students.
Examples:

1. Her first name is Denise.
1. Her surname is Quinton.
2. His name is Gavin Jowitt.

'Her first name's Gillian.' 'Six.' 'That's right.'
'His surname's Jowitt.' 'One.' 'No, two.'

4 Ask about other students.

'What's his surname?' 'I don't know.'
'Is her first name Anne?' 'Yes, that's right.'
'Is her name Barbara?' 'No, it isn't.'

ABCDEFGHIJKLMNOPQRSTUVWXYZ
abcdefghijklmnopqrstuvwxyz

5 Listen and practise.

AHJK   IY   UQW   R
EBCDGPTV   O   FLMNSXZ

6 Listen and write the words.

name, your, hello, right, What, Is, yes, no, my, one, five, three

7 Ask other students to spell a name from Exercise 2.

'Five.' 'J, A, M, E, S, W, H, A, R, T, O, N.'
'Six.' 'G, I, double L, I, A, N, S, H, A, R, P, E.'

8 Spell your name, and choose another student to spell it back to you.

Learn: four; five; six; his; her; first name; surname; I; I don't know; that's right; double; ABCDEFGHIJKLMNOPQRSTUVWXYZ.

1C How are you? *I'm well / fine*

Saying hello and goodbye; *I am*; *I'm*; *are you?*

1 Listen, and practise the conversation.

- Hello, Dan.
- Hi, Mary.
- How are you?
- Fine, thanks. And you?
- I'm fine.
- Well, here's my bus. Bye, Mary.
- Goodbye, Dan. See you.

2 Close your books. Can you remember the conversation?

3 Listen to the recording and complete the conversations.

ALICE: Excuse me. *Is your name* Fred Andrews?
JAKE: *No*, I'm sorry, *it isn't*. It's Jake Barker.
ALICE: *I'm* sorry.

ALICE: Excuse me. Are *you* Fred Andrews?
FRED: *Yes*, I am.
ALICE: Oh, *hello I'm* Alice Watson.
FRED: Oh, yes. How do you do?
ALICE: *How do you do*?

4 Practise the conversations.

5 Listen to the recording and answer.

6 Choose a person to be, and a person to look for, from the list on page 132. Walk round until you find your person.

- Excuse me. Is your name Mickey Mouse?
- No, I'm sorry. It isn't. It's James Bond.

I am (I'm)	am I?
you are (you're)	are you?
he/she/it is (he's / she's / it's)	is he/she/it?

Learn: you; Hi; How are you?; and; Fine, thanks; Goodbye; Bye; See you; Oh; Here's . . . ; me; Excuse me; I'm sorry; How do you do?

1D Where are you from? Wo kommst Du her

Asking and saying where people are from; nationalities; he and she.

1 Where's she from? Where's he from?

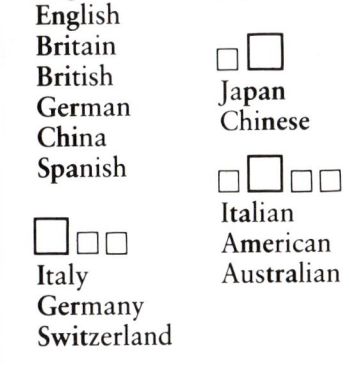

6 Australia 7 Egypt 2 India Japan 1 Scotland 3
5 Italy the United States 4 Russia 8

1. Japan
2. India
3. Scotland
4. the United States
5. Italy
6. Australia
7. from Egypt He's Egyptian
8. Russia Russian [rʌʃə]

2 Where are you from? Ask and answer.

Where are you from?
I'm from India.
I'm from Paris.

3 Use your dictionary.

COUNTRY	NATIONALITY *Sprache+Adjektiv*
Carla's from Italy.	She's Italian.
Manuel's from Spain.	He's Spanish.
Shu-Fang's from China.	He's Chinese (Schainiesd)
Rob's from Australia	He's Australian.
Kenji's from Japan	He's Japanese.
Joyce is from the United States.	She's American.
Sally's from Britain.	She's British
Rosa's from Argentina	She's Argentinian.
Fiona's from Scotland	She's Scottish.
Mohammed's from Algeria	He's Algerian.
Lakshmi's from India.	She's Indian
Milton's from Nigeria	He's Nigerian.
Sarah's from England.	She's English

Germany — German
I'm from France — I'm French
Greece — Greek Griechenland

4 🔊 Pronunciation: stress. Listen and repeat.

□□
England
English
Britain
British
German
China
Spanish

□□□
Japanese

□□
Japan
Chinese

□□□
Italian
American
Australian

□□□
Italy
Germany
Switzerland

5 Listen to the recordings.
1. Write the numbers and the words.
2. Write the letters.

6 Use your real name or invent a person. Answer Susie.

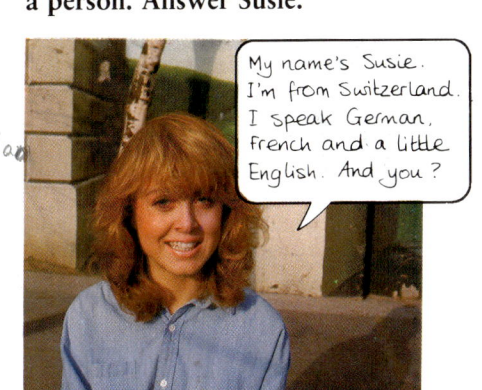

My name's Susie. I'm from Switzerland. I speak German, French and a little English. And you?

I	—	my
you	—	your
he	—	his
she	—	her

Learn: he; she; where; from; speak; a little; Britain; British; the United States; American; English; Where (are you) from?

Learn some more words for countries and nationalities if you want to.

9

Unit 2 You

2A What do you do?

Jobs; *a* and *an*.

1 Complete the sentences.

artist
doctor
electrician
housewife
secretary
shop assistant

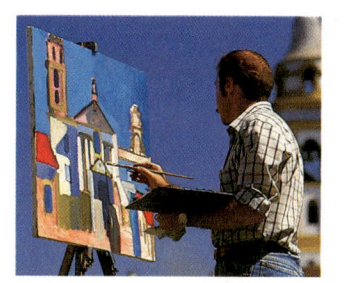

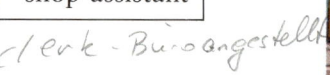

1. He's an **artist**.
2. He's a **shop assistant**.
3. She's a **doctor**.
4. She's a **housewife**.
5. He's an **electrician**.
6. She's a **secretary**.

2 Choose a job or use your job. Say what you do.

'I'm an engineer.'
'I'm a medical student.'
'I'm a photographer.'
'I'm between jobs.'

3 Ask and answer.

'What do you do?'
'I'm a dentist.'
'I'm an artist.'
'I'm a housewife.'

4 Say what other students do.

'She's a doctor.'
'He's an electrician.'

5 Listen and practise.

- What do you do?
- I'm a secretary.
- Are you a doctor?
- No, I'm an artist. She's a doctor.
- Are you a photographer?
- Yes, I am. Are you an artist?
- No, I'm not. I'm a doctor. He's an artist.

6 Choose jobs and work in pairs. Ask and answer.

'Are you a doctor?'
'Yes, I am.' / 'No, I'm not.'

7 Find another pair; ask and answer.

'Is she an artist?'
'Yes, she is.' / 'No, she isn't.'

'Is he an engineer?'
'Yes, he is.' / 'No, he isn't.'

Learn: What do you do?; do; a; an; student; between jobs.

Learn four or more: doctor; secretary; electrician; housewife; shop assistant; artist; engineer; dentist; photographer; medical student.

2B I'm very well, thank you

Formal and informal greetings.

morning *afternoon* *evening* *night*

1 Morning, afternoon, evening or night?
Example:
1. morning or night

2 🔊 Listen. Learn the new words from a dictionary or from your teacher. Listen again and practise.

WOMAN: Good morning, Mr Roberts. How are you?
MAN: Oh, good morning, Dr Wagner. I'm very well, thank you. And you?
WOMAN: I'm fine, thank you.

MAN: Hello, Mary.
WOMAN: Hi, Tom. How are you?
MAN: Fine, thanks. And you?
WOMAN: Not bad – but my daughter's not well today.
MAN: Oh, I'm sorry to hear that.

3 *Good morning* or *Hello*?

Good afternoon or *Hello*?

Good evening or *Hello*?

4 Differences. Read the conversations again and complete the table.

CONVERSATION 1	CONVERSATION 2
1. Good morning	Hello/Hi
2.	Mary
3. How are you?	How are you?
4.	Fine / Not bad
5.	thanks
6.	And you?

5 Stand up, walk around if you can, and greet other students.

Learn: morning; afternoon; evening; night; Good morning; Good afternoon; Good evening; Good night; very; well; I'm very well; not well; not bad; or; man; woman; Dr; Mr.

2C I'm an actress. And you?

> More personal information.

1 🔊 Listen and practise.

1 one	11 eleven
2 two	12 twelve
3 three	13 thirteen
4 four	14 fourteen
5 five	15 fifteen
6 six	16 sixteen
7 seven	17 seventeen
8 eight	18 eighteen
9 nine	19 nineteen
10 ten	20 twenty

2 What number? What letter? Test other students.

1. R	11. B
2. E	12. W
3. N	13. L
4. J	14. P
5. A	15. H
6. V	16. U
7. I	17. O
8. M	18. Y
9. Z	19. Q
10. G	20. S

3 Listening for information. Copy the table; then listen, and fill it in.

NAME	NATIONALITY	JOB	MARRIED/SINGLE	ADDRESS
Bill	British	doctor	don't know	14 Church Street
Lucy	American	artist	married	10 Sutton Road
Jane Webb	British	teacher	single	16 Hirst Close
Gérard	French	electrician	single	19 Ross Street
Annie	Greek	photographer	don't know	17 Cedar Avenue
Philip	Australian	secretary	married	8 Evans Lane

4 Complete the dialogue and practise it.

VIRGINIA: Hello, I'm Virginia. What's your name?
YOU: ....
VIRGINIA: Is that an English name?
YOU: ....
.... ?
VIRGINIA: No, I'm not. I'm Argentinian.
YOU: ...., Virginia?
VIRGINIA: I'm an actress. And you?
YOU: ....
VIRGINIA: That's interesting. Are you married?
YOU: ....
.... ?
VIRGINIA: Yes, I am.

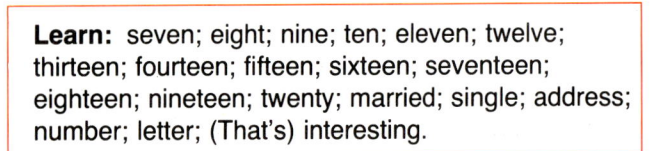

> **Learn:** seven; eight; nine; ten; eleven; twelve; thirteen; fourteen; fifteen; sixteen; seventeen; eighteen; nineteen; twenty; married; single; address; number; letter; (That's) interesting.

2D How old are you?

> Numbers; ages; titles.

1 🔊 Listen and practise.

20 twenty	30 thirty	40 forty
21 twenty-one	34 thirty-four	50 fifty
22 twenty-two	35 thirty-five	60 sixty
23 twenty-three	36 thirty-six	70 seventy
24 twenty-four	37 thirty-seven	80 eighty
25 twenty-five	38 thirty-eight	90 ninety
26 twenty-six	39 thirty-nine	100 a hundred

2 Thir*teen* or *thir*ty? Four*teen* or *for*ty?
Listen and write what you hear.

3 Practise with numbers.
1. Count: '1, 2, 3, . . .'
2. Count in twos: '2, 4, 6, 8, . . .'
3. Count in fives: '5, 10, 15, . . .'
4. Count backwards: '99, 98, 97, . . .'

4 Work in groups or pairs.
1. Say numbers for other students to write.
   'Fifty-six.' _56_
2. Say numbers for other students to add.
   'Thirty-eight and seven?'   'Forty-five.'
3. Say numbers for other students to multiply.
   'Six sevens?'   'Forty-two.'

5 How old?
1. Write down an age for each person.
2. Talk to some other students and agree on the ages.

'I think A is about 50.'
'I think she's about 60.'
'No, 55.'
'OK, 55.'

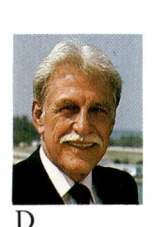

HARRIS AND SANDERS
Photographic Supplies
13 Old High Street, Wembley

Job Application *(Bewerbungen)*

Mr/Mrs/Miss/Ms ....
First name ....
Surname ....
Age *(Alter)* ....
Marital status: single ☐
  married ☐
  Familystatus divorced ☐ *geschieden*
  separated ☐ *getrennt*
  widow(er) ☐ *Witwe (Witwer)*
Nationality ....
Address ....

Form (Formular)

6 Copy and fill in the form.

7 Copy the form again and fill it in with a new identity. Then work with a partner. Ask each other these questions.

1. Mr, Mrs, Miss or Ms?
2. What's your first name?
3. How do you spell it?
4. What's your surname?
5. How do you spell it?
6. How old are you?
7. Where are you from?
8. Are you married?
9. What's your address?

A B C D
E F G H

> **Learn:** *numbers* 21 to 100; How old are you?; divorced; separated; widow; widower; Miss; Mrs; Ms; I think; about; OK; How do you spell it?

13

Unit 3 People

3A Andrew's bag's under the table

Prepositions; possessive *'s*; *Where* questions.

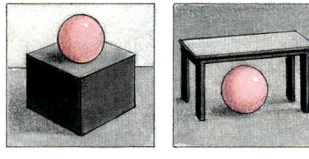

1 *Under,* on, *in* or near ?

1 2 3 4 5 6 7 8

2 Describe the picture. Example:

'His coat's on the chair.'

3 Look at the picture for one minute. Then turn to page 132 and say where things are.

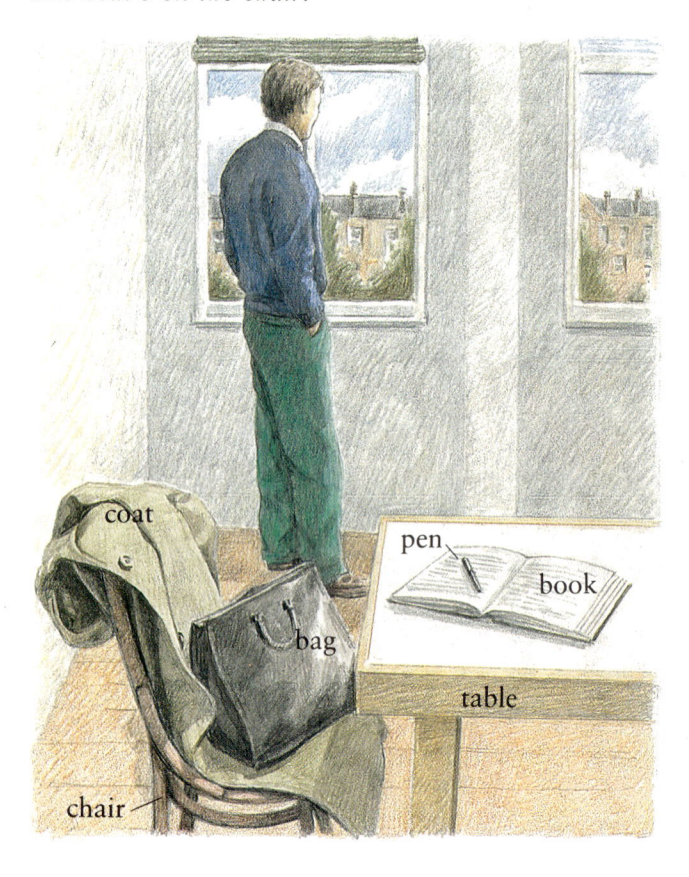

Polly   Ann   Andrew

4 Turn to the page your teacher tells you. Describe your picture for your partner to draw. Example:

'Andrew's bag's under the chair.'

5 Work in groups. Move things around, and let another group say where things are.

'Annie's book's under her chair.'

'Where's Ana's coat?'
'It's on Antonio's chair.'

'Where's Guido's pen?'
'It's on the table near Carla.'

Learn: pen; hat; book; coat; bag; table; chair; on; in; under; near; the.

3B This is Judy

Possessive 's; we are, you are, they are; descriptions; This is . . .

JUDY
This is Judy.
She is tall and fair.
She is very pretty.

SAM
This is Sam.
He is Judy's boyfriend.
He is not very _tall_.
_He's_ dark.
He ist quite good-looking.

ERIC
This is Sam's friend, Eric.
He is _tall_ and _dark/slim_
He is Alice's _boyfriend_
He is _very quite_ good-looking.

ALICE
This is Eric's girlfriend, _Alice_.
She is short and fair. She is pretty.

1 Look at the pictures and complete the descriptions.

2 Pronunciation. Practise:

Judy's	Mary's	Joe's	Harry's	(/z/)
Sam's	Bob's	Anne's	Susan's	(/z/)
Eric's	Margaret's	Jeff's	Kate's	(/s/)
Alice's	Joyce's	Ross's	Des's	(/ɪz/)

3 Use your dictionary. Match the words and the pictures.

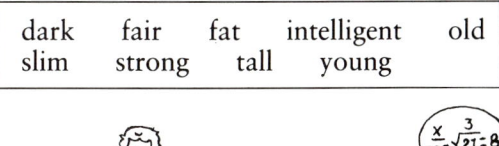

dark	fair	fat	intelligent	old
slim	strong	tall	young	

1 2 3 4 5 6 7 8 9

4 Work with another student. Make sentences about the two of you. Tell the class:

We're not very tall. We're young. We're English.

No, you aren't. You're Mexican.

5 Write about two other students. Example:

Mario and Carla are tall, slim and dark. They are quite young.

we are (we're)	are we?	we are not (aren't)
you are (you're)	are you?	you are not (aren't)
they are (they're)	are they?	they are not (aren't)

Learn: dark; fair; fat; good-looking; intelligent; old; pretty; slim; tall; strong; young; friend; boyfriend; girlfriend; they; we; quite; not very; this.

3C I've got three children

> Families; noun plurals; plural *s'*; *Who* questions; *have got*; *their*.

1 Look at the 'family tree' and complete the sentences. Use your dictionary.

| his | her | wife | husband | brother | sister |

1. John is Polly's *husband*. Polly is John's *wife*.
2. Andrew is Joyce's *brother*. Joyce is Andrew's *sister*.
3. Polly and John are Joyce's parents. Polly is her mother, and John is *her* father.
4. Andrew and Joyce are John's children. Andrew is his son, and Joyce is *his* daughter.

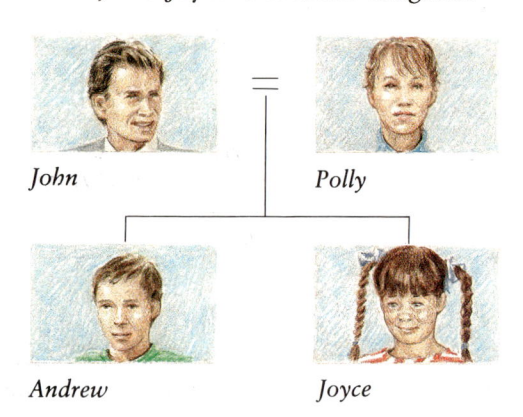

John   Polly
Andrew   Joyce

2 Now look at this family tree. Read the sentences and put in the names. *Stammbaum*

| Eric | Lucy | Ann | Harry |
| Pat | Fred | Alice | Joe |

1. Joe 2. Ann
3. Fred 4. Lucy 5. Alice 6. Harry
7. Eric 8. Pat

Joe's wife's name is Ann. Joe and Ann have got three children: two daughters and a son. Their daughters' names are Alice and Lucy, and their son's name is Fred. Fred and Lucy are not married. Alice's husband's name is Harry. Harry and Alice have got two children: a boy and a girl. Their daughter's name is Pat, and their son's name is Eric.

3 Listening. Look at the family tree in Exercise 1. Listen to the sentences and say *Yes* or *No*. Then look at Exercise 2. Make some sentences for other students. Examples:

'Ann has got two sons.' 'No.'
'Alice's husband's name is Harry.' 'Yes.'

4 Write five or more true sentences about your family. Use some of these words.

boy(s)   brother(s)   girl(s)   mother
parents   child(ren)   father   daughter(s)
husband   son(s)   wife   sister(s)   married
divorced   separated   widow   widower

Examples:

I've got three children, two girls and a boy.
My sister and I are dark, but our brother is fair.
My mother has got four sisters and a brother.
I've got no children.

5 Talk about your family. Say three things, and then answer one question. Examples:

'We've got one child, a daughter. Her name's Helen. She's short and fair.'
'How old is she?'
'Two.'

'My mother's sister has got three sons. They're sixteen, thirteen and twelve. They're in Barcelona.'
'What are their names?'
'Antonio, Juan and Carlos.'

'My sister and I are quite tall, and my brothers are very tall. Our mother isn't very tall.'
'Is your father tall?'
'Yes, very tall.'

Regular plurals		Irregular plurals	
daughter	daughters	child	children
parent	parents	man	men
family	families	woman	women
secretary	secretaries	wife	wives
address	addresses		
six	sixes		

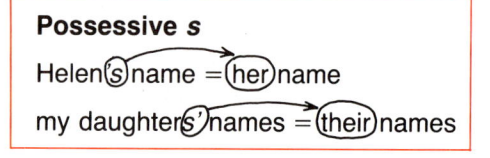

Possessive *s*

Helen*'s* name = *her* name
my daughter*s'* names = *their* names

Learn: father; mother; wife; husband; brother; sister; son; daughter; parent; child; boy; girl; family; I've / they've / he's / she's got; who; their; our.

3D An interview

Conversation practice; *Have you got . . . ?*; *Yes, I have*; *No, I haven't*.

BANK MANAGER: Good morning, Mr Harris.
CUSTOMER: Good morning.
BM: Please sit down.
C: Thank you.
BM: Now, one or two questions . . .
C: Yes, of course.
BM: How old are you, Mr Harris?
C: Thirty-two.
BM: And you're Canadian, aren't you?
C: Yes, that's right.
BM: Are you married?
C: Yes, I am.
BM: What is your wife's name?
C: Monica.
BM: And your wife's age, Mr Harris?
C: Pardon?
BM: How old is Mrs Harris?
C: Oh, she's thirty.
BM: Thirty. And is she Canadian, too?
C: No, she's British.
BM: British, yes. Have you got any children?
C: Yes, three. Two boys and a girl.

(Phone rings)

BM: Excuse me a moment. Hello, Anne. Yes? Yes? Yes, I am. No. Yes. No, I'm sorry, I don't know. No. Yes, all right. Thank you. Goodbye. I'm sorry, Mr Harris. Now, two girls and a boy, you said?
C: No, two boys and a girl.
BM: Oh, yes, I'm sorry. And what are their names?
C: Alan, Jane and Max.
BM: And their ages?
C: Twelve, ten and six.
BM: I see. Now one more question, Mr Harris. What is your job?
C: I'm a university teacher.
BM: A university teacher. Right. Thank you. Now, you want £100,000 to buy a house.
C: That's right.
BM: And how much . . . ?

1 Listen to the conversation. Then see how much you can remember.

2 Pronunciation. Practise these expressions.

one or two questions   Yes, of course.
How old are you?   How old is Mrs Harris?
What is your wife's name?   Yes, I am.
two boys and a girl   What are their names?
Twelve, ten and six.

3 Practise part of the conversation.

4 Ask and answer. Examples:

'Have you got any brothers or sisters?'
'Yes, I have. I've got two brothers.' / 'No, I haven't.'

5 Choose a new name, age, nationality, job, etc. Then work with another student, and interview him or her.

'What is your husband's name, Ms Carter?'   'Eric.'

NAME: Mr Harris / Mr Gordon / Mrs Shaw / Ms Carter / . . .
AGE: 22 / 30 / 41 / 67 / . . .
NATIONALITY: English/Scottish/Australian/ . . .
JOB: teacher/doctor/engineer/secretary/ . . .
WIFE'S/HUSBAND'S NAME: Mary/Alice/Sam/ Eric/ . . .
CHILDREN: a boy and a girl
          two boys and a girl
          two girls and a boy
          ....
CHILDREN'S NAMES: ....
CHILDREN'S AGES: ....

I have (I've) got	have I got?	I have not (haven't) got
you have (you've) got	have you got?	you have not (haven't) got
he/she/it has (he's *etc.*) got	has he *etc.* got?	she *etc.* has not (hasn't) got
we have (we've) got	have we got?	we have not (haven't) got
you have (you've) got	have you got?	you have not (haven't) got
they have (they've) got	have they got?	they have not (haven't) got

Learn: age; (a) moment; aren't you?; any; job; of course; Pardon?; please; question; sit down; teacher; too; What does . . . mean?; Have you got . . . ?; Yes, I have; No, I haven't.

Unit 4 Consolidation

4A Things to remember: Units 1, 2 and 3

I am

I am (I'm)	am I?	I am (I'm) not
you are (you're)	are you?	you are not (aren't)
he is (he's)	is he?	he is not (isn't)
she is (she's)	is she?	she is not (isn't)
it is (it's)	is it?	it is not (isn't)
her name is (her name's)	is her name?	her name is not (isn't)
we are (we're)	are we?	we are not (aren't)
you are (you're)	are you?	you are not (aren't)
they are (they're)	are they?	they are not (aren't)

Examples:
I'm sixteen. (~~I have sixteen.~~)
'**Are** you English?' 'Yes, I **am**.' (~~'Yes, I'm.'~~)
'Is Susan an engineer?' 'Yes, she **is**.' (~~'Yes, she's.' 'Yes, Susan is.'~~)
Are John and his father doctors? (~~Are doctors John and his father?~~)
'You're Canadian, **aren't** you?' 'Yes, that's right.'

I've got

I have (I've) got	have I got?	I have not (haven't) got
you have (you've) got	have you got?	you have not (haven't) got
he/she/it has (he's *etc.*) got	has he *etc.* got?	she *etc.* has not (hasn't) got
we have (we've) got	have we got?	we have not (haven't) got
you have (you've) got	have you got?	you have not (haven't) got
they have (they've) got	have they got?	they have not (haven't) got

Examples:
'**Have** you **got** any sisters or brothers?' 'Yes, I **have**. I've **got** two sisters.' / 'No, I **haven't**.'
'**Has** your mother **got** any sisters?' 'Yes, she **has**. She's **got** two.' / 'No, she **hasn't**.'

A and an

an + a....., e....., i....., o....., u..... (/ʌ/): an engineer, an artist, an architect
a + u..... (/juː/), other letters: a university teacher, a secretary, a name

A, B, C, . . . : pronunciation

/eɪ/: A, H, J, K
/iː/: E, B, C, D, G, P, T, V
/aɪ/: I, Y
/əʊ/: O
/juː/: U, Q, W
/e/: F, L, M, N, S, X, Z
/ɑː(r)/: R

Remember:
A (/eɪ/) and R (/ɑː(r)/)
E (/iː/) and I (/aɪ/)
G (/dʒiː/) and J (/dʒeɪ/)
V (/viː/) and W (/'dʌbljuː/)

Nouns: singular and plural

Regular

boy ⟶ boys
girl ⟶ girls
name ⟶ names
parent ⟶ parents
family ⟶ families
secretary ⟶ secretaries
address ⟶ addresses
six ⟶ sixes

Irregular

child ⟶ child**ren**
man ⟶ men
woman ⟶ women
wife ⟶ wives
housewife ⟶ housewives

Prepositions

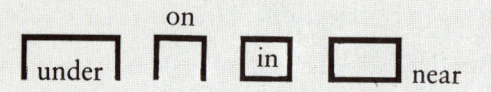

under on in near

Adjectives

John is quite **tall**. Mary is very **tall**.
My daughters are quite **tall**.
  (~~My daughters are quite talls.~~)

18

My, your, his, her . . .

I ———→ my
you ———→ your
he ———→ his
John ———→ John's
she ———→ her
Susan ———→ Susan's
it ———→ (its)
we ———→ our
you ———→ your
they ———→ their
my sons ———→ my sons'

Examples:
My bag is on the chair.
Susan's surname is Perkins.
 (The Susan's surname is Perkins.)

Where, who, what, how: questions and answers

'Where are you from?' 'Egypt.'
'Where's my pen?' 'It's under your book.'
'Who's your doctor?' 'Doctor Wagner.'
'What does *coat* mean?'
'What's your name?' 'Denise Quinton.'
'What do you do?' | 'I'm an artist/electrician/engineer.' ('I'm artist.')
                  | 'I'm a student/teacher/doctor.' ('I'm student.')
'How do you do?' 'How do you do?'
'How are you?' | 'Very well, thank you. And you?' 'Fine, thank you.'
               | 'Not bad, thanks. And you?' 'Fine, thanks.'
               | 'Not very well.' 'I'm sorry to hear that.'
'How old are you?' 'I'm thirty-five.' ('I've got thirty-five.')
'How do you spell it?' 'J, O, W, I, double T.'
'What's your address?' '17 Church Street.'

Excuse me, I'm sorry, Pardon

'Excuse me, is your name Fred Andrews?'
'No, I'm sorry, it's not. It's Jake Barker.'
'Pardon?'
'It's Jake Barker.'
'Oh, I'm sorry.'

Numbers

1 one	11 eleven	20 twenty	30 thirty
2 two	12 twelve	21 twenty-one	40 forty
3 three	13 thirteen	22 twenty-two	50 fifty
4 four	14 fourteen	23 twenty-three	60 sixty
5 five	15 fifteen	24 twenty-four	70 seventy
6 six	16 sixteen	25 twenty-five	80 eighty
7 seven	17 seventeen	26 twenty-six	90 ninety
8 eight	18 eighteen	27 twenty-seven	100 a hundred
9 nine	19 nineteen	28 twenty-eight	
10 ten		29 twenty-nine	

Hello and *goodbye*

Formal
Good morning/afternoon/evening.
Goodbye / Good night.

Informal
Hi / Hello.
Bye / Goodbye / See you / Good night.

Words and expressions

Nouns
name, first name, surname, address, age, job, widow, widower, Britain, the United States, student, teacher, morning, afternoon, evening, night, moment
man (men), woman (women), boy, girl, friend, boyfriend, girlfriend, father, mother, wife (wives), husband, brother, sister, son, daughter, parent, child (children), family
number, letter, pen, hat, book, coat, bag, table, chair, question

Adjectives
double, British, American, English, well, married, single, divorced, separated, dark, fair, fat, slim, young, old, good-looking, intelligent, pretty, tall, strong

Other words and expressions
not, yes, no, a, an, the, any, and, or, Oh, from, speak, do, sit down, about, OK, Dr, Miss, Mr, Mrs, Ms
this, a little, please, between jobs, very, not very, quite, not well, too, Here's . . ., I don't know, That's right, That's interesting, I think, a moment, of course, . . . aren't you?

Optional words to learn
doctor; secretary; electrician; housewife (housewives); shop assistant; artist; engineer; medical student; photographer; dentist.

4B Please write

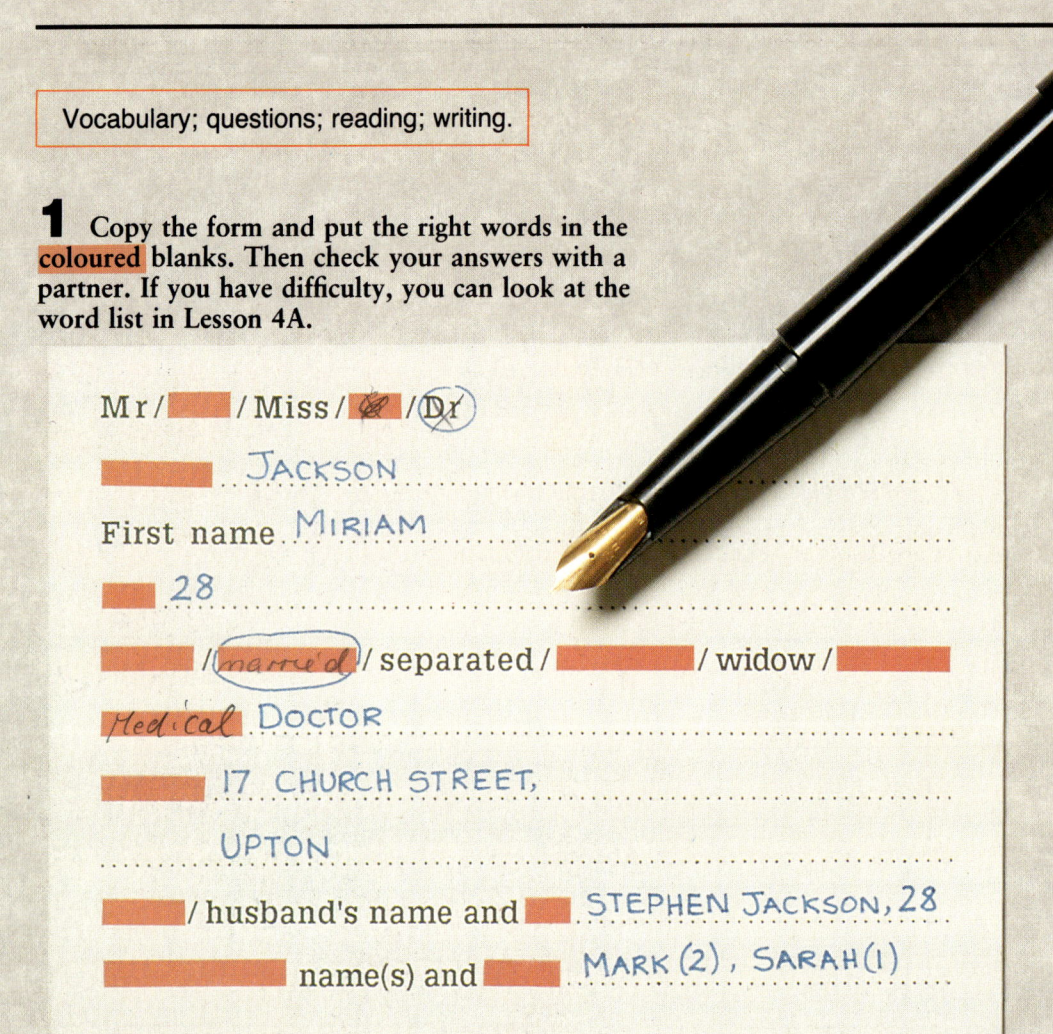

Vocabulary; questions; reading; writing.

1 Copy the form and put the right words in the coloured blanks. Then check your answers with a partner. If you have difficulty, you can look at the word list in Lesson 4A.

```
Mr / ▬▬ / Miss / ⊗ / (Dr)
▬▬      JACKSON
First name  MIRIAM
▬▬  28
▬▬ / (married) / separated / ▬▬ / widow / ▬▬
Medical  DOCTOR
▬▬  17 CHURCH STREET,
    UPTON
▬▬ / husband's name and ▬▬  STEPHEN JACKSON, 28
▬▬          name(s) and ▬▬  MARK (2), SARAH (1)
```

2 Work with a partner. Change the questions on the form into spoken questions. Then listen and check your answers. Example:

Surname: *'What is your surname?'*

3 Put the letter in the right order. Which picture is Teresa's family?

Dear Miriam,

and very intelligent, too. 11
They are dark and very good-looking, 10
We've got two children: 7
I'm Spanish, from Barcelona. 2
Here's a photograph. 14
I am tall and dark, 5
our daughter Rosa is four, 8
My name is Teresa Riera. 1
I speak Catalan, Spanish, and a little French. 12
and my husband Patricio is an artist. 4
I am an English student at a language school. 13
I'm a photographer for a fashion magazine, 3
Please write. 15 Mode
and Patricio is tall and fair. 6
and our son Antonio is two. 9

Yours sincerely,

Teresa

1
2
3
4

4 Write Miriam's answer to Teresa.
Begin: *Dear Teresa,*
        Thank you for . . .

5 Imagine you are someone else. Write a letter to someone in your class. When you receive a letter, try and guess who it is from.

4C I've got a new girlfriend

> Social chat; /θ/ and /ð/; questions; role play.

1 📼 What do you think they say next? Your teacher will help. Listen to check.

2 Listen to these two words from the dialogue:

thanks   mother

Can you say them correctly? And how about these words:

th like *thanks* (/θ/):
think   thirteen   thirty   three

th like *mother* (/ð/):
brother   father   that's   the   their   they

3 Make as many questions as you can.

| What
Who
How
How old
Where | Is
  is
    Are
  are
    Have
      do
    does | John
Ann and her mother
they
  your sister
    your name
  you
      he
  rapid
    she | an engineer
  photographers
    English
do
    spell it
got any children
  got any sisters
your brother
  from
    mean | ? |

4 Who's who? Get your role from the teacher, and find . . .
Example:

- Have you got any brothers?
- Yes, I have.
- What are their names?
- I don't know. They're 34 and 38. One's an engineer.

- Are you an engineer?
- Yes, I am.
- How old are you?
- 38.
- What's your name?

4D Test yourself

LISTENING

1 Copy the form. Then listen, and fill it in.

```
FIRST NAME: Anne
SURNAME: Harris.
AGE: 30
JOB: photographer
ADDRESS: 17 York Gardens, Perth. in Scotland
HUSBAND'S NAME: John Harris. married
HUSBAND'S AGE: 36
HUSBAND'S JOB: dentist
NUMBER OF CHILDREN: 2
CHILDREN'S NAMES AND AGES: Mary (4),
Sam 2
```

2 Listen and choose the best answer.

1. A. Hi!
   B. Good morning.
   C. Goodbye.
2. A. Thanks.
   B. China.
   C. I'm a teacher.
3. A. Very well, thank you.
   B. I'm thirty-two.
   C. How do you do?
4. A. No, I'm sorry, it's not.
   B. He's an engineer.
   C. It's under your book.
5. A. Not very well.
   B. In America.
   C. 17 Church Street.

3 Listen and write the letters.

VOCABULARY

1 Write the numbers in words. Example:

13 thirteen

17 30 51 12 26
99 8   15 11 100

2 Add five more words to each list.

1. student, teacher, secretary, . . .
2. British, Egyptian, Indian, . . .
3. Japan, Spain, the USSR, . . .

GRAMMAR

Put - setze, lege, stelle
order - an die richtige Stelle
Are Lucy and her brother students?

1 Put the words in the right order.

1. got you brothers any have? *Have you got any brothers?*
2. me is Ann name excuse your Smith? *Excuse me, is your name Ann Smith?*
3. Lucy are her students and brother?
4. from where Catherine's is father? *Where is Catherine's father from?*
5. spell name your how do first you? *How do you spell your first name?*

2 Add *s*, *'s*, *s'* or *–*.

1. I've got three brother**s**.
2. My brother**s** are very tall.
3. My sister**'s** husband**'s** name **'s** Steve.
4. My parent**s'** surname is Webb, but my name**'s** Watson.
5. How old are your children?

3 Choose the correct word.

1. My wife and *his/her* brother are in America.
2. My *wife/wife's/wives*' parents are artists.
3. Her brother's *a/an* teacher.
4. We've got two children; *they/their* are very tall.
5. My wife and I are dark, but *our/your/their* children are fair.

PRONUNCIATION

1 Which *th* is different?

1. think, that, three, thanks
2. brother, they, the, think
3. father, thanks, think, thirteen

2 Which word has a different stress? Example:

husband, letter, teacher, (address)

1. married, excuse, goodbye, address
2. family, interesting, secretary, afternoon
3. doctor, hello, double, woman

Unit 5 Where?

5A Home

Houses and flats; *there is* and *there are*.

1 Look at the picture, and put the words with the right letters. Use your dictionary or work with other students. Example:

A. bathroom

| C bedroom | D kitchen | B toilet |
| A bathroom | F living room | E hall |

2 Now put these words with the right numbers.

11 chair	5 bed	3 toilet	13 door
4 window	12 stairs	7 cooker	
16 sofa	10 fridge	14 armchair	
15 television (TV)		cupboard 9	
6 wardrobe	8 sink	1 washbasin	
2 bath			

3 The teacher's home. Listen.

4 Complete the sentences, and make some more sentences about the house in the picture.

1. There are ...two... bedrooms in the house.
2. There is (There's) an armchair ...in... the living room.
3. ...There... is not (isn't) a garage.
4. There ...is one... bathroom.
5. There ...are... two toilets.
6. ...There... ...is... ...a... fridge in the kitchen.

5 Work in pairs.
1. Both students copy the plan.
2. One student furnishes his or her rooms.
3. The other asks questions beginning *Is there a . . . ?* or *Are there any . . . ?*
4. He or she listens to the answers and tries to put the right furniture etc. into the rooms.

Examples:

'Is there a table in the living room?' 'Yes, there is.'
'Is it near the hall?' 'Yes, it is.'
'Is it under the window?' 'No, it isn't.'
'Are there any chairs in the bathroom?' 'Yes, there are.' (Or 'Yes, there are two.')

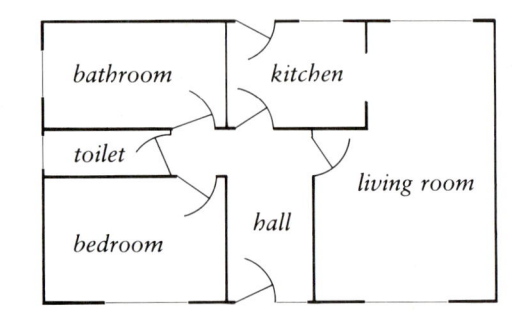

| there is (there's) | is there? | there is not (isn't) |
| there are (–) | are there? | there are not (aren't) |

Learn: there is/are; house; window; door; stairs; room.

Learn three or more: bedroom; kitchen; bathroom; toilet; living room; wall; garage.

Learn three or more: furniture; bed; cooker; sofa; fridge; armchair; television; TV; cupboard; bath; wardrobe.

5B Where do you work?

> Where people live and work; Simple Present tense; *at*, *in* and *on*; phone numbers; *first*, *second*, ...

1 Look at the pictures. Put the words in the right places.

> The Prime Minister lives at 10 Downing Street.
> My sister works in Edinburgh.
> 'Where do you live, Mary?' 'In Aston Street.'
> 'What's your address?' '39 Morrison Avenue.'
> We live in a small flat on the fourth floor.
>
> Mrs L. Williams
> 17 Harcourt Road
> Coventry
> West Midlands CY2 4BJ

ninth (9th) floor
eighth (8th) floor
seventh (7th) floor
sixth (6th) floor
fifth (5th) floor
fourth (4th) floor
third (3rd) floor
second (2nd) floor
first (1st) floor
ground floor

2 *At, in* or *on*?

1. I live ..*at*.. 37 Valley Road.
2. 'Where do you work?' '..*In*.. New York.'
3. My office is ..*on*.. the fourteenth floor.
4. Jake lives ..*in*.. a big old house ..*in*.. Washington.
5. 'Where do you live?' '..*at*.. 116 New Street.'

3 🔊 Listening for information. Copy the table. Then listen to the conversations, and write the correct letters after the names. (There are only three phone numbers.)

NAME	LIVES	PHONE NUMBER
John	D	314 6829
Peter Matthews	F	—
Alice's mother	C	X 314
Mr Billows	E	Z 41758
Mrs Webber	G	417 85
Mrs Simon	A	41632

A at 16 Norris Road, Bedford.
B in a small flat in North London.
C in Birmingham.
D at 116 Market Street.
E in New York.
F on the fourth floor.
G at 60 Hamilton Road, Gloucester.

V 314 6928
W 41632
X 314 6829
Y 41785
Z 41758

4 You all work in the same building; it has got eight floors. Your teacher will tell you your jobs and phone numbers and what floor you work on. Find out who works where; ask for phone numbers.
Example:

'What do you do?'   'What's your phone
'I'm an engineer.'   number?'
'And where do you work?'   '633 4945.'
'I work on the fourth floor.' 'Thanks.'

Now look at the example and complete the sentences.

An engineer works (or *Two engineers work*) *on the fourth floor, and his/her/their phone number is 633 4945.*

1. .... work(s) on the ground floor, and .... phone number is ....
2. .... work(s) on the first floor, and ....
3. .... work(s) on the .... , and ....
4. .... on the .... , and ....
5. .... , and ....
6. ....
7. ....

I live	we live
you live	you live
he/she/it lives	they live

> **Learn:** work; live; at; big; small; flat; street; road; floor; ground floor; first; second; third; fourth; fifth; sixth; seventh; eighth; ninth; phone number.

5C Where's the nearest post office?

Asking for and giving directions.

1 Put the words with the correct pictures.

```
6 phone box    7 supermarket    2 bank    1 post office
3 police station    8 car park    4 bus stop    5 station
```

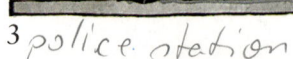

1 post office
2 bank 
3 police station
4 bus stop 
5 station 
6 phone box 
7 supermarket 
8 car park

2 Listen and practise these dialogues.

A: Excuse me. Where's the nearest post office, please?
B: It's over there on the right / left.
A: Oh, thank you very much.
B: Not at all.

* * *

A: Excuse me. Where's the nearest bank, please?
B: I'm sorry, I don't know.
A: Thank you anyway.

3 Complete these dialogues and practise them.

A: .... the manager's office, ...?
B: .... by the reception desk.
A: ....

* * *

A: .... the toilets, ...?
B: Upstairs .... the first floor, first door .... left.
A: .... much.

4 Make up similar conversations in pairs and practise them. You are: a person who lives in your town and a foreign tourist; or a visitor to your school and a student; or a visitor to the planet Mars and a Martian.

Learn: there; over there; right; left; on the right/left; Thank you anyway; Not at all; by; upstairs; downstairs.

Learn four or more: phone box; supermarket; bank; post office; police; police station; car park; bus stop; station.

5D First on the right, second on the left

More asking for and giving directions.

1 Put in the missing words, and put the sentences in the right order in each conversation.

'Thank you very much.'
'................ on the right, then second .... It's next to the post office.'
'................ is it?'
'Excuse me. .... the nearest car park, ...?'
'About five hundred yards.'
'................ .'

* * *

'Yes. It's .... the car park. Go .... for about three hundred ....'
'Thanks very much.'
'................ . Is there a .... near here?'

excuse me	first	how far	not at all
on the left	opposite	please	straight on
swimming pool	where's	yards	

2 Look at the map. Then work with another student and test his or her memory.

'Where's the police station?' 'Opposite the railway station.'
'Where's the car park?' 'I don't remember.'

3 🔊 Listen and follow the directions on the map. Then say where you are.

4 Give directions to other students. Example:

'You are at A. Take the first left, second right, first right, second right, and go straight on for about three hundred metres. Where are you?'

5 Copy the map. Then put in *either* the places in list A *or* the places in list B.

A. a supermarket   B. a church
   a swimming pool   a good restaurant
   a bookshop   a good hotel
   a phone box   a chemist's
   a cheap restaurant   a public toilet
   a cheap hotel

Work in pairs. Ask and give directions (you are at A on the map). Example:

'Excuse me. Is there a bookshop near here, please?'
'Yes. First left, second right, in Station Road.'
'Thank you.'

Learn: here; nearest; good; cheap; opposite; straight on; then; yard; for (. . . yards/metres); How far . . . ?; far; swimming pool; next to; take.

Learn three or more: railway station; bookshop; restaurant; hotel; church; chemist's; public.

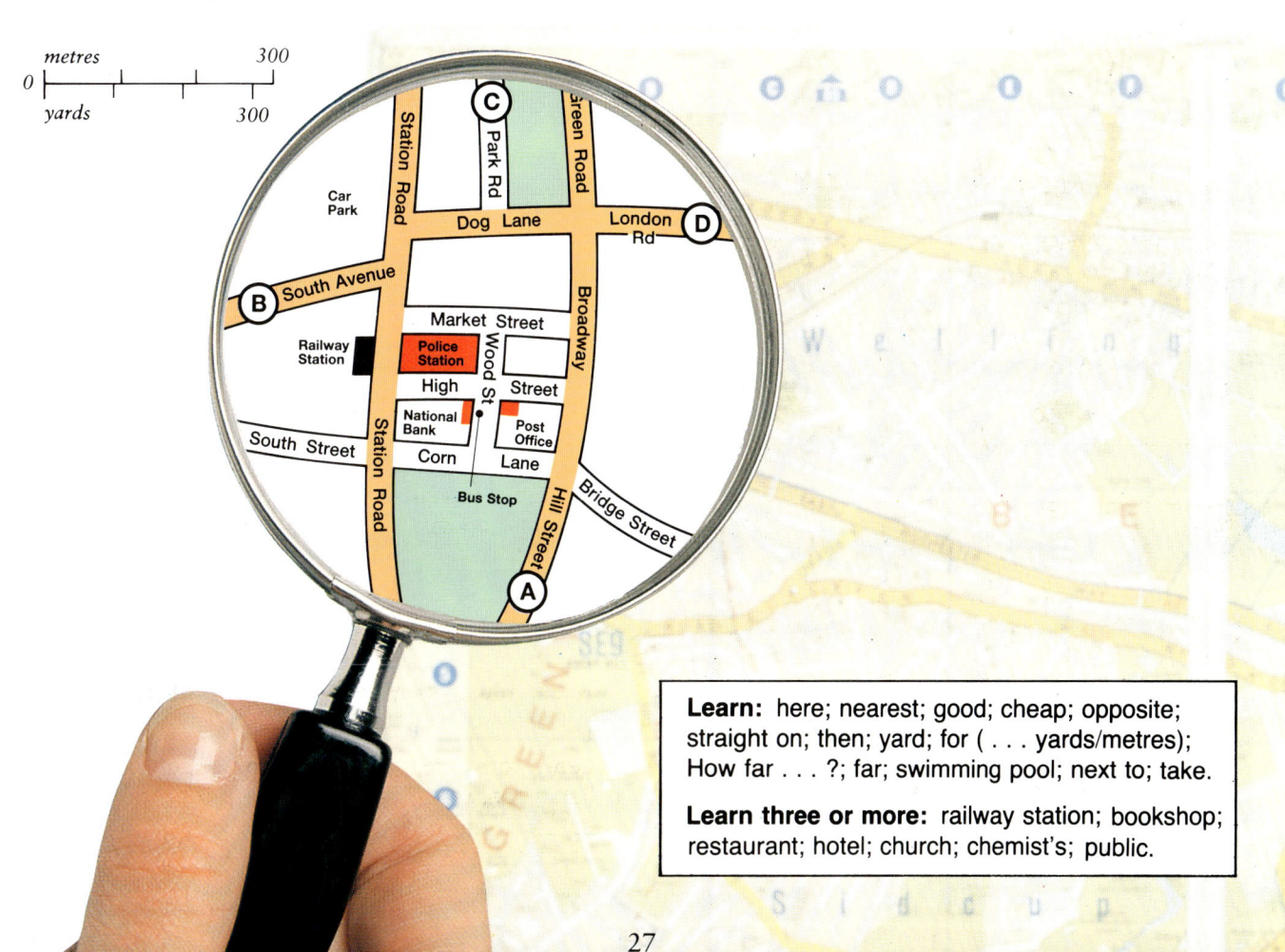

Unit 6 Habits

6A What do you like?

Likes and dislikes; Simple Present tense; *him, her, it* and *them*.

Jackson Pollock: Yellow Island

Vermeer: Young Girl

Mexican mask

Greek statue

1 Look at the pictures and statue. Which one do you like? Examples:

'I like the Greek statue very much.'
'I quite like the mask.'
'The mask is OK.'
'I don't like the Vermeer picture much.'
'I hate the Pollock picture. I don't like it at all.'
'I like the Greek statue the best.'

2 Listen to the music and sounds and say whether you like them or not.

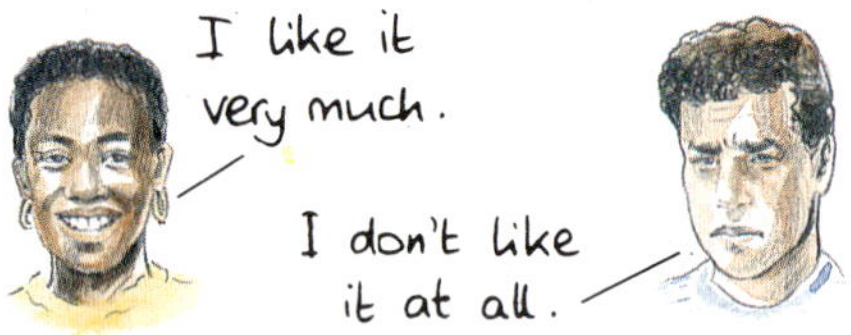

I like it very much.
I don't like it at all.

3 Put in *like, likes, it, them, him* or *her*.

1. I don't _like_ cats, but my brother _likes_ them very much.
2. 'Do you _like_ dogs?' 'Yes, I love _them_.'
3. George _likes_ Mary, but Mary doesn't like _him_.
4. Mary _likes_ dancing and travelling.
5. 'Do you _like_ orange juice?' 'No, I don't like _it_ at all.'
6. I don't dislike opera, but I don't really _like it_.
7. 'Your husband _likes_ cooking, doesn't he?' 'Yes, he does.'
8. My wife hates big dogs, but I love _them_.
9. My wife and I _like_ the sea, but our children don't – they _like_ climbing mountains.
10. 'Do you _like_ Anne?' 'Yes, I _like her_ very much.'

4 Do you like these? Ask other students about one of them.

| big dogs maths whisky mountains the sea cats |
| shopping watching TV cooking dancing writing letters |
| travelling |

'Do you like cooking?'   'Yes, I do.'
'Do you like big dogs?' 'No, I don't.'
                         'I hate it/them.'
                         'I love it/them.'
                         'It depends.'

5 Report to the class. Examples:

'Seven students like cats.'
'Five people like big dogs.'
'Only two people like shopping.'
'Only one person likes maths.'
'Jean-Claude likes whisky very much.'
'Nobody likes cooking.'
'Everybody likes the sea.'

Pronouns

Subject	Object	Subject	Object
I →	me	we →	us
you →	you	you →	you
he →	him	they →	them
she →	her		
it →	it		

Learn: like; hate; love; dislike; him; her; them; it depends; only; nobody; everybody; very much; not much; not at all.

6B Where are you at seven o'clock?

Time; *at* with times; no article in *at home*, *in bed*, etc.

1

It's three o'clock.   It's ten past three.

It's a quarter past three.   It's half past three.

What time is it?

1 2 3 4 5 6 7 8 (9:30)

2

It's twenty-five to four.   It's a quarter to four.

It's ten to four.   It's five to four.

What time is it?

1 2 3 4 5 6 (2:40) 7 (3:45) 8 (9:55)

3 Listening for information. Listen and write down the times you hear.

4 Set your watch to a new time. Ask and answer:

'What time is it?'   'A quarter past twelve.'
'What time is it?'   'Erm, about a quarter to four.'

5 Look at the chart. Complete the sentences. You can use words from the box.

Ingrid (student)

7 9 11 1 3 5 7 9 11 1

George (architect)

on his/her way to school/work	at home	at lunch	at school
at work	but	out	on his/her way back from school/work
in bed			

1. At half past six in the morning, Ingrid is ....
2. At a quarter to eight, George is still ....
3. At nine o'clock, Ingrid is ...., but George is still ....
4. At five past ten, George is ...., and Ingrid is ....
5. At five past one, Ingrid ...., ... George is still ....
6. At a quarter to two, George is ...., and Ingrid is ....
7. At five o'clock, Ingrid is ...., ... George is ....
8. At eight o'clock in the evening, George ....
9. At half past nine in the evening, George is at home or ....
10. At ten to eleven in the evening, Ingrid is ....

6 Work in pairs. Each person chooses a job. Ask the other person four questions about time and try to guess their job. Example:

'Where are you at a quarter to seven in the morning?'
'At work.'
'Where are you at a quarter past eleven in the morning?'
'In bed.'
'Where are you at four o'clock in the afternoon?'
'At home.'
'Where are you at twenty past nine in the evening?'
'At work.'
'Are you a nurse?'
'Yes.'

JOBS
nurse   jazz singer   waiter/waitress   baker   bank manager
school teacher   postman/postwoman

Learn: half; a quarter; past; to; o'clock; time; What time is it?;
but; (at) home; (at) school; (at) work; (in) bed; out; still;
in the morning/afternoon/evening.

29

6C Work

> Routines; more Simple Present tense; *Does he/she . . . ?*; *he/she doesn't*; *at*, *from* and *until* with times.

1 Put the words into the text.

Stan Dixon is a shop assistant. He sells men's clothes in a small shop. It is a tiring job.
   Stan *gets up* at seven o'clock. After *breakfast* he *starts* to work by *bus*. He *starts* work at a quarter past nine; the shop *opens* at half past. Stan *has* lunch at twelve, and then *works* from 12.45 until 5.45.
   On Saturdays, Stan *stops* work at one o'clock.
   On Sundays he *goes* cycling or *plays* tennis.
   Stan does not *stop* his job much.

has	like	breakfast	goes	works	bus
gets up	opens	stops	plays	starts	
goes					

2 Do it yourself. Ask the teacher questions, and write the text about Karen Miller.

Karen Miller is a mechanic. She repairs cars in a garage . . .

What time does she get up?
How .... she go to work?
Does she *have/has* breakfast?
What time .... she start work?
.... time does she *stop/stops* work?
What .... does .... have lunch?
.... supper?
.... work on Saturdays?
What .... do at the weekend?
.... like her job?

3 Learn the days of the week.

MARCH

Monday	5	12	19	26
Tuesday	6	13	20	27
Wednesday	7	14	21	28
Thursday	1	8	15	22	29
Friday	2	9	16	23	30
Saturday	3	10	17	24	31
Sunday	4	11	18	25

on (written beside each day)

sell - verkaufen
tiring - ermüden

4 Write four sentences about yourself using words or expressions from the box.

get up	have breakfast	have lunch	go to school	go to work
on Saturdays	on Sundays	at the weekend		

Now talk to other students. Ask questions as in the examples. Have you written the same sentences?

'What time do you get up?' 'Seven o'clock.'
'What do you do on Saturdays?' 'I play tennis.'

I work	do I work?
you work	do you work?
he/she works	does he/she work?
we work	do we work?
you work	do you work?
they work	do they work?

> **Learn:** have; get up; go; start; stop; breakfast; lunch; supper; from; until; at; (by) bus; (by) car; Monday; Tuesday; Wednesday; Thursday; Friday; Saturday; Sunday; (at the) weekend.

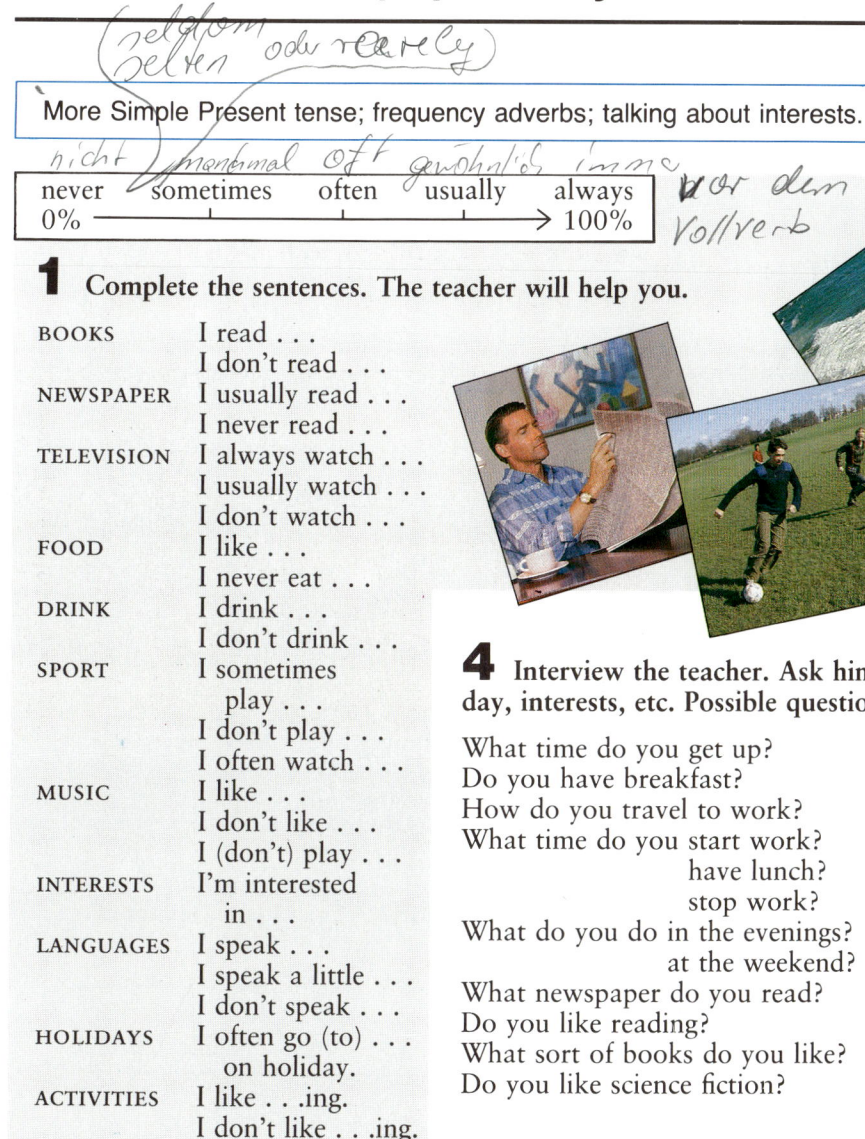

6D What newspaper do you read?

More Simple Present tense; frequency adverbs; talking about interests.

```
never    sometimes    often    usually    always
0% ─────────────────────────────────→ 100%
```

1 Complete the sentences. The teacher will help you.

BOOKS	I read . . .
	I don't read . . .
NEWSPAPER	I usually read . . .
	I never read . . .
TELEVISION	I always watch . . .
	I usually watch . . .
	I don't watch . . .
FOOD	I like . . .
	I never eat . . .
DRINK	I drink . . .
	I don't drink . . .
SPORT	I sometimes play . . .
	I don't play . . .
	I often watch . . .
MUSIC	I like . . .
	I don't like . . .
	I (don't) play . . .
INTERESTS	I'm interested in . . .
LANGUAGES	I speak . . .
	I speak a little . . .
	I don't speak . . .
HOLIDAYS	I often go (to) . . . on holiday.
ACTIVITIES	I like . . . ing.
	I don't like . . . ing.

2 🔊 Listen to the recording. Answer the questions. Examples:

'Are you married?' 'Yes, I am.' / 'No, I'm not.'
'Do you like music?' 'Yes, I do.' / 'No, I don't.'
'What sort of music do you like?' 'Rock.'

3 Where are the stresses?

1. What do you do?
   Where do you live?
   How do you travel to work?
   What time do you start work?
   What time do you stop work?
   What sort of food do you like?
2. What does she do?
   Where does she work?
   How does she go to work?
3. Yes, I do. No, I don't.
   Yes, he does. No, he doesn't.

4 Interview the teacher. Ask him or her questions about his or her day, interests, etc. Possible questions:

What time do you get up?
Do you have breakfast?
How do you travel to work?
What time do you start work?
           have lunch?
           stop work?
What do you do in the evenings?
           at the weekend?
What newspaper do you read?
Do you like reading?
What sort of books do you like?
Do you like science fiction?

Do you like fish?
What sort of food do you like?
Do you like beer?
Do you play tennis?
Do you like skiing?
Do you watch football?
Do you like music?
Do you play an instrument?
Are you interested in politics?
What languages do you speak?
Where do you go on holiday?

5 Interview another student. Spend five minutes with him or her, and try to find:

1. Five negative facts (for example, 'He doesn't play tennis.').
2. Five things that you both have in common (for example, 'We both like the sea.').

6 Write about the student you interviewed.

Simple Present tense		
I play	do I play?	I do not (don't) play
you play	do you play?	you do not (don't) play
he/she/it play**s**	do**es** she *etc*. play?	he *etc*. do**es** not (do**es**n't) play
we play	do we play?	we do not (don't) play
you play	do you play?	you do not (don't) play
they play	do they play?	they do not (don't) play

Learn: newspaper; language; travel; read; play; watch; both; never; sometimes; often; usually; always; interested in; (on) holiday; What sort of . . . ?

Learn three or more: maths; music; rock; science fiction; fish; beer; tennis; skiing; football; instrument; politics.

Unit 7 Counting and measuring

7A How many calories?

Two sorts of nouns (countable and uncountable); food and drink.

2. a litre of .... calories
1. 100ml of .... calories
3. 500g of .... calories
4. an .... calories
5. half a litre of .... calories
6. 100ml of .... calories
7. a .... calories
8. a .... calories
9. a .... calories
10. 500g of .... calories
11. an .... calories
12. 150g of .... calories
13. 50g of .... calories

1 What are the names of the things in the picture? Try to put the words in the right places.

banana	bread	cheese	coffee	egg
ice cream	milk	orange	orange juice
potato	rump steak	tomato	water

2 How many calories? Try to put the numbers with the pictures.

| 0 | 7 | 40 | 40 | 50 | 80 | 90 |
| 115 | 175 | 320 | 636 | 850 | 893 |

3 Listen to the recording of people guessing how many calories there are. Write down the calories they guess for: ice cream, orange, milk, coffee and potato.

4 Can you complete the lists?

C: an egg, a tomato, . . .
U: orange juice, cheese, . . .

5 Two students take turns choosing food from Exercise 1, and adding up the calories. The person who can total closest to 1,500 calories wins.

I'll have 500g of rump steak.

A | B
850 | 893

I'll have 500g of ice cream.

Learn: gram; litre; money; listen to; try; of; half a . . . of . . .

Learn five or more: banana; bread; cheese; coffee; egg; ice cream; milk; orange; (orange) juice; potato; rump steak; tomato; water.

32

7B It's terrible

Prices; nouns without articles; *was* and *were*.

- It's terrible.
- The prices.
- Oh dear.
- Do you know potatoes are eighty pence a kilo?
- Eighty pence a kilo? In our supermarket they're eighty-five.
- It's terrible.
- Oh dear.
- Everything's so expensive.
- Do you know tomatoes are £6.00 a kilo?
- £6.00? In our supermarket they're £6.25.
- No!!!
- Yes!
- It's terrible.
- Milk's seventy-five pence a litre.
- Half a kilo of rump steak is £7.50.
- An orange costs 60p. One orange!
- And cheese!
- I know!
- Do you know, yesterday I was in Patterson's.
- Were you?
- Yes, and cheese was £8.30 a kilo.
- £8.30?
- Yes, and bananas were £2.25.
- It's terrible.

1 Listen to the conversation (books closed) and answer the teacher's questions.

2 Say these words and expressions.

It's **ter**rible
eighty **pence** a **ki**lo
Po**ta**toes are **eigh**ty **pence** a **ki**lo.
In our **su**permarket they're **eigh**ty-**five**.
ex**pen**sive
Everything's **so** ex**pen**sive.
to**ma**toes are **six pounds**
six pounds a **ki**lo
half a **ki**lo
an **or**ange
I **was** in **Pat**terson's
Do you **know**?
ba**na**nas were **two pounds twen**ty-**five**

3 Put in *the* where necessary.

1. There are 424 calories in 100g of .... cheese.
2. Your tomatoes are in ...the... fridge.
3. .... potatoes are not very expensive.
4. There are no calories in .... water.
5. 'Where are .... bananas?' 'On .... table.'
6. .... wine is expensive in Britain.
7. 'We've got one orange and one banana.' 'I'll have .... orange.'
8. Do you like .... tomatoes?

4 Put in *am, is, are, was* or *were*.

1. Yesterday I .... in London.
2. Steak .... very expensive.
3. Yesterday my mother and father .... in Manchester.
4. Oranges .... £1.40 a kilo.
5. In 1960, oranges .... 20p a kilo and a bottle of wine .... 60p.
6. When I .... a child, bananas .... very expensive.
7. My daughter's name .... Helen.
8. .... you American?
9. Where .... you yesterday?
10. 'What do you do?' 'I .... a teacher.'

5 Practise the conversation.

6 Make short conversations in groups of four or five. Begin: *'It's terrible.'*

Learn: price; terrible; Do you know?; pound (£); pence (p); I know; yesterday; kilo; cost; was; were; Oh dear; expensive.

7C Have you got a good memory?

> More countables and uncountables; *there is/are*; *some* and *any*.

1 Countable or uncountable? Put *a/an* before the countable nouns.

car · chair · music
light · lamp · apple
snow · rain · cup
horse · money · ice
potato · glass · lamb
potato · glass · lamb

2 Look at the picture for two minutes. Then close your book. Work with a partner, and make as many sentences as you can with *some*. Examples:

There are some books on the tables.
There's some ice outside the window.

3 Show your sentences to the other students. Then open your book and check. Were any of your sentences wrong? Examples:

'There aren't any horses on the tables. There are some horses on a bed.'
'There isn't any snow on the television; there's some rain.'

Now make four more sentences about things that *aren't* in the picture.

4 🔊 Listen to the questions and write the answers:

Yes, there is.   No, there isn't.
Yes, there's one.   No, there aren't.
Yes, there are.

    I don't know.
    I don't understand.

5 Class survey. Choose one countable and one uncountable. Ask other students: 'Are there any . . . ?' / 'Is there any . . . ?' Keep account of the results.

fair people in your family	cheese in your kitchen
books under your chair	money in your bag
chairs in your bathroom	rain in your country today
horses near your home	snow in your country today
apples in your kitchen	ice in your fridge
doctors in your street	ice cream in your fridge

Yes	?	No
There is some rain.	Is there any rain?	There isn't any rain.
There are some horses.	Are there any horses?	There aren't any horses.

> **Learn:** music; snow; ice; light; rain; lamp; cup; apple; horse; glass; people; outside; some; (I don't) understand.

7D Not enough money

Much and *many*; *too* and *enough*; *a lot of*.

1 Put the words from the box in the right columns. What kind of words go in each column?

How much? Too much Not much Enough A lot of	How many? Too many? Not many Enough A lot of
water light air	cars houses children

milk   tomatoes   potatoes   cheese   bread
wine   rain   hair   men   chairs   people
snow   money

2 Quiz. Put in *How much* or *How many*. Can you answer any of the questions? Make some questions yourself.

1. .... states are there in the USA – 36, 49, 50 or 60?
2. .... Coca-Cola is drunk in the world in one day – one million bottles, 11 million bottles or 110 million bottles?
3. .... planets (Mercury, Venus etc.) are there – 7, 9, 11 or 13?
4. .... keys are there on a piano – 70, 82 or 88?
5. .... air is there in our lungs – half a litre, one and a half litres or two and a half litres?
6. .... Beatles were there – 3, 4 or 5?
7. .... of a person is water – 40%, 60% or 90%?

3 Listen, and choose the right words for each situation. Example:

1. 'not many people'

not much not many a lot of	people cats cigarettes students food money time water girlfriends

4 Talk about the classroom. Begin:

'There isn't much . . .'
'There aren't many . . .'
'There is/are a lot of . . .'

5 Look at the pictures and choose the right words.

not enough too much too many	people toothpaste hair perfume light money cars toilets children chips hair shaving cream numbers

6 Talk about yourself.

'I've got enough / too much / too many . . .'
'I haven't got enough . . .'

Learn: much; many; how much/many; not much/many; too much/many; a lot of; enough; word; person (people); toothpaste; hair; wine; food; cat.

Learn if you want: shaving cream; perfume; chips.

Unit 8 Consolidation

8A Things to remember: Units 5, 6 and 7

There is, there are . . .

| there is (there's) | is there? | there is not (isn't) |
| there are (−) | are there? | there are not (aren't) |

Examples:
There's a big table in my kitchen.
There's some coffee on the table.
Is there a bathroom on the first floor?
'Is there any milk in the fridge?'
  'Yes, there is.' / 'No, there isn't.'
There isn't a garage.
There isn't any ice in your glass.

There are two chairs in the hall.
There are some apples here.
'Are there any oranges?' 'Yes, there are.' /
  'Yes, there's one.' / 'No, there aren't.'
There aren't enough eggs.
There aren't any potatoes.

Stress
There's a **big ta**ble in my **kit**chen.
'**Is** there a (/ɪzðərə/) **bath**room on the **first floor**?'
  'Yes, there **is**.' / 'No, there **isn't**.'
There **isn't** any **ice** in your **glass**.
There **are** (/ðərə/) **two chairs** in the **hall**.
There **are** some (/ðərəsəm/) **ap**ples here.
'**Are** there any **or**anges?' 'Yes, there **are**.' / 'No, there **aren't**.'
There **aren't** enough **eggs**.

Was and were

| I was |
| you were |
| he/she/it was |
| we were |
| you were |
| they were |

Simple Present tense

I play	do I play?	I do not (don't) play
you play	do you play?	you do not (don't) play
he/she/it play**s**	do**es** he *etc*. play?	she *etc*. do**es** not (do**es**n't) play
we play	do we play?	we do not (don't) play
you play	do you play?	you do not (don't) play
they play	do they play?	they do not (don't) play

Examples:
'I live in Curzon Street.' 'Oh? I do, too.'
'Do you like orange juice?' 'Yes, I do.' (~~'Yes, I like.'~~)
'What time does Karen get up?' 'Half past seven.'
'Does she have breakfast?' 'No, she doesn't.' (~~'No, she hasn't.'~~)
'Does she go to work by car?' 'Yes, she does.' (~~'Yes, she goes.'~~)
'Do Sam and Virginia live near you?' 'No, they don't.'

Spelling of *he/she/it* forms

Regular
get ⟶ get**s**
play ⟶ play**s**
live ⟶ live**s**
try ⟶ tr**ies**
watch ⟶ watch**es**

Irregular
have got ⟶ has got
do ⟶ do**es**
go ⟶ go**es**

Stress
'Do you (/dju/) **like orange juice**?'
  'Yes, I **do**.' / 'No, I **don't**.'
What **time** does (/dəz/) **Karen get up**?
'Does she **have** (/dəʃi'hæv/) **break**fast?'
  'Yes, she **does**.' / 'No, she **doesn't**.'

Frequency adverbs

I **never** read science fiction. (~~I read never science fiction.~~)
I **sometimes** watch television in the evening.
She **often** goes to work by bus.
They **usually** have supper at six on Sundays.
John **always** goes to work by car.

Both

We **both** like rock music. (~~We like both rock music.~~ ~~We like rock music both.~~)

Pronouns and possessives

Subject	Object	Possessive
I →	me →	my
you →	you →	your
he →	him →	his
she →	her →	her
it →	it →	its
we →	us →	our
you →	you →	your
they →	them →	their

Articles

a/an: There's **an** apple on the table.
There's **a** book under your chair.
a/an and *some*: There's **a** woman at the reception desk.
There's **some** milk in the fridge.
(There's a milk . . .)
There are **some** books on the table.
no article: **Oranges** were expensive when I was young.
(The oranges were expensive when I was young.)
a and *the*: There's **a** chair in **the** bathroom. Where's **the** car?

Quantifiers with plurals and uncountables

Much with uncountables; *many* with plurals

There **isn't much light** in this room.
How **much air** is there in our lungs?
There **was** too **much snow** at St Moritz.
There **aren't many cars** in the street.
How **many brothers** and **sisters** have you got?
I've got too **many students** in my class.

Enough and *a lot (of)*

We haven't got **enough** ice cream. (. . . enough of . . .)
We've got **a lot of** potatoes. (. . . a lot potatoes.)
'How much would you like?' 'A lot.' ('A lot of.')

Some in affirmatives; *any* in negatives and questions

There are **some** oranges on the table. (. . . any oranges . . .)
I haven't got **any** time this morning. (. . . some time . . .)
Is there **any** ice in the fridge? (. . . some ice . . .)

Prepositions

Places: **by** the reception desk
opposite the railway station
next to the post office
on his way **to** work
on her way back **from** school
outside the window
in England; **in** New York; **in** Park Street, **in** a flat; **in** a big house; **in** the living room
at 23 Park Street
on the second floor

Special expressions: **at** home, **at** work, **at** school, **in** bed
Time: **at** half **past** seven
from nine o'clock **until** a quarter **to** six
on Saturdays
at the weekend
in the morning/afternoon/evening
Travel: **by** bus; **by** car; **on** holiday

Days

Monday (/ˈmʌndi/), Tuesday (/ˈtjuːzdi/),
Wednesday (/ˈwenzdi/), Thursday (/ˈθɜːzdi/),
Friday (/ˈfraɪdi/), Saturday (/ˈsætədi/),
Sunday (/ˈsʌndi/) Note the **s** in 'On Sunday**s**'.

First, second . . .

1st first	4th fourth	7th seventh
2nd second	5th fifth	8th eighth
3rd third	6th sixth	9th ninth

Time

What time is it? Where are you at seven o'clock?
five past six; a quarter past six; half past six
twenty to seven; a quarter to seven; seven o'clock
What time do you get up? (At what time do you get up?)
I have lunch from 12.30 to 1.15.

Likes and dislikes

I like the Greek statue very much.
I quite like the mask. The mask is OK.
I like the Vermeer best.
I hate shopping.
I don't like classical music at all.
'Do you like travelling?' 'It depends.'
Everybody like**s** music. Nobody like**s** rain.

Questions and answers

'Where do you live?' 'In Barcelona.'
'Where do you work?' 'In a shop in George Street.'
'What's your phone number?' 'Seven six two, four three eight five.'
'What newspaper do you read?' '*The Independent*.'
'How do you travel to work?' 'By bus.'
'What sort of books do you like?' 'Science fiction.'
'Are you interested in politics?' 'Yes, I am.'
'Would you like some fruit juice?' 'I'm sorry, I don't understand.'

8A continued

Directions

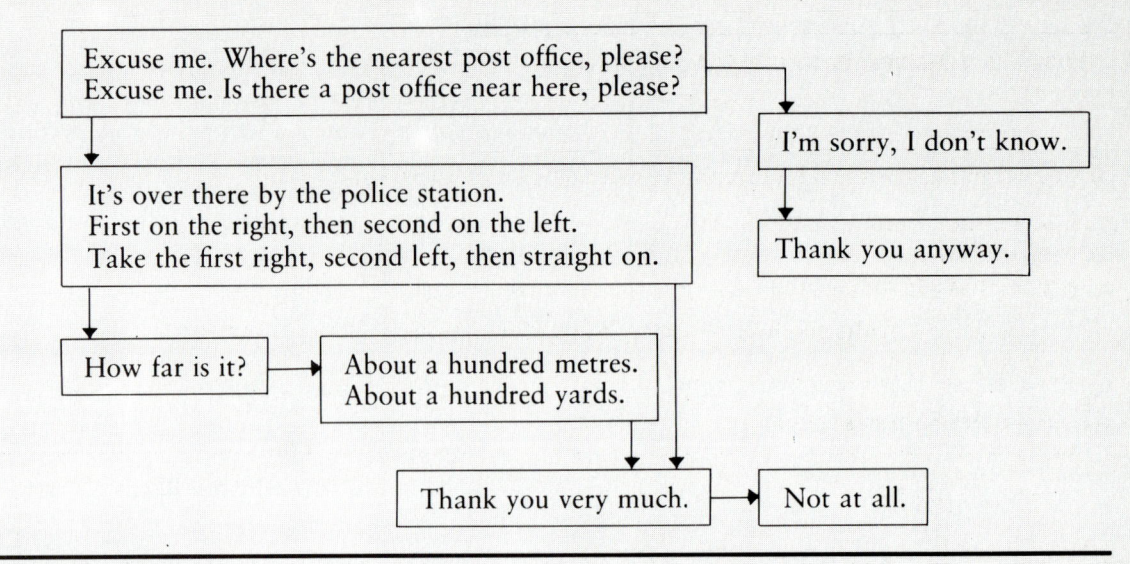

Excuse me. Where's the nearest post office, please?
Excuse me. Is there a post office near here, please?

→ I'm sorry, I don't know.
→ Thank you anyway.

It's over there by the police station.
First on the right, then second on the left.
Take the first right, second left, then straight on.

How far is it? → About a hundred metres.
About a hundred yards.

Thank you very much. → Not at all.

Words and expressions

Countable nouns
house, phone number, car, kilo
window, yard, weekend, lamp
door, swimming pool, newspaper, cup
stairs, home, language, apple
room, school, holiday, horse
flat, bed, gram, person (people)
street, breakfast, litre, word
road, lunch, price, cat
floor, supper, pound (£)
ground floor, bus, pence (p)

Uncountable nouns
time, light
work, rain
money, toothpaste
music, hair
snow, wine
ice, food

Countable or uncountable noun
glass

Verbs
work, stop
live, travel
take, read
like, play
hate, watch
love, listen to
dislike, try
have, understand
get up, cost
go, was/were
start

Adjectives
big
small
nearest
good
cheap
expensive
terrible

Adverbs
upstairs, not much
downstairs, not at all
there, never
here, sometimes
right, often
left, usually
straight on, always
then, out
far, still
only, yesterday
very much

Prepositions
for, by
next to, past
opposite, to
from, of
until, outside
at

Other words and expressions
nobody, It depends, Do you know?, any
everybody, interested in, I know, (too) much/many
both, but, Oh dear, enough
for ... yards/metres, half a ... of ..., some, a lot of

Optional words to learn
Rooms: bedroom; kitchen; bathroom; toilet; living room; wall; garage.
Furniture: furniture (*uncountable*); cooker; sofa; fridge; armchair; television; TV; cupboard; bath; wardrobe.
Places: phone box; supermarket; bank; post office; police station; car park; bus stop; station; railway station; bookshop; restaurant; hotel; church; chemist's.
Interests: maths; rock; science fiction; tennis; skiing; football; instrument; politics.
Food – countable: banana; egg; orange; tomato; chips.
– uncountable: fish; beer; bread; cheese; coffee; ice cream; milk; juice; rump steak; water.
– countable or uncountable: potato.
Other: police (*plural*); public; shaving cream; perfume.

8B What sort of house do you live in?

> Vocabulary (homes, habits); writing; listening.

1 How many words and expressions can you add to these lists?
1. kitchen, bedroom, ...
2. chair, table, ...
3. get up, have breakfast, ...

Now practise the pronunciation of the words and expressions you have written.

2 Write out Teresa's letter.

Dear Miriam,

Thank you for writing, and thank you for the photographs. Mark and Sarah are very pretty!

What sort of [house] do we live in? Well, it's not a [house], it's a [flat]. It's got 4 [bedrooms], 2 [bathrooms], a big [living room] and a big [kitchen]. There is a [park] just opposite our building where the [children] play.

You know Patricio and I both work. We [get up] at [time], and go to work by [bus]. Patricio [paints] [at time] and then [has lunch]. He works again in the afternoon, and [talks to people] at about [time]. I start [work] at [time], and [have lunch] at about [time]. I stop [work] [talking to people] at [time].

A young [woman] comes to look after the [children]. They [have breakfast] at about [time], and say [goodbye] to us. Then they have [lunch], and go to [the playground] in the [park]. They have [dinner] at about [time], and after [dinner] they go to [bed] until [time]. Then they have a bit of [bread] and [jam]. When Patricio and I get home we [play] with them for a while. We have [dinner] at about [time], and the children go to [bed] at [time]. When they are [asleep], Patricio and I [read] or [watch TV], or talk.

What sort of house do you live in? What do you do on Saturdays and Sundays? Please write soon.

All the best, *Teresa*

---

3 🔊 Listen and take notes. Then write Miriam's answer to Teresa.

8C Choose

> A choice of pronunciation, grammar, speaking and listening exercises.

Look at the exercises, decide which ones are useful to you, and do two or more.

PRONUNCIATION

1 Listen. How many words? (Contractions like *isn't* count as two words.)

2 Stress. A lot of words are stressed on the first syllable:

▣□ ▣□□ ▣□□□
armchair **any**way **su**permarket

but some words are stressed on the second syllable:

□▣ □▣□
a**bout** ba**na**na

and some words are stressed on the third syllable:

□□▣
under**stand**

How are these words stressed? Copy the box patterns and see if there are words for each pattern. Then pronounce the words.

cupboard   everybody   excuse   expensive
holiday   interested   kilo   language
newspaper   nobody   opposite   people
person   police   post office   potato
quarter   Saturday   second   seventh
tomato   Wednesday

3 Copy the sentences and underline the stressed syllables, check your answers with the recording, and pronounce the sentences.

1. There are some people at the reception desk.
2. There's some water on your book.
3. Are there any potatoes?
4. Is there any orange juice in the fridge?
5. How many people are there?
6. How much time is there?

GRAMMAR

1 Do you know the names of the things in the bags? Choose a bag; try to find out which bag another student has chosen. Examples:

'Are there any apples in your bag?'
'No, there aren't. Is there any milk in your bag?'
'Yes, there is.'
'How much?'
'A litre.'

first bag    *second bag*

third bag    *fourth bag*

2 Survey. Write three questions: one using *many*, one using *much* and one using *enough*. Walk round asking your questions and noting the answers. Report back to the class, or write the results down and ask your teacher to put them up where everybody can read them. Examples:

'How much television do you watch every week?' 'About three hours.'
'Do you think there are too many cars in this city?' 'No, I think there are too many bicycles.'
'Do you usually have enough time to read the newspaper?' 'Yes, I do.'

SPEAKING AND LISTENING

1 Choose: a sport, a sort of music, and a newspaper. Try to find somebody else in the class who has chosen the same things. Examples:

'Do you play football?'
'No, I don't. Do you like rock music?'
'Yes, I do. Do you read "Le Monde"?'
'Yes, I do.'

2 Match the abbreviations with their meanings, and practise their pronunciation.

Ave   Street
Dr   Road
Rd   Avenue
Sq   Square
St   Drive

Now look at the map and listen. What is the name of the street you arrive in at the end?

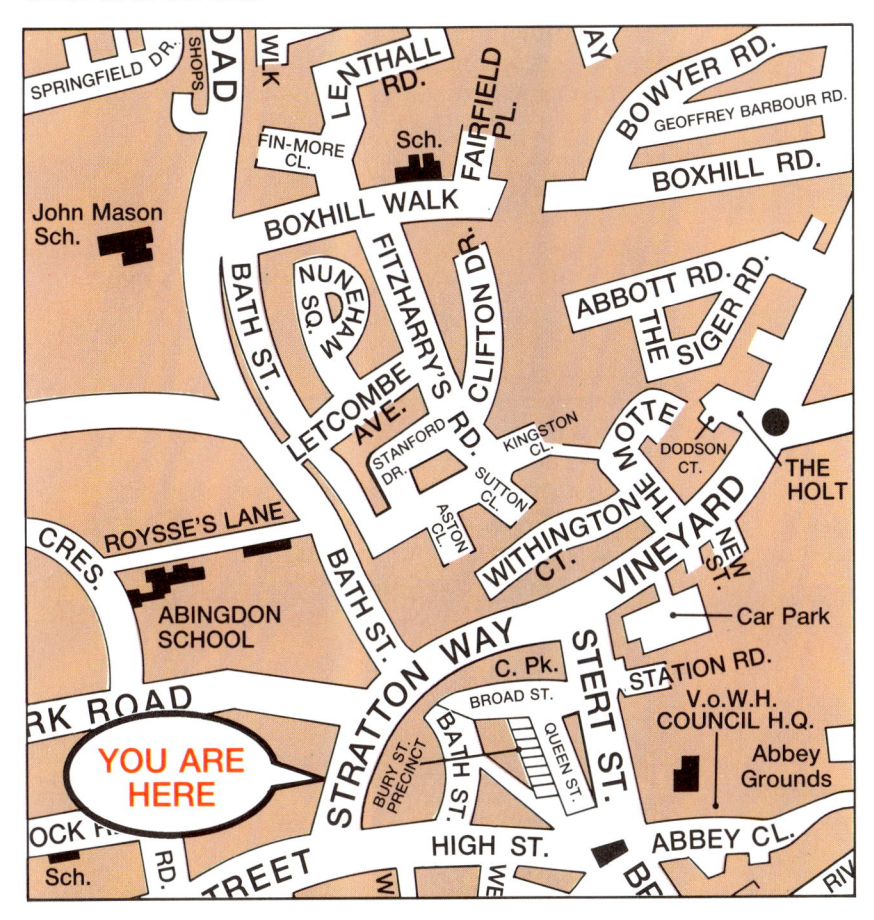

3 Look at the map again; listen to four people giving directions to 2 Clifton Drive. Are any of them wrong?

4 How many people can you fool? Give correct *or* wrong directions to a place in the town. Look at page 38 if you need help in giving directions.

5 Put a word or expression from the box into each blank in the song (you can use your dictionary). Then listen to see if you were right.

dance	everybody	feet
find	go	go	go	know
place	secret	secret
there's a	many	everybody
everybody	want

IF YOU CAN KEEP A SECRET

There's a club where I ...1... dancing,
So ...2... people you can meet.
There's a club where I ...3... dancing,
I get rhythm in my ...4....

Oh, ...5... wants to dance there,
But they don't ...6... where to go.
Oh, ...7... wants to jive there,
It's the very best ...8... I know.

If you can keep a ...9...,
I'll tell tell you where to ...10... the place.
If you can keep a ...11...,
We're going to ...12... the night away.

Well, ...13... wants to dance there . . .
There's a club where I ...14... dancing . . .

8D Test yourself

LISTENING

1 Dictation: listen and write down the conversation.

GRAMMAR

1 Make questions. Example:

where | you | live?

<u>Where do you live ?</u>

1. you | like | classical music?
2. where | your mother | work?

2 Complete the sentences.

1. My father always .... to work by bus. (*go*)
2. Both my parents .... on Saturdays. (*work*)
3. Have you got .... apples? (*some/any*)

3 Write the object pronouns and possessives. Example:

I <u>me, my</u>

you, he, she, we, they

4 Put in the correct words.

1. I live .... 17 Hazel Avenue, Dundee.
2. I live .... the fourth floor.
3. I usually get up .... six o'clock.
4. How .... people are there in your class?
5. How .... money have you got?
6. John and .... wife live in the next house to Marianne and .... husband.

5 Give the plurals. Example:

cat <u>cats</u>

man, woman, child, boy, secretary, person, name, address, wife, house

6 Give the *he/she/it* forms. Example:

get <u>gets</u>

play, live, try, watch, do

7 Put in *a*, *an*, *the*, *some* or – (= no article).

1. There's .... orange on the table.
2. There's .... cheese in the fridge.
3. My sister's .... student.
4. What time do you have .... lunch?
5. .... food is expensive.
6. Where's .... nearest post office, please?

VOCABULARY

1 Put four more words in each of these lists.

1. father, brother, . . .
2. Monday, . . .
3. first, second, . . .

2 Write the names of:

1. two big things
2. two small things
3. two cheap things
4. two expensive things

LANGUAGE IN USE

1 Write questions for these answers. Example:

Jean Sheppard. <u>What's your name ?</u>

1. Japan.
2. I'm 35.
3. 42 Feynman Road.
4. Twenty past seven.
5. First on the right, then second on the left.
6. About a hundred metres.
7. Seven six two, four three eight five.
8. I'm sorry, I don't know.

PRONUNCIATION

1 Which sound is different? Example:

like   by   ninth   (live)

1. door   floor   start   small
2. bread   reads   pence   very
3. work   third   person   hair

2 Which syllable is stressed? Example:

<u>brea</u>kfast

opposite, Saturday, sometimes, newspaper, understand

WRITING

> **PENFRIEND WANTED:**
> I am an Australian girl. I am 18. I like music, swimming and reading. I speak English and German. Please write to Anna Schultz, Box 31266, Sydney, Australia.

1 Read the advertisement and write a short letter to Anna Schultz. Tell her:
– your name, nationality and age
– what you do
– where you are from
– about your home and family
– about your interests.
Begin:
Dear Anna Schultz,
I am ...

SPEAKING

1 Interview the teacher. Ask him/her questions and fill in the form.

UNIVERSAL IMPORT/EXPORT

PERSONAL DETAILS

Name ....
Address ....
....
Telephone ....
Age ....
Married/Single/Divorced/Widowed ....
Children ....
Languages ....
House/Flat ....
Floor ....
How many bedrooms ....
How many people ....

2 Answer the teacher's questions.

Unit 9 Appearances

9A Sheila has got long dark hair

Have got; describing people.

1 Read the sentences in the box and complete the descriptions. Use your dictionary. Which name goes with which picture?

Sheila has got long dark hair.	Mary has not got grey hair.
Lucy has got short hair.	Sheila has not got blue eyes.
Mary has got green eyes.	Lucy has not got brown eyes or fair hair.

Sheila has got .... hair and .... eyes.
Mary .... got .... hair and ....
Lucy .... and ....

2 Copy and complete the table.

| I .... got |
| You have .... |
| He/She/It .... |
| We .... |
| They .... |

3 Ask the teacher questions.

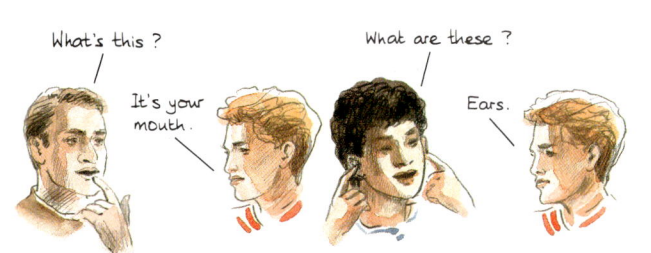

What's this? / It's your mouth.
What are these? / Ears.

4 Do what the teacher tells you. Then test other students. Do they know these words?

arm   ears   eyes   face   foot   hair   hand
left   leg   mouth   nose   right

Touch your right eye.
Touch your left ear.

5 Talk about yourself and other people. Example:

'I've got small hands. My mother's got pretty hair.'

Can you remember what other students said? Example:

'Maria's got brown eyes. Her father's got small ears.'

6 Write three sentences with *and*, and three with *but*. Ask the teacher for words. Examples:

I have got blue eyes, and my mother has, too. I have got straight hair, but Chris has got curly hair.

Learn: eye; nose; ear; mouth; face; arm; hand; foot (feet); leg; long; short; brown; green; blue; grey; these; What's this?; What are these?

9B A red sweater and blue jeans

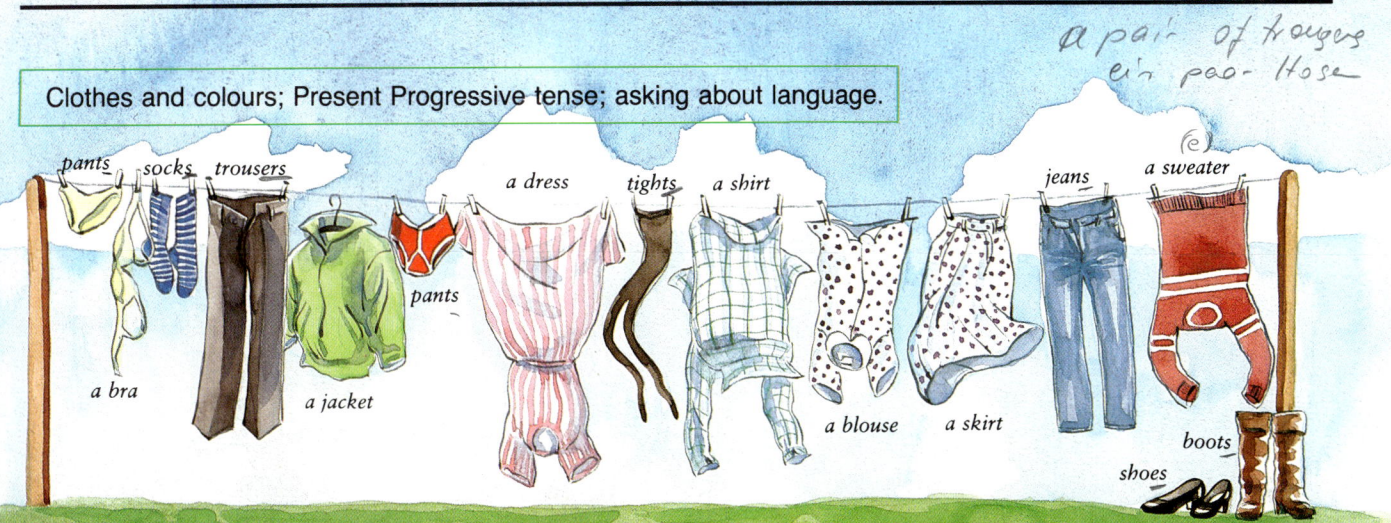

Clothes and colours; Present Progressive tense; asking about language.

pants socks trousers a dress tights a shirt jeans a sweater
a bra pants a jacket a blouse a skirt shoes boots

Red
Orange
Pink
Yellow
Green
Blue
Purple
Brown
Light Green
Dark Green
Light Blue
Dark Blue
Black
White

1 Can you find something red in the classroom? Something blue? Something orange? . . . Examples:

'This is red.'   'That's blue.'
'These are orange.'   'My book is red.'

2 Look at the pictures.

Pat is wearing a white sweater, a green blouse, and a red and black skirt.

Make some more sentences about Keith, Annie and Robert.

'Keith is wearing . . .'

Pat   Keith   Annie   Robert

3 Ask the teacher questions.

'What's this called in English?'
'What are these called?'
'How do you say *boucles d'oreille* in English?'   'Ear-rings.'
'How do you say *rosa*?'   'Pink.'
'How do you pronounce b-l-o-u-s-e?'

4 Listen to the recording and answer the questions.

'Are you wearing a sweater?'   'Yes, I am.'
'Who's wearing brown shoes?'   'I am.'

5 Look at another student. Then close your eyes and describe him/her. Example:

'Carlos is wearing blue jeans and a black shirt. I can't remember the colour of his shoes.'

6 Work with another student. One of you thinks of another person in the class. The other tries to find out who it is, in eight questions beginning *'Is he/she wearing . . . ?'* Example:

'It's a man.'
'Is he wearing jeans?'   'No, he isn't.'
'Is he wearing glasses?'   'Yes, he is.'

I am wearing	we are wearing
you are wearing	you are wearing
he/she is wearing	they are wearing

are you wearing?
is he/she wearing? *etc.*

Learn: *the names of the colours*; light; dark; colour; wear; something; that (= not this); (I can't) remember; What's this called?; What are these called?; How do you say . . . ?; How do you pronounce . . . ?

Learn four or more: pants; bra; sock; jeans; jacket; dress; tights; shirt; blouse; skirt; trousers; sweater; boot; shoe; glasses; bow tie; ear-rings.

9C I look like my father

> Simple Present questions, negatives; resemblances; *all* and *both*; skills practice.

1 Listen to the recording. Who is speaking? Read the text and put the names with the pictures.

| Alice   Ann   Joe   Philip   Alice's father   Alice's mother |
| Uncle George and family   Uncle Edward |

My name's Alice. I've got a sister (her name's Ann), and two brothers, Joe and Philip. We've all got fair hair and blue eyes, and we're all slim except Joe – he's very fat. Ann's very pretty, and she's got lots of boyfriends. I've only got one boyfriend: his name's Kevin, and he's very nice.

I look a bit like my father – I've got his long nose and big mouth – but I've got my mother's personality. Joe and Phil both look more like Mum.

We've got two uncles and an aunt. Uncle George and Aunt Agnes have got three young children. Uncle Edward is only thirteen, so he hasn't got any children, but he's got a rabbit.

2 What are your family like? Who looks like who? Examples:

'In my family we're all tall, and we all wear glasses.'
'Carlos and I have both got dark hair.'
'I look a bit like my father.'
'My brother looks very like me.'
'Ana looks quite like Aunt Maria.'
'I've got my mother's eyes, but I've got my father's personality.'

3 Listening for information. Copy the table. Then listen to the recording and fill in the table.

	HEIGHT	HAIR COLOUR	FACE	EYES	GOOD-LOOKING?
Steve's wife	5 ft 8				don't know
Lorna's mum			pale		
Ruth's friend					
Katy's son					
Sue's husband					

4 Prepare questions and answers for an interview. Examples:

How many people are there in your family?

Have you got any . . . ?   Yes, I have. / No, I haven't.
How many . . . have you got?
Has your . . . got any . . . ?   Yes, she has. / No, he hasn't.
How many . . . has your . . . got?

Do you look like . . . ?   Yes, I do. / No, I don't.
Who do you look like?
Does . . . look like . . . ?   Yes, he does. / No, she doesn't.

What colour is/are your . . .'s . . . ?
How old is . . . ?
Is . . . good-looking?   Yes, she is. / No, he isn't.

5 Interview another student and report to the class. Example:

'Carlos has got three brothers. They all look like their mother, but they've got their father's personality. His brother Diego has got four children . . .'

> **Learn:** uncle; aunt; look like; like; all; nice; except; a bit; more; lots of; What colour is/are . . . ?

9D Dear Mr Bell . . .

Skills practice; intonation.

1 Read the letter and look at the picture of Paul Sanders. Can you find two differences?

> Flat 6
> Monument House
> Castle Street
> Newcastle NE1 2HH
>
> September 12, 1990
>
> Dear Mr Bell,
>
> I am coming to Edinburgh by train next Tuesday, arriving at Waverley Station at 11.40 a.m. Can you meet me?
>
> I am sorry that I have not got a photograph, but here is a description. I am 32, quite short, with dark hair and a small beard. I have got blue eyes. I will be wearing a white shirt, a dark blue sweater and light grey trousers.
>
> I look forward to seeing you.
>
> Yours sincerely,
> Paul Sanders

> Mr J.C. Bell
> 366 Ulster Drive
> Edinburgh EH8 7BJ

2 Read the conversations and then listen to the three recordings with your books closed. Which is the correct recording?

'Hello, Mr Sanders. I'm John Bell. Did you have a good journey?'
'Not bad, thanks. But I'm not Mr Sanders.'
'Oh, I am sorry.'

'Paul Sanders?'
'Sorry.'

'Paul Sanders?'
'Yes. Hello. Mr Bell?'
'Yes, I'm John Bell. How was your journey?'
'Terrible.'
'Oh, I am sorry. Well, my car's outside. Let's go . . .'

3 Practise these sentences.

Paul Sanders?
Mr Bell?
Oh, I am sorry.

Now practise the conversations in groups of four.

4 You are going on a holiday or a business trip. Write a letter to a person you don't know, asking him/her to meet you at the station or airport, and giving a description of yourself. Sign the letter with a false name. Give your letter to the teacher.

5 The teacher will give you a letter. Read it, then go and meet the person who wrote it.

Learn: letter; train; station; journey; look (at); arrive (at); meet; next; short; bad; with; a.m.; p.m.; Dear . . . ; Yours sincerely; Let's go.

Unit 10 Wanting things

10A I'm hungry

Feelings; places; be and have; sentences with when.

1 Put the adjectives with the right pictures. Use your dictionary.

hungry   tired   ill   happy   cold   dirty   bored   unhappy   thirsty   hot

1. She is 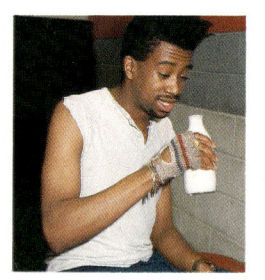 ....   2. He is  ....   3. She is  ....   4. He is  ....   5. She is ....

6. He is  ....   7. She is  ....   8. He is  ....   9. She is 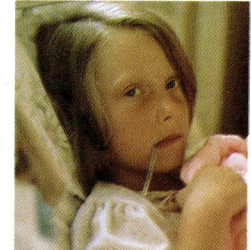 ....   10. She is ....

2 Say how you feel now. Examples:

'I'm very hungry.'
'I'm quite tired.'
'I'm a bit cold.'
'I'm not very happy.'
'I'm not at all thirsty.'

3 Mime one of the adjectives for the class.

You're unhappy.

4 Say these words and expressions.

hungry   happy   unhappy
house   home   at home
hotel   Hilton Hotel   holiday
on holiday   hair   have   half
hundred   a hundred   him
her

5 Have you got a good memory? Look at the sentences for two minutes. Then close your book and answer the teacher's questions.

When Fred's hungry he goes to a restaurant.
When Lucy's hungry she has bread and cheese.
When Fred's thirsty he has a beer.
When Lucy's thirsty she has a drink of water.
When Fred's bored he goes to the cinema.
When Lucy's bored she goes to see friends.
When Fred's hot he goes to the swimming pool.
When Lucy's hot she has a drink of water.
When Fred's dirty he has a bath.
When Lucy's dirty she has a shower.
When Fred's happy he goes shopping.
When Lucy's happy she telephones all her friends.
When Fred's unhappy he goes to bed.
When Lucy's unhappy she goes shopping.
When Fred's ill he goes to the doctor.
When Lucy's ill she goes to bed.

6 What do you do when you're happy, unhappy, tired, bored, etc.?

7 You're in one of these places. Do a mime; the class will say where you are.

at a swimming pool   at a disco   at a restaurant
in bed   in the bathroom   at a car park
at the doctor's   at the dentist's   at a supermarket
at a clothes shop   at home   at school
at a bus stop   at a station   at a hotel

> **Learn:** water; hungry; thirsty; hot; cold; happy; unhappy; bored; tired; ill; dirty; not at all (*with adjectives*); when (*conjunction*); (have a) bath; (have a) shower; go shopping.
>
> **Learn some of these if you want:** restaurant; hotel; cinema.

10B Have you got anything in blue?

> How to buy clothes and shoes; *a ... one*.

1 Here are three conversations (two in clothes shops, one in a shoe shop). Match the sentences to their places in the conversations.

a. I'm just looking.
b. Can I help you?

1. a
2. b

---

a. Here's a lovely one.
b. What size?
c. Yes, I'm looking for a sweater.
d. Well, yellow doesn't really suit me. Have you got anything in blue?
e. Can I help you?

f. Can I try them on?
g. Here's a nice one in blue. And here's another one.
h. £23.99.
i. Yes, of course.
j. How much are they?

1. e
2. c
3. b
4. Fourteen.
5. a
6. d
7. g
8. i
9. f
10. h
11. j

---

a. These are a bit small. Have you got them in a larger size?
b. Yes, these fit very well. I'll take them, please.
c. No, I'm afraid I haven't. Would you like to try these?
d. I'll just see.
e. Yes, please.

2 🔊 Listen to the three conversations. Use your dictionary or ask your teacher about the new words. Then practise the customer's part in each conversation.

3 Change things (clothes, colours, sizes) in the second conversation and practise the new conversation with another student.

Men's clothes				
British	37–38	39–40	41–42	43–44
Continental	94–97	99–102	104–107	109–112
American	38	40	42	44

Men's shoes						
British	7	8	9	10	11	12	13
Continental	41	42	43	44	45½	47	48
American	8	9	10	11	12	13	14

Women's clothes						
British	10	12	14	16	18	20	22
Continental	38	40	42	44	46	48	50
American	8	10	12	14	16	18	20

Women's shoes						
British	3	4	5	6	7	8	9
Continental	35½	36½	38	39½	40½	42	43
American	4½	5½	6½	7½	8½	9½	10½

> **Learn:** size; shop (*noun*); clothes; help; look for; try (on); take; large; other; another; anything; really; I'm afraid; well; Can I ...?; a ... one; Would you like?
>
> **Choose two or more other words or expressions from the lesson to learn.**

10C Buying things

> Prepositions; *this, that, these, those*; the language of shopping.

1 Look at the picture on page 133 for three minutes. Then:
a. write down the names of all the things you can remember (time limit two minutes).
b. look at the picture again and complete the following sentences.
c. write two more sentences about the picture.

1. There is a .... in front of the ....
2. There is a .... on the ....
3. There are some .... under the ....
4. There is a .... outside the ....
5. The .... is by the ....
6. The .... is behind the ....
7. The .... is in the ....
8. The .... is between the .... and the ....

2 Practise saying these sentences. Put them with the right pictures.

How much is this?   This is nice.
How much are these?   I like these.
How much is that?   I don't like that very
How much are those?   much.
                          Those aren't very nice.

3 Listening to fast speech. How many words are there in each sentence? What are they? (Contractions like *there's* count as two words.)

4 Can you put the beginnings and ends of the sentences together? Do you know all the expressions?

How much is   for some coffee.
How much are   nice colour!
I'm looking   looking.
I'm just   you?
Can I look   these shoes?
What a   round?
What nice   that dictionary?
Can I help   size?
Sorry – we've got   trousers!
What   nothing in blue.

* * *

I'd like to look   us, please?
Would you like   grams of blue cheese.
Can I   colour.
I'd like 500   try it on?
I like this   at some watches.
I'll take   to try it on?
Have you got anything   them.
Can you help   a red one.
I'd like   in blue?

5 Work with one or two other students. Prepare a conversation in a shop, in which somebody tries to buy something unusual. Use some of the expressions from Exercises 2 and 4.

> **Learn:** thing; watch (*noun*); buy; those; behind; between; in front of; us; nothing; Can I look round?; How much is/are . . . ?; What (a) nice . . . !; I'd like (to).
>
> **Choose two or more other words or expressions from the lesson to learn.**

10D Travelling

> The language of travelling.

1 Look at the four conversations. Which conversation goes with which picture?

1. TRAVELLER: I'd like .... singles to Norwich, ...
   CLERK: .... £26.40, ...
   TRAVELLER: Twenty-six pounds, ten, twenty, ..., forty.
   CLERK: ....
   TRAVELLER: ....

2. TRAVELLER: .... time is the .... train to Oxford, please?
   CLERK: There's one .... 3.45, change .... Didcot, arriving .... Oxford .... 5.04, or there's a direct .... at 3.49, arriving .... 4.50.
   TRAVELLER: .... platform for the 3.49?
   CLERK: .... 6.
   TRAVELLER: .... much.

3. CLERK: How would you like it?
   TRAVELLER: .... ?
   CLERK: How would you like it?
   TRAVELLER: I'm ...., I don't .... Could you .... more slowly, please?
   CLERK: How would you .... your money? In tens?
   TRAVELLER: Oh, er, four fives and the rest .... tens, ...
   CLERK: Fifty, one, two, three and twenty pence. And here's your receipt.
   TRAVELLER: Thank you.

4. RECEPTIONIST: Can I .... you?
   TRAVELLER: Yes, I'd .... a room, please.
   RECEPT.: Single or double?
   TRAVELLER: Single, please.
   RECEPT.: For .... night?
   TRAVELLER: No, two nights.
   RECEPT.: With bath .... with shower?
   TRAVELLER: With bath, please. How much .... the room?
   RECEPT.: £68 a night, including breakfast.
   TRAVELLER: Can I pay by credit card?
   RECEPT.: Yes, of .... We take American Express, Access or Visa. Could you register, please?
   TRAVELLER: .... ?
   RECEPT.: Could you fill in the form, ... ?
   TRAVELLER: Oh, yes.
   RECEPT.: Your room .... is 403. Have a good stay.
   TRAVELLER: ....

A

B

C

D

2 🎧 Choose one or more of the conversations to study. What are the missing words, do you think? Listen to the recording and complete the conversation with your teacher's help. Then ask the teacher about the new words, or find them in a dictionary.

3 Practise your conversation with another student.

4 Think of some other things to say in the same situation. Ask the teacher.

5 Change as many things as possible in your conversation; write and practise a new conversation for the same situation.

> **Learn:** which; Could you speak more slowly, please?
>
> **Choose ten or more other words and expressions to learn.**

Unit 11 People's pasts

11A She never studied . . .

People's past lives; Simple Past tense.

	ANGELA	SARAH
school	✗ 4 schools ages 11–16	♥ one school ages 11–16
studied	before exams until age 14	every day
music	rock	classical
instrument	guitar	violin
TV	science fiction, cartoons	news, historical dramas
sport	snooker	tennis
age 16	rock group	bank, string quartet
ages 16–20	4 different rock groups	the same bank, the same string quartet
now	rock star	deputy manager at bank, string quartet
income	£1,000,000/year	£22,000/year

1 Look at the chart and find any new words in your dictionary. Then try to complete the text; use the chart, and the words in the box. Listen to check your answers.

> changed   hated   listened   played
> started   stopped   studied   watched

When Angela was younger, she ...1... school. She ...2... schools three times between the ages of 11 and 16. She never ...3... except before exams, and she ...4... studying altogether when she was fourteen. At home, she ...5... to rock music and ...6... science fiction and cartoons on TV. In the evenings and at weekends, she ...7... the guitar, or ...8... snooker with friends.

When she was sixteen, she ...9... a rock group. She was in four different rock groups in the next four years.

Now Angela is a rock star, and she earns £1,000,000 a year. She says, 'I love my work, but I'm sorry I ...10... studying at school.'

2 Look at the way to write regular past tenses:

1. Most regular verbs:
   listen + **ed** = listen**ed**
2. Verb ending in e:
   hate + **d** = hate**d**
3. Short verbs ending in consonant + vowel + consonant:
   stop + **ped** = stop**ped**
4. Verbs ending in consonant + y:
   stud~~y~~ + **ied** = stud**ied**

Now write about Sarah's past, working from the chart. Your teacher can help you with any new words you need.

3 Say these regular past tense verbs.

1. arrived   lived   listened   played   studied
2. disliked   helped   liked   pronounced   watched
3. depended   hated   started

4 Copy the grid in Exercise 1 and write notes about some of your own past. You can change things, or add different notes and pictures if you want.

5 Take another student's notes and tell the class about his or her past. Don't say the student's name!

> When this person was younger, she quite liked school, except for languages. She started a job in a hospital in 1985 ...

> Is it Dolores?

Learn: thousand; million; news (*uncountable*); income; day; sport; earn; study; change; different; the same; before; every.

11B When I was a small child . . .

People's childhoods; *was* and *were*.

1 Use your dictionary to read the first text and complete the other texts (blanks can mean one or more words). Practise reading some of the sentences.

1. A Zulu speaks:
'I was born in a brick house in Soweto, near Johannesburg in South Africa. We were poor. My mother was a maid and my father was a factory worker. He died when I was six. I was always hungry, and nearly always unhappy, when I was a small child. Life was very hard. White people were terrible to us.'

2. A Maori speaks:
'I .... born in a wooden house in a village near Rotorua in New Zealand. We .... not poor, but we .... not rich. My mother and father .... farmers. I .... never hungry when I .... a small child; I .... quite happy, really. Life .... not hard, but white people .... not always kind to me.'

3. A Dakota Indian speaks:
'............ in a cloth *tipi* near Sisseton, South Dakota .... United States. .... poor. .... farmers. .... sometimes hungry .... a small child, but .... happy. My mother .... good cook, and my father .... good teacher. .... hard, and white people .... not usually .... us.'

2 Copy the grid; then listen to the three people and complete it.

NAME	AGE	BROTHERS	SISTERS	PLACE OF BIRTH	CHILDHOOD
Adrian Webber				India England Edinburgh	varied and quite happy very unhappy very happy
Lorna Higgs				Austria Oslo Oxford	quite miserable quite interesting quite mixed, really
Sue Ward				Tadcaster Manchester Hong Kong	very unhappy very happy varied and happy

3 How many questions can you make?

When you were a small child,

| was
were | you
your parents
life
you and your family
your mother
your father
your school
other people | happy
ever hungry
hard
poor
rich
at home from 9 to 5
out a lot
good
kind to you | ? |

4 Choose one question from Exercise 3, and ask as many people as you can; or make up your own question. Begin: '*When you were a small child, was/were . . .*' Examples:

'*When you were a small child, were you happy?*'
'*Yes, I was.*' / '*No, I wasn't.*' / '*I was quite happy.*'

Past tense of *be*

I was	was I?	I was not (wasn't)
you were	were you?	you were not (weren't)
he/she/it was	was he/she/it?	he/she/it was not (wasn't)
we were	were we?	we were not (weren't)
you were	were you?	you were not (weren't)
they were	were they?	they were not (weren't)

Learn: life; village; (was/were) born; die; poor; rich; hard; kind (to); nearly.

11C They didn't drink tea

> Life in the past; Simple Past tense negatives and questions; *ago*.

1 These pictures show life in the country in Europe 500 years ago. Make fifteen sentences about people who lived in Europe, or in your country, at that time; use *didn't*, *wasn't* and *weren't*. Examples:

'Five hundred years ago, they didn't drink tea.'
'They didn't have passports.'
'They didn't know about America five hundred years ago.'
'Most people weren't very tall.'
'There wasn't any paper money.'

2 Write seven sentences about changes in your life. Read one or two of them to the class. Examples:

I didn't like cheese when I was a small child, but now I do.
I played tennis when I was ten, but now I don't.
We didn't have a television then, but now we've got one.
There weren't any pocket calculators then, but now there are millions of them.

3 Work in groups. Write a questionnaire to find out about life forty or fifty years ago in the country where you are studying. Then find some older people and get answers to your questions. Examples:

1. *How did children travel to school fifty years ago?*
2. *Did your family have a television?*
3. *What was your favourite sport?*

Report the results of your questionnaire back to the class.

Simple Past tense		
I changed	did I change?	I did not (didn't) change
you changed	did you change?	you did not (didn't) change
he/she/it changed	did she *etc.* change?	he *etc.* did not (didn't) change
we changed	did we change?	we did not (didn't) change
you changed	did you change?	you did not (didn't) change
they changed	did they change?	they did not (didn't) change

> **Learn:** tea; passport; paper; pocket; calculator; year; America; Europe; know about (knew); most; favourite; then; now; ago.

11D Danced till half past one

> Talking about past events; Simple Past of irregular verbs.

1 Match the present and past forms of these irregular verbs.

go   tell   get   can   do   come   hear   (wake)   have   say   know
(woke)   could   went   heard   said   told   came   had   did   got   knew

2 Close your book and listen to the dialogue. See how much you can remember. Then read the dialogue and the text. Ask your teacher about new words.

May 14 Tuesday

Lovely time with Frank at the disco. Danced till half past one. Then went to his place for a drink. We kissed a bit. Got home at 3 a.m. again. Couldn't find my key, so climbed in through a window. V. tired this morning. Daddy asked a lot of stupid questions, as usual.

FATHER: What time did you come home last night, then, June?
JUNE: Oh, I don't know. About half past twelve, I think.
FATHER: Half past twelve? I didn't hear you.
JUNE: Well, I came in quietly. I didn't want to wake you up.
FATHER: You didn't go to that damned disco, did you?
JUNE: Disco, Daddy? Oh, no. You know I don't like loud music. No, I went to a folk concert with Alice and Mary. It was very good. There was one singer . . .
FATHER: Why did you come back so late? The concert didn't go on till midnight, did it?
JUNE: No, but we went to Alice's place and had coffee, and then we started talking about politics, you know. Alice's boyfriend – he's the President of the Students' Union Conservative Club . . .

3 Find the differences. Example:

June said (that) she went to a folk concert, but actually she went to a disco.
OR: June told her father (that) she...

4 Turn to the page that your teacher tells you. Write ONLY the other half of the conversation. Then find a partner and practise the new conversation.

> **Learn:** tell (told); come (came); say (said); ask; kiss; want; get (got); get home; hear (heard); wake up (woke); talk; last night; late; again; actually; this morning; why.

Unit 12 Consolidation

12A Things to remember: Units 9, 10 and 11

Present Progressive tense
I'**m looking** for a blue sweater.
'**Are** George and Tom **wearing** their blue jackets?'
  'Yes, they **are**.' / 'No, they **aren't**.'

Simple Past tense

I stopped	did I stop?	I did not (didn't) stop
you stopped	did you stop?	you did not (didn't) stop
he/she/it stopped	did she *etc.* stop?	he *etc.* did not (didn't) stop
we stopped	did we stop?	we did not (didn't) stop
you stopped	did you stop?	you did not (didn't) stop
they stopped	did they stop?	they did not (didn't) stop
the cars stopped	did the cars stop?	the cars did not (didn't) stop

Examples:
When Angela was younger, she **hated** school.
I **didn't like** cheese when I was a small child, but I do now.
  (~~I liked not cheese ... I not liked cheese ... I didn't liked cheese ...~~)
'**Did** your family **have** a television when you were a child?' 'Yes, we **did**.' / 'No, we **didn't**.'
'**Did** you **like** school when you were a child?' 'Yes, I **did**.' (~~'Yes, I liked.'~~)

Spelling of regular verbs
1. Most regular verbs:
   listen + **ed** = listen**ed**
2. Verbs ending in -*e*:
   hate + **d** = hate**d**
3. Short verbs ending in one vowel + one consonant:
   stop + **ped** = stop**ped**
4. Verbs ending in consonant + -*y*:
   stud~~y~~ + **ied** = stud**ied**

Pronunciation of regular verbs
1. /d/ after vowels and /b/, /l/, /g/, /v/, /ð/, /z/, /ʒ/, /m/, /n/, /ŋ/, /dʒ/
2. /t/ after /p/, /k/, /tʃ/, /f/, /θ/, /s/, /ʃ/
3. /ɪd/ after /t/ and /d/

Which verbs learnt so far are irregular?

Infinitive	Past tense	Infinitive	Past tense	Infinitive	Past tense
be	was, were	have got	had	sit down	sat down
can	could	know	knew (/nju:/)	speak	spoke
come	came	mean	meant (/ment/)	take	took
cost	cost	meet	met	tell	told
do	did	read	read (/red/)	think	thought (/θɔ:t/)
get	got	say	said (/sed/)	understand	understood
go	went	see	saw (/sɔ:/)	wear	wore
have	had				

The past tense of *be*: *was* and *were*

I was	was I?	I was not (wasn't)
you were	were you?	you were not (weren't)
he/she/it was	was she *etc.*?	he *etc.* was not (wasn't)
we were	were we?	we were not (weren't)
you were	were you?	you were not (weren't)
they were	were they?	they were not (weren't)

Examples:
'When you **were** a small child, **were** you happy?'
  'Yes, I **was**.' / 'No, I **wasn't**.' / 'I **was** quite happy.'
We **weren't** poor, but we **weren't** rich.
My mother **was** a good cook.
It **was** very good. There **was** one singer ...

Pronunciation
We were (/wə/) **poor**. I was (/wəz/) always **hungry**.
Were (/wə/) you ever **hungry**?
Yes, I was (/wɒz/). No, I wasn't (/'wɒznt/).
Were (/wə/) your parents **poor**?
Yes, they were (/wɜ:/). No, they weren't (/wɜ:nt/).

Have and has; be and have

| I have |
| you have |
| she/he/it has |
| we have |
| you have |
| they have |

Examples:
When Lucy **is** hungry she **has** bread and cheese.
 (~~When Lucy has hungry . . .~~ ~~. . . she takes bread . . .~~)
When I**'m** thirsty I **have** a glass of orange juice.
 (~~When I have thirsty . . .~~ ~~. . . I've a glass . . .~~)
When I**'m** dirty I **have** a bath / a shower.
What colour **are** her eyes?

Examples:
This cheese is terrible.
These tomatoes are very nice.
'I like **those** ear-rings.' 'Thank you!'
How much is **that**?

When

When Fred's hungry he goes to a restaurant.
When Lucy's dirty she has a shower.

Tell and say

June **told** her father she went to a folk concert.
OR June **told** her father that she went to a folk concert.
 (~~June said her father she went to a folk concert.~~)
June **said** she went to Alice's place.
OR June **said** that she went to Alice's place.
 (~~June told that she went to Alice's place.~~)

Both and all

We **both** wear glasses.
We've **both** got red cars.
We're **all** tall.
They've **all** got dark hair.

Asking about English

'What's this?' 'It's an umbrella.'
'What are these?' 'Train tickets.'
What's this called in English?
'How do you say *arroyo* in English?' 'I can't remember.'
How do you pronounce k-n-e-w?
Could you speak more slowly, please?

Appearances and clothes

Lucy has got short grey hair and blue eyes.
Pat is wearing a white sweater and a green blouse.
My sister looks very like my mother; I look more like my aunt.
What colour eyes has your mother got?
'Who do you look like?' 'I look a bit like my father.'
I've got my mother's eyes, but I've got my father's personality.

Shopping

'Can I help you?' 'I'm just looking.'
'I'm looking for a sweater.' 'Here's a lovely one.'
What a lovely sweater! (~~What lovely sweater!~~)
What nice shoes!
Those aren't very nice. I don't like that very much.
Can I look round?
Can I try them on?
'Have you got anything in black?' 'I'll just see.'
'No, I'm afraid I haven't. Would you like to try these?' (~~Would you like try these?~~)
How much are they? How much is it?
I'll take them, please.
I'd like a red one.
I'd like to look at some watches.
 (~~I'd like look at some watches.~~)

Writing formal letters

Castle Street
Newcastle NE1 2HH
September 12, 1990

Dear Mr Bell,

I am arriving at Waverley Station, Edinburgh . . .

. . .

I look forward to seeing you.

Yours sincerely,

Paul Sanders

12A continued

Words and expressions

Countable nouns

eye	aunt	watch
nose	letter	income
ear	train	day
mouth	station	life
face	journey	village
arm	bath	passport
hand	shower	pocket
foot (feet)	size	calculator
leg	shop	year
colour	clothes	America
uncle	thing	Europe

Uncountable nouns
water
news
tea

Countable or uncountable nouns
paper
sport

Adjectives

long	white	tired
short	nice	ill
brown	next	dirty
green	short	large
blue	bad	different
grey	hungry	the same
red	thirsty	poor
pink	hot	rich
orange	cold	hard
yellow	happy	kind (to)
purple	unhappy	favourite
black	bored	

Verbs

wear (wore)	buy (bought)	say (said)
remember	earn	ask
look like	study	kiss
look (at)	change	want
arrive (at)	was/were born	get (got)
meet (met)	die	get home
help	know about (knew)	hear (heard)
look for	tell (told)	wake up (woke)
try (on)	come (came)	talk
take (took)		

Adverbs

light	then
dark	now
more	ago
a bit	last night
not at all	this morning
really	late
well	again
nearly	actually

Prepositions
like
except
with
behind
between
in front of
before

Other words and expressions

us	those	million	have a shower
something	lots of	What colour is/are . . . ?	go shopping
anything	other	a.m.	Let's go
nothing	another	p.m.	a . . . one
all	every	when	which
that	most	have a bath	why
these	thousand		

Optional words and expressions to learn
pants; bra; sock; jeans; jacket; dress; tights; shirt; blouse; skirt; trousers; sweater; boot; shoe; glasses; bow tie; ear-rings; restaurant; hotel; cinema.

12B On Saturday

> Writing.

1 Write about what you did on Saturday. Then read another student's writing; say one good thing about it and ask one question. Examples:

'You play tennis – that's interesting. Where did you go shopping?'
'Where do you work on Saturdays? I liked that film, too.'

2 Turn to page 133 and look at the story. Notice how these words and expressions are used.

| and | and then | but | in the afternoon |
| in the evening | until | when | |

Now look at your own text (from Exercise 1) and see if you can put in any words from the box.

3 Look at the pictures and notes, and write a story. Use your imagination; and put in some words from the box in Exercise 2.

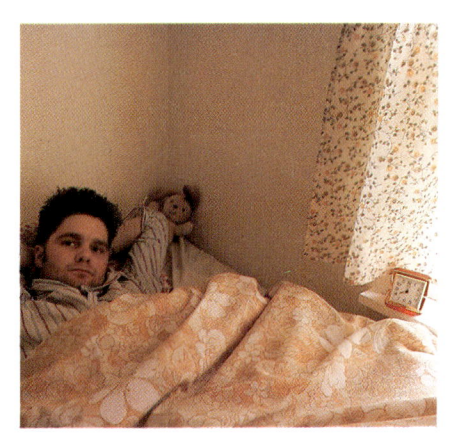

woke up at 8
didn't get up until 9
shower, breakfast, newspaper
met friend in park
post office, lunch with friend
television
swimming pool
cinema

12C Choose

> A choice of pronunciation, listening and speaking exercises.

Look at the exercises, decide which ones are useful to you, and do two or more.

PRONUNCIATION

1 Difficult words. Can you pronounce all of these?

/ð/:	the there then mother brother with this that these those
/θ/:	thank thirty thirsty Thursday third three thousand
/ɪz/:	watches oranges languages villages buses houses
/ʌ/:	brother son mother love money some once young touch cupboard
/ɪ/:	English women orange village
/e/:	many any friend sweater breakfast
/aɪ/:	night light right write eye quiet
/ɔː/:	daughter quarter water you're sure
(l):	half could
(various problems):	child woman people tired wrong watch year enough aunt listen

Ask your teacher how to pronounce other words.

How do you pronounce t-h-r-o-u-g-h?

Is this correct: "Zaturday"?

LISTENING

1 🔊 Listening for information. Listen to the telephone conversations.

Who do you think saw Peter Anderson – the first caller (Mrs Collins), the second (Mr Sands), or the third (Mr Harris)?

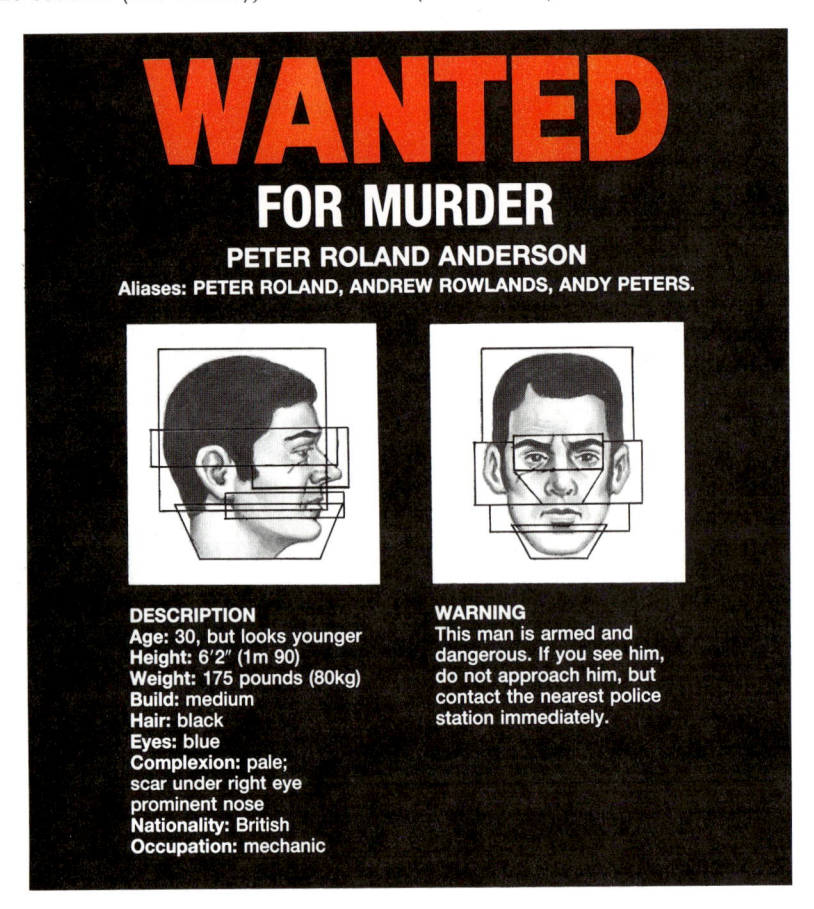

WANTED FOR MURDER

PETER ROLAND ANDERSON

Aliases: PETER ROLAND, ANDREW ROWLANDS, ANDY PETERS.

DESCRIPTION
Age: 30, but looks younger
Height: 6'2" (1m 90)
Weight: 175 pounds (80kg)
Build: medium
Hair: black
Eyes: blue
Complexion: pale; scar under right eye prominent nose
Nationality: British
Occupation: mechanic

WARNING
This man is armed and dangerous. If you see him, do not approach him, but contact the nearest police station immediately.

2 🔊 Put *I*, *I'm*, *I've*, *you*, *your* or *me* into each blank in the song; listen to the song. Close your book and try to remember.

PLEASE WRITE

.... wonder what you're doing now.
Are .... making a new friend?
.... got to see .... again somehow.
.... don't want this love to end.
Oh baby, please write.
Why don't .... write?
.... waiting to get .... letter, baby.

Please write.
Why don't .... write?
It means so much to ....

.... tried to call .... on the phone,
But nobody knew .... name.
Oh, ... can feel .... love run cold.
But listen to what I'm saying, baby.

SPEAKING

1 Work in groups of 3–4 people. Tell the others what you did yesterday evening or last weekend. You must speak for two minutes. You must tell the group one thing that is not true. See if they can tell you what it is.

Then I went to see my old friend the President ...

Not true !!!

2 Work in groups. Show the other students photos of your family and friends, and talk about them.

This is my sister. She's 23.
This is my mother.
What nice eyes!
She's very pretty.
This is my brother. He's got blue eyes.
Who's that?

3 What are you wearing?
1. Do you know the names of all the different clothes you are wearing? Check up.
2. Observe another student for one minute. Then turn your back and try to say everything that he/she is wearing.

4 Revision sketch. Work in groups of 4–6. Roles:

Mr Harris
Mrs Harris
Their child Alex
Bank manager
Wanted man or woman
Policeman or policewoman

Write and practise a sketch, using the English you have learnt in Units 1–11. In your sketch, you must use five or more of these sentences:

First on the right, second on the left.
It's terrible.
I'm hungry.
Two boys and a girl.
I quite like it.
Tall, dark and good-looking.
What time is the next train?
Hands up!

12D Test yourself

LISTENING

1 Listen to the conversation and choose the correct answers.

1. Phone number: (a) 67482   (b) 64482   (c) 61483
2. Caller's name: (a) Mary   (b) Helen   (c) Sally
3. Caller asks for: (a) Mary   (b) Helen   (c) Sally
4. Film is at: (a) 7.15   (b) 7.45   (c) 7.00
5. Name of film: (a) *Gone with the Wind*   (b) *Ben Hur*   (c) *King Kong*
6. Cinema is in: (a) Oxford   (b) Cambridge   (c) London
7. Meet at: (a) station   (b) cinema   (c) pub

2 Listen to the conversation and answer the questions.

1. What colour are the woman's ear-rings?
2. What colour are her eyes?
3. Is her hair short or long?

GRAMMAR

1 Put the words in order. Example:

school where you to go did ?
Where did you go to school?

1. brother got blue has your eyes ?
2. glasses wear we both .
3. tired they very are all .

2 Choose the correct word.

1. My sister *is/has* got very long hair.
2. What colour *are/have* your eyes?
3. *Are/Have* you cold?
4. When I *am/have* dirty I *am/have* a bath.

3 Give the past of these verbs. Examples:

like *liked*   go *went*

1. stop, play, hate, study, work, live
2. come, know, say, see, speak, take

4 Make these sentences negative. Example:

I hated my school.
I did not hate my school.

1. I liked cheese when I was a child.
2. Peter got up at ten o'clock yesterday.
3. My mother was a teacher.

5 Make questions. Example:

They lived in Ireland. (*Where . . . ?*)
Where did they live?

1. She got up at six o'clock. (*What time . . . ?*)
2. We played football at school. (*Did . . . ?*)

6 Ask for more information. Example:

Chris likes music. (*What sort . . . ?*)
What sort (of music) does she like?

1. I saw Alice yesterday. (*Where . . . ?*)
2. I've got two brothers. (*. . . sisters?*)
3. Lucy's coming to see us. (*When . . . ?*)

7 Put in *this, that, these* or *those*.

1. 'Which ones do you want?' '............ blue ones over there.'
2. Look at .... new car in front of Anne's house.
3. Are you at home .... evening?

VOCABULARY

1 Put four more words in each of these lists.

1. tall, nice, . . .
2. red, green, . . .
3. trousers, shirt, . . .
4. living room, . . .
5. eye, foot, . . .
6. station, bank, . . .

2 Write the names of:

1. four things that you like
2. four things that you don't like

LANGUAGE IN USE

1 Write questions for these answers. Example:

Mary Lewis. <u>What's your name ?</u>

1. £3.75
2. It's an umbrella.
3. They're train tickets.
4. Blue.
5. I'm just looking.
6. Yes, of course.
7. I'm afraid I haven't.
8. No, I don't.
9. I'm sorry, I can't remember.

PRONUNCIATION

1 Which word is different? Example:

like   by   ninth   (live)

1. size   grey   life   eye
2. buy   tired   rich   kind
3. wear   ear   hear   nearly
4. earn   third   where   dirty
5. purple   thirsty   journey there

2 Which syllable is stressed? Example:

<u>break</u>fast

colour; income; village; passport; calculator; America; Europe; remember; arrive; orange; different; favourite; except; behind; between; before; something; another; thousand; actually.

WRITING

1 Write this letter with all the lines in the right places.

Yours sincerely,
Can you meet me?
Dear Mrs Anderson,
37 Lucerne Road
Thank you very much for your letter.
Peter Morris
Edinburgh EH9 7BK
I am arriving at Newton Station
   at 9.35 a.m. next Saturday.
14 January 1990

SPEAKING

1 Act out this conversation. Your teacher will take the other part.

CLOTHES SHOP
Go into a clothes shop and ask the price of the blue sweater in the shop window. Ask to try it on. It is too big. Try another one. It's OK. Ask if they have any other colours. Choose a colour and buy the sweater.

Unit 13 Differences

13A I can sing, but I can't draw

Can and *can't* for abilities.

1 Which of these things can you do? Which of them can't you do? Example:

'I can sing, but I can't draw.'

> draw   drive   make cakes
> play chess   play tennis
> play the violin   run a mile
> see well without glasses
> sing   speak Chinese
> speak German   type

2 🔊 Say these sentences after the recording.

1. I can **sing**.
2. I **can't** draw.
3. I can **type**.
4. **Yes**, I can.
5. **No**, I can't.

3 Can you swim / cook / play the piano / dance / go without sleep / sleep in the daytime? Ask two other people, and report their answers to the class. Make sentences with *but*.

'Can you dance?'   'Yes, I can.' / 'No, I can't.'
'Diego can dance, but Alice can't.'
'Solange can dance, but she can't cook.'

4 Listen, and write *can* or *can't*.

5 In groups: find a person for each job. Tell the class about it. Example:

'Preeda can do the first job. He can't play the guitar, but he can play the flute. He can cook and drive, and he likes children.'

Help us with our children and travel around the world. If you can play the guitar or another instrument, cook, and drive, phone Whitfield at 689 6328.

Typist required, excellent pay, one week nights, two weeks days. Musician appreciated. Write to Box 635, Oxford OX6 82J.

Please Help! We are moving to India in six months time and need a good home for our parrot Leroy. He's well behaved and very clean. Loves classical music. If interested please contact Richard...

Travelling companion/driver required for American writer; speaking English, other languages. Chess player appreciated. Excellent pay. Write to Box 492, Newton Tribune.

Take 2 Italian boys, 8 and 10, on holiday in June. Some cooking but no cleaning. Swimming, tennis, windsurfing. Very good pay. Phone Guidotti 2783440 evenings.

Can

I can go (~~I can to go~~)
you can go
he/she/it can go (~~he/she/it cans go~~)
we can go
you can go
they can go

can I go? (~~do I can go?~~)

I cannot (can't) go

Learn: sleep (*noun*); glasses; can (could); cook; dance; drive (drove); make (made); run (ran); see (saw); sleep (slept); swim (swam); write (wrote); without.

Learn some of these if you want: cake; chess; piano; tennis; violin; type; in the daytime; go without sleep.

13B Better than all the others

I can . . . better than . . . ; good at + . . . ing.

WHAT CAN THEY DO?	PLAY TENNIS	DRAW	COUNT	SPELL	RUN 100m	MAKE CAKES	SPEAK ENGLISH
The Queen	🎾🎾🎾🎾	🌹	1 2 3	abcde	43 secs	🧁	3 words
The Prime Minister	🎾🎾🎾	🌹🌹	1 2	ab	35 secs	🧁🧁🧁	10 words
The Foreign Minister	🎾	🌹	1	abc	5 mins	–	–
The Minister of Education	🎾🎾	🌹🌹🌹	3 1 4 2	a	–	🧁🧁	1 word
The Minister of Finance	🎾🎾🎾🎾	🌹🌹	0	abcd	22 secs	🧁🧁🧁🧁🧁	400 words

1 True or false? Look at the table.

1. The Queen can spell very well.
2. The Foreign Minister can count quite well.
3. The Minister of Finance can't speak English.
4. The Prime Minister can't count.
5. The Queen can make cakes better than the Minister of Finance.
6. The Minister of Education can draw better than the Queen.
7. The Prime Minister can run faster than the Minister of Education.
8. The Minister of Education can spell better than the Foreign Minister.
9. The Queen can spell better than all the others.

2 True or false? Listen to the recording.

3 Pronunciations of the letter *a*. Say these words after the recording or your teacher.

1. make   cake   play   late   rain
2. finance   am   cat   back   hand
3. faster   glasses   car   bath   half
4. draw   all   walk   saw   tall   talk

Now look at these words: 1, 2, 3 or 4? Decide how to pronounce them and then check with your teacher or the recording.

a. past _3_
b. age
c. apple
d. bag
e. call
f. artist
g. pass
h. Spain
i. law
j. paper

4 Talk about now and when you were younger; use *than* and *but*.

'My father can speak Spanish better now than he could when I was younger.'
'I could swim better when I was younger than I can now.'
'I was good at maths when I was younger, but I'm not now.'
'I'm better at running now than I was when I was younger.'
'When I was younger I couldn't cook at all, but now I can cook quite well.'

5 In teams: try to remember other students' sentences. One point for each correct one.

> Michel can ski better now than he could when he was younger.

> You're right. / I'm afraid you're wrong.

Learn: count; draw (drew); sing (sang); ski; foreign; better; fast; faster; than; good at . . . ing.

13C I'm much taller than my mother

Comparative and superlative adjectives.

More beautiful **slimmer** **fatter** **OLDER**

1 Look at the list of adjectives. Can you see any rules? Which adjectives are irregular? What are the comparative and superlative of these words?

long _longer longest_

dark   near   hungry   intelligent
cold   big   nice   expensive

	ADJECTIVE	COMPARATIVE	SUPERLATIVE
1.	old	older	oldest
	short	shorter	shortest
	cheap	cheaper	cheapest
	fair	fairer	fairest
2.	fat	fatter	fattest
	slim	slimmer	slimmest
3.	happy	happier	happiest
	easy	easier	easiest
4.	late	later	latest
	fine	finer	finest
5.	good	better	best
	bad	worse	worst
	far	farther	farthest
6.	interesting	more interesting	most interesting
	beautiful	more beautiful	most beautiful
	difficult	more difficult	most difficult

2 Compare people you know.

A is (much)	taller shorter older younger slimmer *etc.*	than B.

'I'm much taller than my mother.'
'Mario's a bit older than his brother.'

In your family, who is the oldest / the youngest / the shortest / the best at English?

3 Compare countries (warm/cold/big/small/cheap/expensive/noisy/quiet) or cars (big/small/fast/slow/expensive/cheap/comfortable/economical/good). Examples:

'Japan is much more expensive than Greece.'
'A Volkswagen is much cheaper than a Mercedes.'

4 Choose a question, and ask as many other students as you can. Report the answers.

Who's the	best singer
	funniest comedian
	most beautiful actress
	best-looking actor
	most interesting writer
	most intelligent
	  politician
		in the world?
		in this/your
		  country?

What's the	most beautiful nicest most interesting most boring	place (that) you know?

Learn: world; place; better; best; worse; worst; easy; difficult; funny; beautiful; slow; boring; more; most.

Choose two or more to learn: politician; singer; comedian; actress; actor; writer.

13D The same or different?

> More comparisons; *the same as* and *different from*; *as . . . as*.

1 The same or different? Use your dictionary; write three sentences with *the same as* and three sentences with *different from*. Examples:

Three o'clock in the afternoon is the same as 15.00.

A café is different from a pub.

1. 7 × 12 and 3 × 28
2. Britain and England
3. The Netherlands and Holland
4. The USSR and Russia
5. Peking and Beijing
6. three o'clock and 15.00
7. a café and a pub
8. handsome and pretty
9. a woman and a wife
10. a pen and a pencil
11. 4,718 and 4.718
12. a cooker and a cook
13. a typewriter and a typist
14. a telephone number and a phone number
15. a restaurant and a hotel

2 Compare some of these people and things. Use (*not*) *as . . . as . . .* Examples:

I'm as good-looking as a film star.

A Volkswagen is not as quiet as a Rolls-Royce.

```
I/me        a film star    a Volkswagen
a Rolls-Royce    the President    Bach
an elephant    a cat    Canada
rock music    Kenya    a piano
```

```
tall    heavy    good-looking
strong    old    fast    economical
cold    warm    cheap    expensive
big    noisy    quiet    comfortable
intelligent    nice
```

3 Listen to the recording. How many words are there in each sentence? What are they? (Contractions like *I'm* count as two words.)

4 Work in groups. In each group, make a detailed comparison between two people, or two countries, or two cars, or two other things. Write at least eight sentences.

"How do you mean I'm as fit as a man of thirty – I **am** thirty!"

> **As and than**
> I can run faster *than* my brother.
> My brother can't run *as* fast *as* me.
> My brother can run *as* fast *as* my father.
> Peking is the same *as* Beijing.

> **Learn:** pencil; restaurant; hotel; economical; comfortable; noisy; quiet; warm; heavy; fast; handsome; typewriter.
>
> **Learn if you want:** typist; film star; president; piano; rock (music); cooker; pub.

Unit 14 Personal information

14A How old are you?

Ages, weights and measures.

statue by Degas

dinosaur

Le Mans Sports Bentley

early telephone

Great Pyramid of Giza

1 Look at the pictures. How old do you think the different things are? How heavy? How big? Examples:

'I think the dinosaur is 75 million years old.'
'I think the car is 3 metres long.'
'I think the pyramid is 120 metres high.'
'I think the statue weighs 50 kilos.'
'I think the dinosaur weighed 30 tonnes.'

2 Listen to the descriptions. What is the person describing – the dinosaur, the car, the pyramid, the statue or the telephone?

3 Say the numbers.

75   57   48   21   99
151   278   984   602
1,000   1,500   75,000   1,000,000   6,000,000

4 Make sentences about yourself and other people. Examples:

'I'm 1m 65.'
'My husband is 1m 85, and he weighs 70 kilos.'
'I weigh about 55 kilos.'
'My baby's six months old.'
'My mother's 66, but she looks older.'
'I'm 34, and I look my age.'
'I'm over 21.'

5 Ask some other students.

'How old/tall are you?'
'How much do you weigh?'

6 Describe somebody. The class must try to say who it is.

'She's a bit taller than me – about 1m 75. She weighs about 60 kilos. She's as old as me – over 20 and under 30. She's got dark hair.'

---

1 inch = 2½cm
12 inches = 1 foot (30cm)
1 pound = about 450gm
2.2 pounds = 1 kilogram

Learn: height; weight; metre; month; pound; think (thought); weigh; high; over (= 'more than'); under (= 'less than').

14B You look shy

People's appearance and personality.

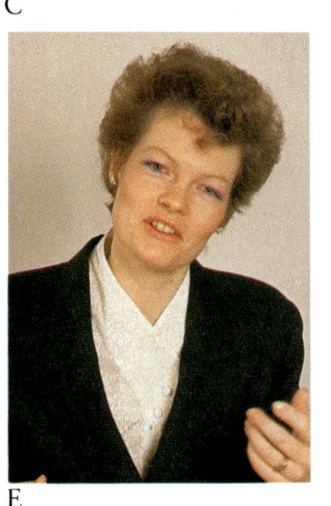

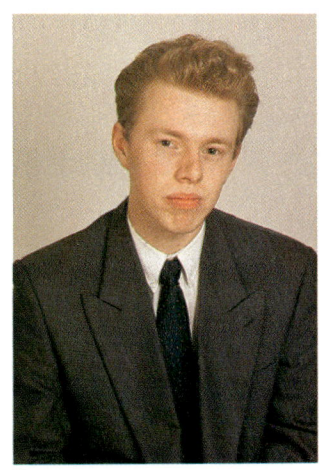

A B C D E F

1 What do they do? Look at the pictures. The six people are: a *criminal*, a *poet*, a *footballer*, a *secretary*, a *scientist* and a *politician*. Discuss who does what. Examples:

'I think C is a poet.' 'I don't agree. I think C's a criminal.'
'D looks like a scientist.' 'No, E looks more like a scientist.'

2 What are they like? Look at the pictures and discuss the people's personalities. Useful words:

| kind   shy   sensitive   self-confident |
| intelligent   stupid   bad-tempered   calm |
| friendly   nervy   optimistic   pessimistic |

Examples:

'What is B like, do you think?' 'Very shy.'
'I think A looks quite friendly.' 'I don't agree. A looks very bad-tempered to me.'

3 Say some things about yourself and other people. Ask about other people. Examples:

'I look shy, but I'm not.'
'What's your sister like?' 'She's quite bad-tempered.'

4 Look at the personality chart. What can you say about Harry and Claire? Use *not at all*, *not very*, *a bit*, *quite*, *very* and *extremely*. Examples:

'Harry's a bit pessimistic.'   H = Harry
'Claire's extremely self-confident.'   C = Claire

CALM	H		C	NERVY
PATIENT	H	C		IMPATIENT
SHY		H	C	SELF-C.
QUIET		H	C	TALKATIVE
OPT.	C		H	PESS.

5 Copy the chart. Work with a partner. Fill in the chart for yourself and your partner. Then compare charts with your partner and see what he/she has written. Report to the class. Example:

'Celia thinks I'm a bit nervy, but I think I'm extremely calm. I think Celia's quite talkative, but she doesn't agree. We both agree that I'm more optimistic than her.'

'What **is** she **like**?' 'She's very shy.'
'What **does** he **look like**?' 'He looks like a scientist.'

Learn: agree; look; extremely; that (*conjunction*).

Learn four or more of these: calm; nervy; patient; impatient; optimistic; pessimistic; shy; self-confident; sensitive; stupid; bad-tempered; friendly; talkative.

14C When is your birthday?

Dates.

1 Pronounce the names of the months.

January February March April May
June July August September October
November December

And can you pronounce these?

week   month   year

2 Can you say the numbers?

1st first	10th	30th
2nd	11th	31st
3rd	12th twelfth	40th
4th	13th	52nd
5th	14th	63rd
6th	18th	70th
7th	20th twentieth	99th
8th	21st twenty-first	100th
9th	22nd twenty-second	

3 Ask and answer.

'What's the eighth month?'   'August.'

4 When is your birthday? Examples:

'My birthday is on March the twenty-first.'
  (OR: '... the twenty-first of March.')
'My birthday is on November the third.'
  (OR: '... the third of November.')
'My birthday is today.'   'Happy Birthday!'

5 How to say and write dates.

WRITE	SAY
14 Jan(uary) 1990 14.1.90 (GB) 1.14.90 (US)	January the fourteenth, nineteen ninety (GB) January fourteenth ... (US)
5 Apr(il) 1892	April the fifth, eighteen ninety-two
9 Dec(ember) 1600	December the ninth, sixteen hundred
5 Nov(ember) 1804	November the fifth, eighteen hundred and four OR: ... eighteen oh four

Say these dates:

14 Jan 1978   17 May 1936   30 Dec 1983
3 Aug 1066   10 Oct 1906   3 Mar 1860
21 Sept 1980   20 July 1840   1 April 1900

What is today's date? What about tomorrow, the day after tomorrow, yesterday, and the day before yesterday?

6 Listen to the recording and write the dates.

7 Can you match the dates and the pictures? (There are too many dates.)

12 Oct 1492   6 May 1525   4 July 1776
8 June 1876   17 Dec 1903   17 Jan 1910
29 May 1953   22 Nov 1963   20 July 1969
6 Oct 1980

Columbus reached America on ...

J. F. Kennedy was assassinated on ...

Mount Everest was climbed for the first time on ...

The United States declared its independence from Britain on ...

The first person walked on the moon on ...

The first heavier-than-air flight took place on ...

Learn: *the names of the months; ordinal numbers from* tenth *to* hundredth; week; birthday; date; new; today; tomorrow; the day before yesterday; the day after tomorrow; after; Happy Birthday.

14D Could I speak to Dan?

Telephoning.

1 Make questions.

1. Dan's | phone number?
2. Sue's | phone number?
3. When | Sue's birthday?
4. How old | Sue?
5. Sue | as old | Dan?
6. time | party?
7. What sort | food | Sue | want?
8. What sort | CDs | she | want?
9. How many brothers | Sue | ?
10. What sort | job | Sue | do?
11. Sue's | boss's | name?
12. Dan | as old | Sue's boss?
13. Dan's hair | same colour | John's?

2 Listen to the conversations and answer the questions in Exercise 1.

BEN: Brighton ....
SUE: Hello. Could I speak to Dan, please?
BEN: Just a moment. Dan! . . . Dan! . . . I'm sorry. He's not in. Can I take a message?
SUE: Yes. Could you ask him to phone me? It's Sue.
BEN: OK.
SUE: Thanks very much. Bye.
BEN: You're welcome. Bye.

* * *

SUE: Brighton ....
DAN: Hello. This is Dan. Is that Sue?
SUE: Yes. Hi, Dan. Listen. It's my birthday on ....
DAN: Yes? How old are you?
SUE: Never mind. Well, ...
DAN: Yes? You're .... as old as me. You don't look it.
SUE: Yes, well, I'm having a party. Would you like to come?
DAN: Yes. Great. What time?
SUE: Oh, ... o'clock.
DAN: Can I bring something?
SUE: Something to eat, if you like. ...., ... Or a bottle of wine. And some CDs.
DAN: OK. What sort?
SUE: It doesn't matter. Something good for ....
DAN: Who's coming?
SUE: Oh, about twenty people. Jim and Bob. .... my brothers. My boss and the girls from the ....
DAN: Your boss?
SUE: Yes, ... He's really nice. He's very young. Only .... Tall and .... I like him.
DAN: Do you? Yes. Great. OK. Thanks. See you on Saturday, then.
SUE: Right. See you. Bye, Dan.
DAN: Bye.

3 Practise these sentences.

Could I **speak** to **Dan**, please?
Just a **moment**.
Can I **take** a **message**?
Could you **ask** him to **phone** me?
I'm **having** a **party**.
Would you **like** to **come**?

4 Ask other people's phone numbers and give yours.

'What's your phone number?'
'Milan three oh seven double two eight six.'

5 Work in groups of three. Prepare and practise two short telephone conversations. (A telephones B and asks to speak to C; A invites C to a party.)

Learn: party; boss; eat (ate); (tele)phone (*verb*); bring (brought); This is . . . ; Is that . . . ?; Could I speak to . . . ?; He's not in; Can I take a message?; You're welcome; It doesn't matter.

Unit 15 Present and future

15A What's happening?

Present Progressive tense.

1 Who is the man talking to? What does she think is happening in the room? What is really happening? What is she doing? Examples:

'Some people are dancing.'
'Somebody is lying on the floor.'

Hello, darling . . . Yes . . . Are you having a good time? . . . How's your mother? . . . What? . . . What do you mean, 'What's happening?' . . . Oh, the noise . . . Yes, it's the TV – I'm watching something good on the TV . . . What? . . .

2 What is your wife/husband/father/mother/boyfriend/girlfriend/boss, etc. doing just now? Useful expressions: *I think, I know, probably*.

'I think my boyfriend's working. My mother's shopping. John's probably getting up.'

3 Pronouncing the letter *e*. Say these words.

1. red   dress   get
2. he   eat   sleep

1 or 2? Decide how to pronounce these words, and then check with your teacher.

went   meat   men   bed
be   left   reading   mean
me   speak

1 or 2?

many   friend   head   any

4 Prepare questions about the picture. Examples:

'What is the woman in the red dress doing?'
'What is the man with glasses doing?'
'Is anybody smoking?'

Can you answer all the questions?

5 Memory test. Work in groups. One group asks its questions from Exercise 4; another group tries to answer with books closed.

Present Progressive tense		
I am (I'm) talking	am I talking?	I am (I'm) not talking
you are (you're) talking	are you talking?	you are not (aren't) talking
he/she is (he's/she's) talking	is he/she talking?	he/she is not (isn't) talking
we are (we're) talking	are we talking?	we are not (aren't) talking
you are (you're) talking	are you talking?	you are not (aren't) talking
they are (they're) talking	are they talking?	they are not (aren't) talking

Learn: head; noise; happen; lie (lying, lay); stand (stood); sit (sat); drink (drank); smoke; shave; shop (*verb*); answer (*verb*); somebody; anybody; probably; have a good time.

15B The Universal Holiday Postcard Machine

Present Progressive tense; weather; places.

1 Spelling. Make the *-ing* form.

1. sing *singing*   work ....   3. stop *stopping*   shop ....
   play *playing*   start ....   sit *sitting*   run ....
   stand ....   eat ....   get ....   begin ....
   read ....   go ....

                                4. lie *lying*   die ....

2. make *making*   dance ....
   smoke *smoking*   drive ....
   write ....   like ....

2 It's easy to write holiday postcards! Write one now and send it to a friend.

Dear ..N..
   Well, here we are in ..T.. ..W.., and we are having a/an ..A.. time. I am sitting/lying ..Pr.. ..Pl.., writing postcards, drinking ..D.. and looking at ..L.. ..N.. is ..V.., and ..PN.. are ..V.. ..Pr.. ..Pl... Tomorrow we are going to ..T... I'm sure it will be ..A.. Wish you were here,
Love, ..N..

POSTCARD DICTIONARY

N (*name*)
John
Mary
Alexandra
Mother
etc.

T (*town, city, village*)
Rome
Manchester
Honolulu
etc.

W (*weather*)
The sun is shining
It is raining
It is snowing
There is a hurricane
etc.

A (*adjective*)
wonderful   terrible
beautiful   awful
lovely   horrible
exciting   catastrophic
interesting   boring
magnificent   *etc.*

Pr (*preposition*)
in
on
at
under
by
near
opposite
etc.

Pl (*place*)
my room
their room
the bar
the beach
a café
a tree
a mountain
etc.

D (*drink*)
coffee
beer
wine
etc.

L (*things to look at*)
the sea
the mountains
the tourists
the rain
the sheep
etc.

V (*verb*)
shopping
sightseeing
sleeping
drinking beer
dancing
playing cards
having a bath
etc.

PN (*plural noun*)
the children
Mummy and Daddy
George and Sue
etc.

Learn: postcard; town; city; sun; sea; mountain; weather; Love; send (sent); sure.

Learn some more words from the lesson if you want to.

15C Who's doing what when?

> Present Progressive tense with future meaning; plans and invitations.

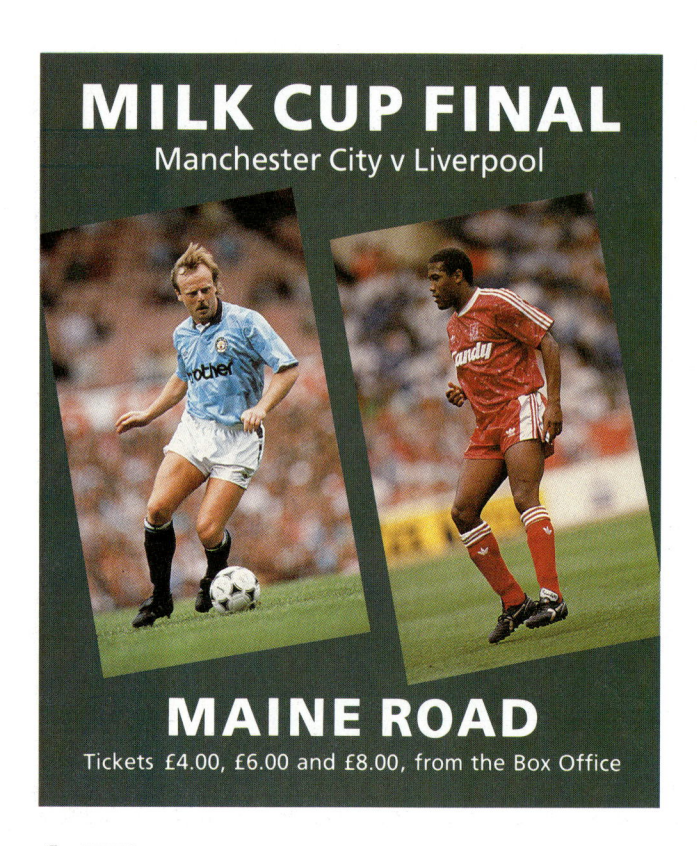

MILK CUP FINAL
Manchester City v Liverpool
MAINE ROAD
Tickets £4.00, £6.00 and £8.00, from the Box Office

MICHAEL BENTLEY
in concert
at the PALACE THEATRE
Tickets are £6.00, £7.50 and £9.50
(available from the Palace box office)

1 Listen to the conversation and fill in the missing information.

WHO?	WHAT?	WHEN?
Michael Bentley	is ....ing at the Palace	on .... evening.
City	are playing at home	....
Jane	is working	....
Bill	is ....ing	on Wednesday evening.
Jane's granny	is probably coming	....
Jane	is	on Tuesday evening.

2 Can you think of some things that are happening during the next week or so (concerts, football matches, ...)? What are you doing this evening, next weekend, for your next holiday?

3 Listen to the recording. How many words do you hear in each sentence? (Contractions like *I'm* count as two words.)

4 Complete this conversation and practise it in pairs. You can make some changes if you want to.

A: Are you doing anything this evening?
B: I'm not sure. Why?
A: Well, would you like to .... with me?
B: I'd love to, but I'm probably ....ing.
A: Well, what about tomorrow? Are you free?
B: Perhaps. ....
A: ....

> **Learn:** (football) match; concert; free; perhaps; I'd love to; What about . . . ?

15D We're leaving on Monday

Talking about the future; prepositions of time.

(Janet and Bill are talking on Monday April 19th, at nine o'clock in the morning.)

JANET: Is everything all right?
BILL: Yes, I think so. I'm picking up the visas on Wednesday morning and the tickets in the afternoon, and I'm getting the traveller's cheques from the bank tomorrow.
JANET: Oh, good. Don't forget that the children are going to stay with Mother on the 22nd – you're driving them.
BILL: Oh, yes. How long for?
JANET: Just for two days. Back on Friday night.
BILL: That isn't long.
JANET: Darling – you know it's John's birthday on the 24th.
BILL: So it is. We must have him home for his birthday. What are we giving him?
JANET: A bike.
BILL: Oh yes, that's right. When are you going to do the packing?
JANET: At the weekend, at the last possible moment. You're going to help, I hope.
BILL: Oh yes. Yes, of course.
JANET: And then on Monday we're off! British Airways Flight 011 to Australia. For three months! I'm so excited!
BILL: OK. Remember Peter and Sally are coming this evening.
JANET: No, they aren't. It's tomorrow.
BILL: Well, somebody's coming this evening.
JANET: Your father. And Mary Rawson's telephoning this afternoon. She wants to ask you about insurance.
BILL: Well, I'm sorry, but I'm leaving in about two minutes. I have to be at the office in half an hour, and I won't be back before six.
JANET: All right. I'll give Mary your love.
BILL: OK. Bye, darling. Have a nice day.
JANET: You too. Bye-bye.

1 Put these events in the right order as fast as you can.

A Bill's visit to the bank
B John's birthday
C Mary Rawson's phone call
D Bill picking up the tickets
E children leaving to stay with their grandmother
F family leaving for Australia
G Bill picking up the visas
H Peter and Sally's visit
I Bill leaving for the office
J Janet packing (with Bill's help)
K Bill coming back from the office
L Bill's father's visit

2 Janet and Bill are talking at nine o'clock on Monday April 19th. They can talk about the future in two or three different ways. Examples:

on the 22nd = on Thursday = in three days
at ten o'clock = in an hour
at ten past nine = in ten minutes

How could Bill and Janet say these differently?

on Wednesday   on the 24th   in a week
at eleven o'clock   in three hours
in twenty minutes   in four days   at 9.05

3 How soon are the following: your birthday; Christmas; the end of your English course; the end of this lesson? (Use *in*.)

4 Put *at, on, in, for* or no preposition.

1. What are you doing .... the weekend?
2. I'm seeing Carlo .... Tuesday.
3. My mother's telephoning .... three o'clock.
4. 'Can I talk to you?' 'Sorry, I'm leaving .... five minutes.'
5. I think it's going to rain .... this afternoon.
6. We're going to Dakar in June .... three weeks.
7. Would you like to go out with me .... Monday evening?
8. Telephone me .... tomorrow if you have time.
9. 'I'm going to Norway .... August.' 'That's nice. How long .... ?'

5 Are you going on a journey soon? If so, tell the class about it. If not, imagine that you are going on a journey (a really interesting one) next week, and tell the class about it.

Learn: minute; hour; half an hour; ticket; forget (forgot); get (got) (= obtain); give (gave); leave (left); stay; long (= a long time); back.

Unit 16 Consolidation

16A Things to remember: Units 13, 14 and 15

Present Progressive tense

I am (I'm) eating	am I eating?
you are (you're) eating	are you eating?
he/she/it is (he's/she's/it's) eating	is he *etc.* eating?
we are (we're) eating	are we eating?
you are (you're) eating	are you eating?
they are (they're) eating	are they eating?

I am (I'm) not eating
you are not (aren't) eating
she *etc.* is not (isn't) eating
we are not (aren't) eating
you are not (aren't) eating
they are not (aren't) eating

Examples:
Some people **are dancing**.
What **is** the woman in the red dress **doing**?
   (What is doing the woman . . . ?)
John **is** probably **getting** up now.

Spelling of *-ing* forms

ORDINARY VERBS:	sing ⟶ sing**ing** eat ⟶ eat**ing**
ENDING IN *-e*:	make ⟶ mak**ing** (makeing) write ⟶ writ**ing**
ENDING IN ONE VOWEL + ONE CONSONANT:	stop ⟶ stop**ping** sit ⟶ sit**ting** run ⟶ run**ning**
ENDING IN *-ie*:	lie ⟶ **ly**ing

Talking about the future

Are you **doing** anything this evening?
I'**m working** next Thursday.
   (I work next Thursday.)
We'**re leaving** on Monday.
We'**re going** to Australia for three months.
Jane's granny **is** probably **coming** on Thursday.

Can

I can go (I can to go)
you can go
he/she/it can go (he/she/it cans go)
we can go
you can go
they can go
can I go? (do I can go?)
I cannot (can't) go

Examples:
I **can** sing, but I **can't** dance.
Diego **can** dance, but Alice **can't**.
'**Can** you swim?'   'Yes, I **can**.'
'**Can** you cook?'   'No, I **can't**.'

Pronunciation and stress

I can (/kən/) swim, but I can't
   (/kɑːnt/) dance.
Yes, I can (/kæn/).

Comparative and superlative adjectives

	ADJECTIVE	COMPARATIVE	SUPERLATIVE
SHORT ADJECTIVES:	short cheap young	shorter cheaper younger (/ˈjʌŋə(r)/)	shortest cheapest youngest (/ˈjʌŋɪst/)
ENDING IN ONE VOWEL + ONE CONSONANT:	fat slim big	fatter slimmer bigger	fattest slimmest biggest
ENDING IN *-e*:	late	later	latest
ENDING IN *-y*:	happy	happier	happiest
IRREGULAR:	good bad far	better worse farther	best worst farthest
LONG ADJECTIVES:	interesting beautiful	**more** interesting **more** beautiful	**most** interesting **most** beautiful

Ways of comparing

I'm **taller than** my mother.
I'm **much** taller than my brother.
He's fatter **than me**.
Mario's **a bit** older than his brother.
I can speak English **better than** my father.
My father can speak Spanish **better** now **than** he could when I was younger.

I'm **the tallest** in my family.
What's **the most beautiful** place (that) you know?

I'm **as good-looking as** a film star.
A Volkswagen is not **as quiet as** a Rolls-Royce.
He can't run as fast as **me**.

Peking is **the same as** Beijing.
England is **not the same as** Britain.
A pen is **different from** a pencil.

As and than

faster **than**
more beautiful **than**
as fast **as**
the same **as**

Be like, look (like)

What **is** she **like**? (How is she?)
She's a bit shy, but very nice.

He **looks like** a footballer.
I think he **looks more like** a businessman.
She **looks like** her mother.

She **looks** bad-tempered.
You **look** tired.

Ages, heights and weights

The Great Pyramid **is** 4,500 years **old**.
It is 135 metres **high**.
The car **is** 4 metres **long**.
The statue **weighs** three kilos.

Lucy is four months **old**.
Her mother **is** 40 (years old).
I **am** 1 metre 91.
I **weigh** 85 kilos.

She's **over** 21 and **under** 30.

How old/tall are you?
How much do you weigh?

British and US measures

1 inch = 2½cm
12 inches = 1 foot (30cm)
1 pound = about 450gm
2.2 pounds = 1 kilogram

Large numbers

100: a hundred OR one hundred
125: a/one hundred and twenty-five
 (US a/one hundred twenty-five)
300: three hundred
 (three hundreds)
1,000: a/one thousand
1,467: one thousand, four hundred and sixty-seven
4,000: four thousand
 (four thousands)
1,000,000: a/one million
1,400,000: one million, four hundred thousand

Ordinal numbers

10th: tenth
11th: eleventh
12th: twelfth
13th: thirteenth
20th: twentieth (/ˈtwentɪəθ/)
21st: twenty-first
22nd: twenty-second
30th: thirtieth
100th: hundredth

Dates

WRITE	SAY
14 Jan(uary) 1990	January the fourteenth, nineteen ninety (GB)
14.1.90 (GB)	
1.14.90 (US)	January fourteenth ... (US)
5 Apr(il) 1892	April the fifth, eighteen ninety-two
9 Dec(ember) 1600	December the ninth, sixteen hundred
14 May 1906	May the fourteenth, nineteen hundred and six OR: ... nineteen oh six

Question expression + object

What sort of food do your children like?
How many children have you got?

Prepositions

on June 22nd
on Thursday
in three days
at ten o'clock
in an hour
the girl **in** jeans
the man **with** a beard
good **at** maths/running *etc.*
the highest mountain **in** the world

Agree

I agree. (I am agree.)
He doesn't agree.
We both agree.

Telephoning

Can/Could I speak to ...?
This is ...
Is that ...?
He/She's not in.
Can I take a message?

16A continued

Inviting; answering invitations

Are you doing anything this evening?
Would you like to see a film?
I don't know, I'm a bit tired.
I don't really want to go out tonight.
Well, what about tomorrow?
I'd love to, but I'm probably going to a concert in London.

Let's do something at the weekend.
Are you free?
Perhaps.
Yes, why not?
See you about two o'clock.
Right, see you then.

Words and expressions

Nouns
sleep
glasses
world
place
pencil
restaurant
hotel
typewriter
height
weight
metre
month
pound (*weight*)
week
birthday
date
party
boss
head
noise
postcard
town
city
sun
sea
mountain
weather
(football) match
concert
minute
hour
half an hour
ticket

Verbs
can (could)
cook
dance
drive (drove)
make (made)
run (ran)
see (saw)
sleep (slept)
swim (swam)
write (wrote)
count
draw (drew)
sing (sang)
ski
think (thought)
weigh
agree
look
eat (ate)
(tele)phone
bring (brought)
happen
lie (lying, lay)
stand (stood)
sit (sat)
drink (drank)
smoke
shave
shop
answer
send (sent)
forget (forgot)
get (got)
give (gave)
leave (left)
stay

Adjectives
foreign
better
best
worse
worst
easy
difficult
funny
beautiful
slow
boring
economical
comfortable
noisy
quiet
warm
heavy
fast
handsome
high
new
sure
free

Adverbs
better
fast
faster
extremely
probably
perhaps
long
back

Prepositions
without
than
over (= more than)
under (= less than)
after

Months
January
February
March
April
May
June
July
August
September
October
November
December

Other words and expressions
somebody
anybody
today
tomorrow
the day before yesterday
the day after tomorrow
good at . . .ing
that (*conjunction*)
Happy Birthday
You're welcome
It doesn't matter
have a good time
Love (*end of a letter*)

Optional words and expressions to learn
cake; chess; piano; tennis; violin; politician; singer; comedian; actress; actor; writer; typist; film star; president; rock (music); cooker; pub; type; calm; nervy; patient; impatient; optimistic; pessimistic; shy; self-confident; sensitive; stupid; bad-tempered; talkative; in the daytime; go without sleep.

16B Present tenses

The difference between the two present tenses.

1 Look at the table and examples, and choose the best rules for each tense.

PRESENT PROGRESSIVE TENSE	SIMPLE PRESENT TENSE
I am working, you are working *etc.* am I working? *etc.* I am not working *etc.*	I work, you work, he/she works *etc.* do I/you work? does he/she work? *etc.* I/you do not work, he/she does not work *etc.*
'Are you free now?' 'Sorry, **I'm studying**.' 'Look. Helen**'s wearing** a lovely dress.' The cat**'s eating** your steak. What **are** you **doing** tomorrow? He**'s** not **working** on Saturday. We**'re spending** Christmas with Ann and Peter again this year.	I always **study** from five to seven o'clock. Helen often **wears** red. Cats **eat** meat. What **do** you **do** at weekends? He never **works** on Saturdays. We always **stay** with Ann and Peter at Christmas.

Rules
We use the Present Progressive to talk about:
1. ....
2. ....

Rules
We use the Simple Present to talk about:
1. ....
2. ....

A things that are happening now, these days
B things that are always true
C things that happen often, usually, always, never, *etc.*
D plans for the future

2 Put in the correct tense.

1. 'Can you help me for a minute?' 'I'm sorry, I ....' (*'m working / work*)
2. .... on Saturdays? (*Are you working / Do you work*)
3. 'Have you got a light?' 'Sorry, ...' (*I'm not smoking / I don't smoke*)
4. How many languages ....? (*are you speaking / do you speak*)
5. Why .... a sweater? It isn't cold. (*are you wearing / do you wear*)
6. My father .... August in Ireland. (*is always spending / always spends*)
7. Robert .... football most weekends. (*is playing / plays*)
8. 'Where's Lucy?' 'She ....' (*'s shopping / shops*)
9. 'What ....?' 'Chocolate.' (*are you eating / do you eat*)
10. '................ English?' 'Yes, a bit.' (*Are you speaking / Do you speak*)
11. The children .... with Granny this week. (*are staying / stay*)
12. 'Is John in the bathroom?' 'No, he's outside. He .... the car.' (*'s cleaning / cleans*)

3 📼 Listen to the recording and answer the questions.

4 What are they doing? Listen to the conversation and circle any of these verbs that you hear.

sending   spending   standing   staying
playing   having   working   watching
washing   doing   reading   eating   writing
raining   cleaning   drinking   thinking
looking   cooking   going

5 Who is doing what? First copy the table, then listen again and fill it in.

JANE	
POLLY	
JANE'S MOTHER	
BILL	
THE BABY	
SUE	
FRANK	

79

16C   Choose

> A choice of vocabulary, pronunciation, listening and speaking exercises.

Look at the exercises, decide which ones are useful to you, and do two or more.

VOCABULARY

1 Which one is different?

1. Monday, Wednesday, Friday, Sunday
2. Britain, Brazil, Australia, Japan
3. station, hotel, restaurant, phone box
4. beer, cheese, bread, banana
5. aunt, sister, father, girlfriend
6. bus, train, horse, car
7. short, big, large, tall
8. dark, long, grey, big
9. blue, brown, black, green
10. sun, rain, snow, weather

2 Choose a word from Units 1–15 and draw it. Other students will try to say what it is.

I think it's a sofa.
Is it a bed?
Perhaps it's a horse.
I don't know.

LISTENING

1 Listen to the song (*Anything You Can Do, I Can Do Better*). You will hear most of these comparatives. Which two do you *not* hear?

better   older   greater   higher   cheaper   shorter   softer   longer   faster

2 Look at the picture and listen to the recording. How many differences can you find?

PRONUNCIATION

1 Pronunciation of the letter *i*. Say these words.

1. sit   in   big
2. wine   five   night   right
3. first   shirt

Now decide how to pronounce these words. Are they in group 1, 2 or 3? Check with your teacher or the recording.

girl   like   arrive   tights   white
skirt   light   with   fin   bird   stir
slight   bright   excite   ride   skip

2 Word stress.
1. Copy the names from the box. Under each word draw a ～～～ for stress. Example: England.
2. Listen and check your answers.
3. Listen again. Circle the vowel where you hear /ə/. Example: Engl(a)nd.

Pronounce the words.

| England | Brazil | Italy | Russia | Japan |
| America | Lebanon | Canada | Africa |
| London |

SPEAKING

1 Prepare questions for an interview with an English-speaking stranger. Some ideas for questions:

How old . . . ?   What did you . . . ?   . . . favourite . . . ?
Are you . . . ?   What was . . . ?   What sort of . . . ?
Where do . . . ?   What do you . . . ?   Can you . . . ?
Where were you . . . ?   Have you got a/any . . . ?   Do you like . . . ?
Where did you . . . ?   How many . . . ?   Do you know . . . ?

Prepare 'follow-up' questions for some of your questions. Examples:

'Have you got a car?'
'Yes, I have.'
'What sort of car? What colour is it? Do you drive to work? . . . '

'Did you study languages at school?'
'Yes, I did.'
'What languages?'

2 Work in groups of three or four. Some of you are shop assistants; and some of you want to buy things.

Prepare and practise a sketch. Use all the English you can.

16D Test yourself

LISTENING

1 Listen to the conversation and answer the questions.

1. How many bedrooms are there?
2. Is the kitchen big or small?
3. Is there a toilet downstairs?
4. Is there a garage?
5. How much is the rent?

2 Listen and answer these questions about the speaker.

1. How old is she?
2. Where was she born?
3. What is her best friend's name?
4. What happened when she was seven?
5. When did she begin to like school?
6. How old are her sister and brothers?
7. Where is her sister working now?
8. Does she see her little brother very often?

GRAMMAR

1 Write five things that are happening in your school or home now. Example:

Some students are playing table-tennis.

2 Give the *-ing* forms. Example:

play *playing*

work; write; stop; sit; eat; run; lie; make.

3 Choose the correct forms.

1. .... John tomorrow? (*Are you seeing / Do you see*)
2. .... on Saturdays? (*Are you working / Do you work*)
3. What .... with my bicycle? (*are you doing / do you do*)
4. 'Have you got a cigarette?' 'Sorry, I ....' (*'m not smoking / don't smoke*)

4 Give the comparative and superlative. Example:

old *older   oldest*

young; big; important; interesting; fat; happy; late; good.

5 Complete the sentences using the words in brackets (and any other words that you need).

1. She can run .... I can. (*faster*)
2. These oranges cost .... the others. (*the same*)
3. 'I think it's a really good film.' 'No, I ....' (*not agree*)
4. Do you think she .... her mother? (*look like*)
5. 'What ....?' 'She's a bit shy, but very nice.' (*like*)

6 Write the object pronouns. Example:

I *me*

you; he; she; it; we; they.

7 Write sentences beginning:

1. What sort of . . .
2. How much . . .
3. How many . . .
4. I can . . .
5. I can't . . .
6. He weighs . . .
7. How tall . . .

VOCABULARY

1 Write these numbers in words.

14; 40; 100; 234; 6,798; 1,000,000; 12th; 20th; 100th.

2 Which word is different?

1. hour   birthday   week   month
2. eat   drink   draw   noisy
3. goodbye   think   remember   forget
4. noisy   comfortable   quiet   ticket
5. ski   swim   run   answer
6. city   town   station   village

3 Put in the right preposition.

1. We're leaving .... Monday: we're going to Australia .... three months.
2. I'm not free now, but I can see you .... an hour, ... ten o'clock.
3. I'm the tallest .... my family.
4. She's over 21 and .... 30.
5. Who's the girl .... jeans and a red sweater?
6. I was very bad .... maths at school.
7. Which is the hottest country .... the world?

LANGUAGE IN USE

1 Complete these conversational exchanges.

1. 'Agresti, kunsti sifnit?'   'I'm sorry, I don't ....'
2. 'What's that girl's name?'   'I'm sorry, I don't ....'
3. 'What does *shut* ....?'   'The same as *closed*.'
4. '............ do?'   'I'm a photographer.'
5. '............ do?'   'How do you do?'
6. '............?'   'Fine, thanks.'
7. '............?'   'I'm afraid she's not in. Can I take a ....?'
8. 'Are you doing anything this evening?'   '............'
9. 'I don't really want to go out tonight.'   'Well, ... tomorrow?'
10. 'Would you like to see a film tomorrow?'   '............'
11. 'See you about two o'clock.'   '............'

PRONUNCIATION

1 Which word is different?

1. high   height   weigh   lie
2. cook   look   pound   could
3. easy   head   heavy   weather
4. metre   best   ski   leave
5. any   many   send   place
6. town   slow   smoke   post
7. month   boss   shop   got
8. warm   thought   got   saw

2 Which syllable is stressed?

typewriter; birthday; postcard; mountain; concert; telephone; forget; foreign; comfortable; economical; handsome; extremely; tomorrow; today; perhaps; without.

WRITING

1 Write about the differences between you and another person in your family (100–200 words).

SPEAKING

1 Act out this conversation. The teacher will take the other part.

TELEPHONE CALL
Telephone a friend. You want to ask him/her to go and see a film with you. Try to find an evening when you are both free.

Unit 17 Ordering and asking

17A I'll have roast beef

> Eating in a restaurant; *no* = *not any*; *some* and *something* in offers and requests.

1 Try to put the sentences in order. Then listen and check your answers.

'Yes, sir. Over here, by the window.'
'Have you got a table for two?'

'How would you like your steak?'
'Oh, all right then. I'll have a rump steak.'
'I'll start with soup, please, and then I'll have roast beef.'
'I'm sorry, madam, there's no more roast beef.'
'Rare, please.'

'Vegetables, sir?'
'Chicken for me, please.'
'Mushrooms and a green salad, please.'
'And for you, sir?'

2 The conversations continue. Try to guess what goes in the blanks. Then listen and check.

'............ you .... something to ....?'
'Just .... water, please.'
'Certainly, madam.'
'I'll .... a lager, ... And .... you .... me some water, too?'
'............ course, sir.'

* * *

'How's the chicken?'
'Not too bad. .... about .... steak?'
'A bit tough. The vegetables are ...., though.'

* * *

'Is .... all right?'
'Oh, yes, excellent, ... you.'
'............ good.'

* * *

'............ I .... you a little more coffee?'
'No, thank you.' 'Yes, ...'

* * *

'............ you .... us the bill, please?'
'............, madam.'
'Is service included?'
'No, ...'

3 Listen to the questions on the tape, and try to remember the answers. Example:

'Have you got a table for two?'
'Yes, sir. Over here, by the window.'

4 Make up your own restaurant conversations and practise them.

> **Learn:** (the) bill; everything; all right; for (you, *etc.*); though; just; then; certainly; how; I'll have; a little more; no more; Is service included?
>
> **Learn some of these if you want:** soup; (roast) beef; (rump) steak; chicken; vegetable; mushroom; salad; lager; coffee; tough; rare; excellent; over here; not too bad.

84

17B Could you lend me some sugar?

Lending and borrowing.

1 Read the story and complete the conversation. Practise the complete conversation with a partner.

Hello.
Excuse me. My name's Alan. I live downstairs.
I'm sorry to trouble you, but could you lend me some sugar?
Yes, of course. Just a minute.
Here you are.
Thanks very much.

2 Match the questions and answers. You can find more than one answer to each question.

QUESTIONS
1. Sorry to trouble you, but could you lend me some bread?
2. Could you lend me a dictionary?
3. Could you show me some black sweaters, please?
4. Excuse me. Have you got a light, please?
5. Could you possibly lend me your car for half an hour?
6. Could I borrow your keys for a moment?
7. Could I borrow your umbrella, please?
8. Have you got a cigarette?

ANSWERS
a. I think so . . . Yes, here you are.
b. Yes, of course. Just a minute.
c. I'm sorry. I need it/them.
d. I'm afraid I haven't got one.
e. I'm afraid I haven't got any.
f. Sorry, I don't smoke.
g. I'm sorry, I'm afraid I can't.

Look at the questions again; find two very polite questions and two very casual questions.

3 Ask the teacher the names of some of your possessions. Examples:

'What's this?'
'What's this called in English, please?'
'Is this a pen or a pencil?'
'Is this a lighter?'

4 Ask other students to lend, give or show you things. Examples:

'Could you lend me your Practice Book for a moment?'
'Yes, here you are.' / *'I'm sorry. I haven't got one.'*

'Could you possibly lend me your watch?'
'Yes, of course. Here you are.' / *'I'm sorry, I need it.'*

Now ask for your possessions back. Example:

'Could I have my watch back, please?'
'Yes, of course. Here you are. Thanks.'

Learn: cigarette; lend (lent); borrow; show; need; (I'm) sorry to trouble you; Could you possibly lend me . . . ?; Here you are; Just a moment/minute; Have you got a light?

Learn if you want to: sugar; bread (*uncountable*); dictionary; key; umbrella; *some of the possessions you lent or borrowed in Exercise 4.*

17C   Somewhere different

> Making suggestions; agreeing, disagreeing and negotiating.

1 What are they talking about? Look at the pictures; then listen to the recording.

[Picture 1: Turkey – holiday?]

[Picture 2: think ... expensive ... time / package holidays ... Ted ... cheap ... phone]

[Picture 3: you? / good ... cheap ... different]

[Picture 4: different ... doesn't cost too much / Fine ... phone tomorrow]

2 Can you remember? Try and put words and expressions in each blank from the dialogue. Then listen again to check.

1. .... go to Turkey for our holiday
2. Yeah, OK, ... ?
3. Hey, ..., ... think about this.
4. .... we can get package holidays
5. ...., darling?
6. I think ....
7. ...., ..., Sarah, find out about it.
8. .... I'll phone tomorrow morning.

3 Can you fill in the blanks and put this conversation in order?

BOB: ...., ... ask her to come with us – can you phone her?
BOB: .... I'll get the paper and see what's on.
BOB: .... go to the cinema tonight?
SUSAN: Yes, ... ? The last film we saw was months ago. I'll phone.
SUSAN: I'd love to, but Anne is coming for supper.

4 Listen to the recording. How many words are there? What are they? (Contractions like *don't* count as two words.)

5 Work in groups of four to try and solve the problem.

You are a group of eighteen-year-olds. Your parents have agreed to give you holiday money for six weeks if:
- you all travel together
- you spend two weeks learning something: for example, a new sport; a new skill (typing, bricklaying, ...); a foreign language; ...
- you camp in the mountains or at the seaside for two weeks.

Agree on how and where you will spend your six weeks.

> **Learn:** idea; paper; find out (found); spend (spent); wait (a minute); let's; Why don't we . . . ?; Why not?; Well, . . . ; all right; fine; about; somewhere; with.

17D Meet me at eight

> Writing: inviting and replying; Shall we . . . ?

1 Read the notes. Ask your teacher for help with any difficult words or expressions.

2 Write similar notes to other students. Reply to the notes that you get. Fill up your diary for the next week with a list of appointments.

Dear Polly,
What a nice idea! See you at 6.30.
Yours, Sally

Dear Sally,
Let's have a drink after the class. Shall we meet at the pub at 6.30?
Yours, Polly

Dear Carlos,
Why don't we go and see 'Rock, rock, rock of ages' tomorrow evening? Let's meet at the station at 6.55. OK?
Yours, Annie

Dear Annie,
Sorry. I can't go this evening. Perhaps another day?
Yours, Carlos

Dear Jonathan,
Thank you. I would very much like to have dinner with you on Friday.
Yours, Susan

Dear Alex,
Meet me at seven o'clock at the usual place. Don't tell Carola.
Love, Judy

JANET — LUNCH TODAY? JOE.

Dear Oliver,
Meet me at Joe's house. It's very important.
Yours, Al

Dear Susan,
Would you like to have dinner with me at the Ritz next Friday? I'll call for you in the Rolls about 7.30.
Yours, Jonathan

Dear Joe,
I'm afraid I'm not free today. How about tomorrow?
Janet

DEAR AL, OK. WHERE'S JOE'S HOUSE? OLIVER

DEAR JANE, LET'S CATCH A PLANE TO SPAIN. LOVE, FRED

Sorry, Fred. I'm going with Ted.

JUNE
1 Sun 8.00 cinema with Mario
2 Mon
3 Tues
4 Wed Lunch with Barbara, 1.15
5 Thurs Dentist 10.30
6 Fri Dinner with George and Catherine
7 Sat Henry's party
8 Sun
9 Mon Meeting with M.C.

> **Learn:** dinner; pub; plane; usual; important; Shall we . . . ?; catch (caught); catch a plane/train/*etc.*; Yours (*at the end of a letter*).

Unit 18 More about the past

18A Where was Galileo born?

More about people's pasts.

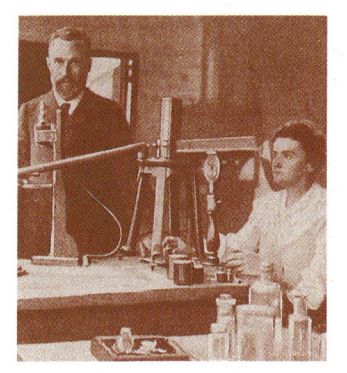

Galileo *Amelia Earhart* *Marie and Pierre Curie* *Ho Chi Minh*

1 Match four of the phrases with each picture. You can use a dictionary.

A
born in Paris, France and Warsaw, Poland
born in Annam, Vietnam
born in Atchison, Kansas, USA
born in Pisa, Italy

B
student in Saigon
student at the University of Pisa, Italy
student at Columbia University, New York
students at the Sorbonne, Paris

C
mathematician, astronomer and physicist
politician and poet
professors of physics
pilot and writer

D
first woman to fly a plane across the Atlantic
people who discovered radium
founder of the People's Republic of Vietnam
man who discovered sunspots

2 Look at the example; then choose one of the other people and turn the phrases into complete sentences. Example:

Ho Chi Minh was born in Annam, Vietnam. He was a student in Saigon. He was a politician and poet, and the founder of the People's Republic of Vietnam.

3 🔊 First, read through the questions and try to guess some of the answers. Next, listen to the recording, and then see how many of the questions you can answer.

1. Galileo was born in the (a) *15th* (b) *16th* (c) *17th* century.
2. Was he a professor at Pisa? (a) *Yes.* (b) *No.* (c) *We don't know.*
3. Students came to Galileo (a) *to hear his lectures* (b) *to work with him* (c) *to study sunspots.*
4. Amelia Earhart stopped studying at (a) *18* (b) *22* (c) *33.*
5. She stopped studying because she (a) *didn't have enough money* (b) *wanted to fly* (c) *wanted to work.*
6. She paid for her flying lessons (a) *with her father's help* (b) *with a lorry driver's help* (c) *by doing several jobs.*
7. She worked as a lorry driver because (a) *the money was good* (b) *there was plenty of free time* (c) *she liked driving.*
8. Her Atlantic flight finished in (a) *Newfoundland* (b) *Iceland* (c) *Ireland.*
9. Which places did Ho Chi Minh visit? (a) *South Africa* (b) *the USSR* (c) *England* (d) *France.*
10. He worked as a photographer in (a) *North Africa* (b) *the USA* (c) *Paris.*
11. The Curies met in (a) *Poland* (b) *Paris* (c) *Germany.*
12. In 1903, (a) *Marie Curie* (b) *Pierre Curie* (c) *both of them* got the Nobel Prize.

4 Prepare a short talk (2–3 minutes) about somebody's life. Give your talk, and then ask the other students questions to see how much they can remember.

Learn: century; learn (learnt); fly (flew); pay (paid); pay for something; because; plenty of; round; round the world; across; together; (at a) university; the first man/woman/person to . . .; who; the woman/man/person who . . .

Learn these if you want to: republic; Atlantic; free time; finish.

88

18B America invades Britain!

> Connecting sentences into stories.

1 Read the text and put the pictures in the correct order. Use your dictionary where necessary, but try not to use it too much.

Here is a piece of history that British people don't learn at school.

In 1778 the British had the strongest navy in the world. They laughed at the small navy of their American colonies, ……1…… were fighting to be free of Britain.

One American captain thought he would like to show the British ……2…… size was not everything. ……3…… this is what he did.

On the night of April 24, 1778, Captain John Paul Jones quietly brought his ship *Ranger* to Whitehaven, in the north-west of England. As soon ……4…… he arrived, he took a group of his men to one of the inns in the town, broke into it, ……5…… had a drink with them.

……6…… they started work. ……7…… , they went to the fort and destroyed the guns. ……8…… , they began burning British ships. The British sailors woke up and started fighting against the Americans, ……9…… they could not stop Jones and his men.

……10…… , the Americans left Whitehaven and sailed to the south of Scotland, ……11…… they carried out more attacks.

After Jones' visit, the British stopped laughing at the small American navy.

2 Complete the text with the words and expressions from the box. (There are two words too many.)

and	as	because	but	finally
first of all	next	so	that	then
where	who	why		

3 Pronunciation: linking. Read these phrases and sentences aloud. Be careful to join the words as shown.

1. Here is a piece of history
2. They laughed at the small navy
3. to be free of Britain
4. as soon as he arrived
5. he took a group of his men
6. to one of the inns in the town
7. broke into it
8. first of all

4 Choose a section of the story (one sentence or more) and read it aloud.

5 Write a short story using some of the words in the box from Exercise 2 (as many as you can). You can write about a journey, a holiday, a party, a strange thing that happened to you, a historical event, or anything else you like.

> **Learn:** piece; north; south; west; east; so; first of all; next; finally; where.

18C Who? What? Which? How? Where? When?

> Question-word questions.

1 Put one of these words into each question: *Who, What, Which, How, Where, When.* Can you answer any of the questions? The picture will help.

HISTORY QUIZ

1. .... did Louis Blériot travel from France to England in 1909?
2. .... animals did Hannibal take across the Alps when he invaded Italy?
3. .... in Israel was Jesus Christ born?
4. .... was the name of the man who built the Eiffel Tower?
5. Copernicus disagreed with Ptolemy. .... about?
6. .... was 'New Amsterdam'?
7. .... did the Second World War start (month and year)?
8. .... led the 'Long March' in China?
9. .... starred in the film *The Sound of Music*?
10. .... of these was not a member of the Beatles: John Lennon, Mick Jagger, George Harrison, Ringo Starr, Paul McCartney?
11. .... wrote the James Bond novels?
12. .... of these sports was Pele famous for: baseball, running, football, tennis?

2 Can you make a better quiz than the one in Exercise 1? Work in groups. Make at least ten questions, and use all of the question words.

> **Learn:** when; animal; film; build (built); disagree; lead (led); famous.

18D Washed and shaved, had breakfast

Talking about the past; understanding spoken English; building sentences.

AL'S DAY

JAKE'S DAY

1 Look at the pictures. Which of these things did both Al and Jake do? Which did neither Al nor Jake do? Examples:

'Both Al and Jake robbed a bank.'
'Neither Al nor Jake went to bed early.'

got up late   washed   shaved   had breakfast
robbed a bank   wore masks   carried guns
had lunch at the Ritz   went to a football match
bought flowers   went to an art gallery
listened to the radio   took the dog for a walk
went to bed early

2 Listen to Al's statement to the police. Can you find anything that is not true? Example (practise the pronunciation):

'He told the policeman that he got up at **eight** o'clock, but actually he got up at **ten** o'clock.'

3 Listen to Jake. Can you find any differences between his statement and Al's? Example (practise the pronunciation):

'Al said that they went to an **art gallery** together, but Jake said that they went to a **football match**.'

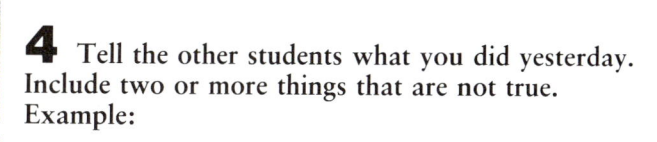

4 Tell the other students what you did yesterday. Include two or more things that are not true. Example:

... then I went to have lunch with the President.

Not true!

No, you didn't!

You had lunch with Pedro.

Learn: policeman; gun; flower; radio; dog; walk (*noun and verb*); wash; carry; early; true; listen to the radio; watch TV.

Unit 19 Getting to know you

19A Is this seat free?

Permission (asking, giving, refusing); starting conversations; *Do you mind if . . . ?*

1 Look at the pictures. What do you think the people are saying in each picture?

2 Pronunciation. Say these words and expressions.

a. Is this seat free?
b. seat sit   eat it   sheep ship
c. heat need cheap steam steel leak
   seek peach keep
d. win spit hit pick lip

3 Work with another student. You are on a train, and you want to sit down, open the window, etc. Ask and answer.

ASK FOR PERMISSION	REFUSE PERMISSION
Do you mind if I sit here?	I'm sorry. It's not free.
Do you mind if I open the window?	Well, it's a bit cold.
Do you mind if I smoke?	Well, I'd rather you didn't.
Do you mind if I look at your paper?	Well, I'm reading it myself, actually.
	GIVE PERMISSION
	Not at all.
	No, please do.
	Go ahead.

4 🔊 Close your books, listen to the recording and answer.
a. Refuse permission.
b. Give permission.

5 Improvisation. Work in groups of between four and six. You are sitting together on a train. Begin a conversation.
OR: Work in pairs. You are both in a coffee-bar, a pub or a park. Begin a conversation.

Learn: seat; myself; open; mind; Do you mind if . . . ?; for a moment; please do; go ahead; I'd rather you didn't.

92

19B How often do you come here?

> Frequency; showing interest; comparing interests and habits; reply questions; *So . . . I.*

♥ *I always come here on Sunday mornings.*
♦ Oh, do you? So do I.
♦ *I'm Pisces.*
♥ Are you? So am I.
♥ Do you like 'Top of the Pops'?
♦ *I never watch it.*
♥ My brother . . .
♦ Does he?
♥ I go to the cinema at least once a week.

♦ *How often do you . . . ?*
♥ Every two or three days . . .
♦ *I've got a . . .*
♦ *Oh, have you? . . .*
♦ Do you ever go to the opera?
♥ Oh, yes, I love opera.
♦ So do I. Actually, I've got two tickets for 'Carmen' tonight.
♥ Oh, have you?
♦ Would you like to go with me?
♥ *I'd love to.*
♦ *Let's have a drink before it starts.*
♥ Why not?

1 Ask and answer.

How often do you:
go to the hairdresser / watch TV /
travel by train / go on holiday / go for a walk /
go to the cinema / listen to music at home /
go skiing / write letters / drink coffee?

| Very often. | Sometimes. | Hardly ever. |
| Quite often. | Occasionally. | Never. |

Once	a day.
Twice	a week.
Three times	a month.
	a year.

Every day/week/month/Tuesday.
Every three days / six weeks.

2 Word order. Write sentences like the examples.

I never go to the cinema.
I often listen to records.
I go skiing twice a year.
I travel by train every Tuesday.

3 Reply questions. Match sentences and answers. Practise the intonation. Then close your books and answer the recorded sentences.

My sister's a doctor.
My brother's got five children.
Maria likes fast cars.
It's raining again.
I slept badly last night.
I love skiing.
My father can speak five languages.
I'm tired.

Oh yes?	Has he?
Really?	Are you?
Do you?	Can he?
Is it?	Does she?
Is she?	Did you?

4 Match the sentences and the answers. (Two answers for each sentence.)

I like fish.
I'm tired.
I've got too much work.
I can speak German.

So can I.	I haven't.
I don't.	So am I.
So have I.	I can't.
I'm not.	So do I.

5 Compare real or imaginary interests and habits. Tell your partner things about yourself. Your partner will answer beginning '. . . you? So . . . I.' or '. . . you? I . . .n't/not.' Examples:

'I've got a pink Rolls-Royce.'
'Have you? So have I. I've got a yellow one, too.'
'Really? I don't like yellow, but . . .'

'I go skiing twice a year.'
'Do you? I don't; I can't ski. But I've got a brother who skis very well.'
'Oh, yes? . . .'

> **Learn:** cinema; go to the cinema; go for a walk; tonight; occasionally; hardly ever; once; twice; three times *etc.*; once a week/month *etc.*; every day/week *etc.*; every three days *etc.*; badly; How often . . . ?; So (do/am/have I *etc.*).

19C What do you think of . . . ?

Opinions; *What do you think of . . . ?*; Present Perfect tense.

1 Look at the questions in the picture. Choose possible answers from these.

Yes, I do.   Terrible!   Cheesecake.
Yes, I went to Senegal last year.
No, I don't.   Yes, lots of times.   Not bad.
We played it at my school.   No, never.
No, I haven't.   Great!   Not much.
I saw it in Paris three years ago.

Speech bubbles in picture:
How do you like this place?
Have you seen 'Carmen' before?
What's your favourite food?
Have you ever played baseball?

What do you think of the government?
Have you ever been to Africa?
Do you like modern jazz?

2 Look at the table of verb forms and choose words to complete the sentences.

1. 'Have you .... *Carmen* before?' 'Yes, I .... it three years ago.'
2. 'Have you ever .... to America?' 'Yes, I .... to California last summer.'
3. 'Have you ever .... fish curry?' 'No, I haven't.'
4. 'Do you like modern jazz?' 'I don't know. I haven't .... much.'
5. 'Do you like driving?' 'Actually, I've never .... to drive.'
6. 'Have another drink.' 'No, thanks. I've .... enough.'
7. 'I .... my job last week.' 'I've .... my job three times this year.'
8. 'Have you ever .... in a shop?' 'Yes, I .... in my uncle's shop every summer when I was younger.'
9. 'Have you ever .... in a car crash?' 'Yes, I .... in a bad crash when I was eighteen.'
10. 'I've .... in three different countries.' 'I've always .... here – I've never wanted to live anywhere else.'

3 Class survey. Write three questions:
a. One question beginning *'What do you think of . . . ?'*
b. One question beginning *'What's/Who's your favourite . . . ?'*
c. One question beginning *'Have you ever . . . ?'*

4 Ask other students your questions. Example:

'What do you think of classical music?'   'Not much.'
'Who's your favourite musician?'   'Tracy Chapman.'
'Have you ever heard her in person?'   'Yes, I have.' / 'No, I haven't.'

Then report to the class. Example:

'Seven people like classical music, three think it isn't bad, and two think it's terrible. Favourite musicians are: Tracy Chapman, . . . One person has heard her favourite musician in person.'

Present Perfect tense	
I have ('ve) been	we have ('ve) been
you have ('ve) been	you have ('ve) been
he/she/it has ('s) been	they have ('ve) been
have I been?	have we been?
have you been?	have you been?
has he/she/it been?	have they been?
I have not (haven't) been	
you have not (haven't) been	
he/she/it has not (hasn't) been	
we have not (haven't) been	
you have not (haven't) been	
they have not (haven't) been	

Verb forms		
INFINITIVE	PAST TENSE	PAST PARTICIPLE
be	was/were	been
have	had	had
see	saw	seen
hear	heard	heard
eat	ate	eaten
learn	learnt	learnt
go	went	gone/been
change	changed	changed
work	worked	worked
live	lived	lived

Learn: great; ever; anywhere; anywhere else; *past participles of the irregular verbs in the table.*

19D   I've only known her for twenty-four hours, but . . .

> Present Perfect tense; *How long*, *for* and *since*.

1 Can you complete the sentences in the two torn letters? These words and expressions will help.

LETTER 1	LETTER 2
sure he's He's	we've got music
I am: man	Pisces. known her
known him am I.	woman. we've always
smile He's	in love

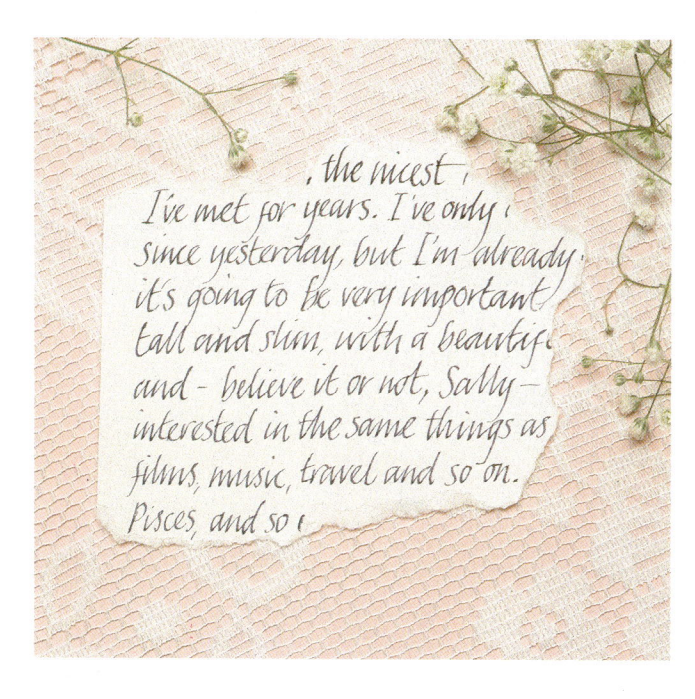

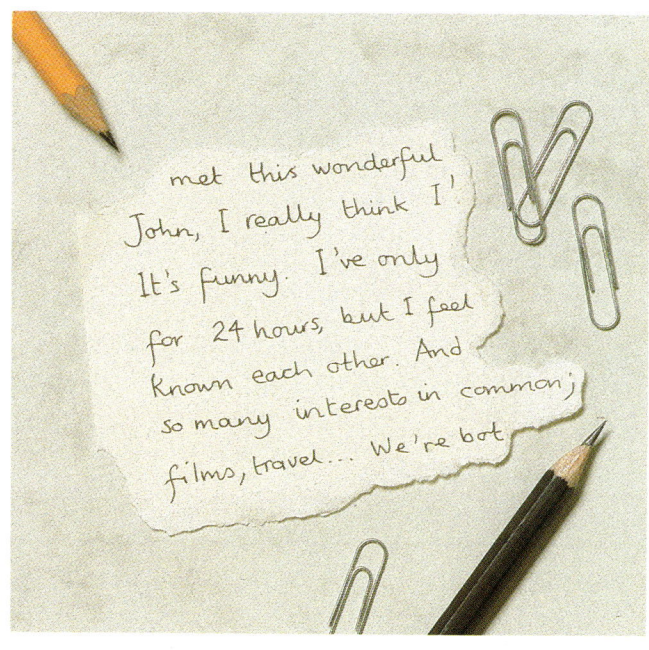

Letter 1 (excerpt): . . . , the nicest . . . I've met for years. I've only . . . since yesterday, but I'm already . . . it's going to be very important . . . tall and slim, with a beautiful . . . and – believe it or not, Sally – interested in the same things as . . . films, music, travel and so on. . . . Pisces, and so . . .

Letter 2 (excerpt): . . . met this wonderful . . . John, I really think I' . . . It's funny. I've only . . . for 24 hours, but I feel . . . known each other. And . . . so many interests in common; films, travel . . . We're bot . . .

2 *Since* and *for*.

since yesterday = for 24 hours
for 400 years = since the 16th century
since last Tuesday = for ....
since last .... = for five days
since 1977 = for ....
.... I was born = all my life
.... = since my birthday
since nine o'clock = ...
since last July = ...
for ten years = ...

3 Make questions with *How long* and ask a partner. Write down four of the answers. Examples:

How long have you | lived in this town/city?
 | been in this class?
 | been married?
 | been learning English?
 | been studying karate / the violin etc.?
 | had that watch/sweater/ring etc.?
 | had long/short hair?
 | known your friend Maria etc.?

4 Give your partner's answers to the teacher, who will shuffle the papers and pass them round. Try to guess who answered the questions.

> **Learn:** smile (*noun*); believe; feel (felt, felt); funny; wonderful; already; since; for (*with time*); all my life; in love; and so on; each other.

Unit 20 Consolidation

20A Things to remember: Units 17, 18 and 19

Present Perfect tense

I have ('ve) been	have I been?	I have not (haven't) been
you have ('ve) been	have you been?	you have not (haven't) been
he/she/it has ('s) been	has he *etc*. been?	she *etc*. has not (hasn't) been
we have ('ve) been	have we been?	we have not (haven't) been
you have ('ve) been	have you been?	you have not (haven't) been
they have ('ve) been	have they been?	they have not (haven't) been

Examples:
'Have you ever **been** to Africa?' 'Yes, I **have**.'
'Have you **seen** *Carmen* before?' 'No, I **haven't**.'
I've never **learnt** to drive.
I've **changed** my job three times this year.
How long **have** you **lived** in this town?
  (How long do you live in this town?)
How long **have** you **known** Maria?
  (How long do you know Maria?)
How long **have** you **been** learning English?
I've **been** in this class for three weeks.
  (I am in this class for three weeks.)
  (I've been in this class since three weeks.)
I've **known** her since 1986.
  (I know her since 1986.)

Since and *for*
since yesterday = **for** 24 hours
since the 16th century = **for** 400 years

Present Perfect and Simple Past
– I've **changed** my job three times **this year**.
  I **changed** my job three times **last year**.
– **Have** you **seen** *Carmen* **before**?
  I **saw** it **three years ago**.
– **Have** you **ever worked** in a shop?
  I **worked** in my uncle's shop **when I was younger**.

Infinitive, past tense and past participle

INFINITIVE	PAST TENSE	PAST PARTICIPLE
Regular verbs		
work	worked	worked
live	lived	lived
stop	stopped	stopped
try	tried	tried
play	played	played
Irregular verbs		
be	was/were	been
bring	brought	brought
buy	bought	bought
catch	caught	caught
come	came	come
cost	cost	cost
draw	drew	drawn
drink	drank	drunk
eat	ate	eaten

(For a complete list of irregular verbs from Units 1–24, see page 136.)

Verbs with two objects
Could you bring **me** some water?
Can I give **you** a little more coffee?
Could you lend **me** some sugar?
Could you show **me** some black sweaters, please?

Imperatives
Meet me at seven o'clock.
Don't tell Carola.

Reported speech; *say* and *tell*
He **told** the policeman that he got up at eight o'clock.
  (He told that he got up ....)
He **said that** they went to an art gallery.
  (He said the policeman that ....)

Question words
How did Louis Blériot travel from France to England? (How travelled ....?)
When did the Second World War start?
  (When started ....?)
What animals did Hannibal take across the Alps?
Where was Jesus Christ born?
  (Where was born Jesus Christ?)

Question word as subject
Who wrote the James Bond novels?
  (Who did write ....?)

Which of ... ?
Which of these was not a member of the Beatles? (Who of these ....?)
Which of these sports was Pele famous for?

Determiners and pronouns
I'm sorry, there's **no more** roast beef.
Would you like **something** to drink?
Could you bring me **some** water?
Is everything all right?
   (Are everything . . . ?)

Articles
He was **a** student in Saigon.
   (He was student . . .)
She was **a** pilot and writer.
She was **the** first woman to fly a plane across the Atlantic.
He was **the** man who discovered sunspots.

Frequency adverbs and adverbials
How often do you go to the cinema?
Do you ever go to the opera?

I	always very often quite often sometimes occasionally hardly ever never	come here on Sunday mornings.
I come here	every day. every three days. once a day. twice a week. three times a year.	

Joining subjects
Both Al **and** Jake robbed a bank.
Neither Al **nor** Jake went to bed early.

Joining sentences
Then they started work. **First of all** they went to the fort and destroyed the guns. **Next,** they began burning British ships . . . **Finally,** the Americans left Whitehaven . . .

Joining clauses into sentences
The British sailors woke up **and** started fighting, **but** they could not stop Jones and his men.
One American captain wanted to show the British **that** size was not everything.
They laughed at the small navy of the Americans, **who** were fighting to be free of Britain.
The Americans left Whitehaven and sailed to Scotland, **where** they carried out more attacks.
As soon as he arrived, he took a group of his men to an inn.
Amelia Earhart stopped studying **because** she wanted to learn to fly.

Showing interest: reply questions
'I'm Pisces.'   '**Are** you?'
'I've got a . . .'   'Oh, **have** you?'
'My father **can** speak five languages.'   '**Can** he?'
'I love skiing.'   '**Do** you?'
'I **slept** badly last night.'   'Oh, **did** you?'

So am I etc.
'I've got a pink Rolls-Royce.'   'So **have** I.'
   'I **haven't**.'
'I'm tired.'   'So **am** I.'   'I'm **not**.'
'Mary **can** swim.'   'So **can** Alice.'   'Louise **can't**.'
'I go skiing twice a year.'   'So **do** I.'   'I **don't**.'
'John **phoned** last night.'   'So **did** your mother.'

Lending and borrowing
I'm sorry to trouble you, but could you lend me some sugar?
Could you possibly lend me your car?
Could I borrow your keys **for a moment**?
Yes, **here you are**.
Yes, **of course**.
I'm sorry, **I need it/them**.
I'm afraid I haven't got one/any.
I'm sorry, **I'm afraid** I can't.

Lend and *borrow*
Could you **lend** me some sugar?
Could I **borrow** some sugar?
   (Could I borrow you some sugar?)

Suggestions; inviting; replying to invitations
Let's have a drink.
Shall we meet at 6.30?
Why don't we go and see a film?
Would you like to have dinner with me?
What a nice idea!
Why not?
I'm afraid I'm not free today. **How about** tomorrow?

Ordering and asking
I'll start with soup, please, and then **I'll have** roast beef.
Chicken **for me**, please.
Could you bring me some water?
Just some water, please.
a little more coffee
Could you bring us the bill, please?
Is service included?

20A continued

Asking for and giving permission: Do you mind if . . . ?

Do you mind if I | sit here?
 | open the window?
 | smoke?
 | look at your paper?

Not at all.   I'm sorry, it's not free.
No, please do.   Well, it's a bit cold.
Go ahead.   Well, I'd rather you didn't.
                         Well, I'm reading it myself, actually.

Opinions

'How do you like this place?'   'Great / Not bad / Not much / Terrible.'
Do you like modern jazz?
What do you think of the government?
What's your favourite food?

Asking about English

What's this?
What's this called in English, please?
Is this a pen or a pencil?
Is this a lighter?

Pronunciation: linking

Here is a piece of history.
as soon as he arrived
first of all

Pronunciation: contrastive stress

He said he got up at **eight** o'clock, but actually he got up at **ten** o'clock.
Al said they went to an **art gallery**, but **Jake** said they went to a **football match**.

Words and expressions

Nouns
bill
cigarette
idea
paper (= newspaper)
dinner
pub
plane
century
university
piece
animal
film
policeman
gun
flower
radio
dog
walk
seat
cinema
smile

Adverbs
though
just
then
certainly
so
first of all
next
finally
early
tonight
occasionally
hardly ever
once
twice
three times *etc.*
once a week *etc.*
every day *etc.*
every three days *etc.*
badly
ever
already
all my life

Verbs
lend (lent, lent)
borrow
show (showed, shown)
need
find out (found, found)
spend (spent, spent)
wait
catch (caught, caught)
learn (learnt, learnt)
fly (flew, flown)
pay (paid, paid)
build (built, built)
disagree
lead (led, led)
walk
wash
carry
open
mind
believe
feel (felt, felt)

Other words and expressions
north
south
east
west
something
everything
somewhere
anywhere
anywhere else
how
How often . . . ?
because
who
where
all right
no more
plenty of
Just a moment/minute
for a moment
Have you got a light?
wait a minute
Well, . . .
all right
catch a plane *etc.*
listen to the radio
watch TV
go to the cinema
go for a walk
pay for (*something*)
Yours (*end of a letter*)
round the world
at a university
in love
the first woman *etc.* to . . .
the man *etc.* who . . .
and so on
each other

Adjectives
fine
usual
important
famous
true
great
funny
wonderful

Prepositions
round
across
since
for (*person*)
for (*time*)
about
with

Optional words and expressions to learn

soup; (roast) beef; (rump) steak; chicken; vegetable; mushroom; salad; lager; coffee; sugar; bread; excellent; over here; not too bad; tough; rare; dictionary; key; umbrella; republic; Atlantic; free time; finish.

20B Past, Perfect and Present

> The differences between the Simple Past, the Present Perfect and the Simple Present.

1 Look at the table and examples, and choose the best rules for each tense.

PRESENT PERFECT TENSE	SIMPLE PAST TENSE
I have seen, you have seen *etc.* have I seen? *etc.* I have not seen *etc.*	I saw, you saw *etc.* did I see? did you see? *etc.* I did not see, you did not see *etc.*
I've changed my job three times this year. **Have** you **seen** *Carmen* before? **Have** you ever **been** to America? She **has** never **learnt** to drive.	**I changed** my job last week. **I saw** *Carmen* three years ago. **Did** you **go** to California last summer? She **learnt** to fly when she was eighteen.

Rules
We use the Present Perfect:

Rules
We use the Simple Past:

A when we are thinking of a period of time that is finished.
B when we are thinking of a period of time that is not finished.
C when we mean 'at any time up to now'.
D with *ever, never, before, this week/month/year* etc., *since*.
E with *ago, yesterday, last week/month/year* etc., *then, when*.

2 Present Perfect or Simple Past?

1. .... this book before? (*Have you read / Did you read*)
2. Yes, I .... it last year. (*have read / read*)
3. 'Do you know where Alice is?' 'She's at home. I .... her yesterday.' (*have seen / saw*)
4. .... to Alaska? (*Have you ever been / Did you ever go*)
5. I .... to eight different schools when I was a child. (*have been / went*)
6. 'Do you like Chaplin?' 'Actually, I .... any of his films.' (*have never seen / never saw*)
7. Ann .... to a lot of parties this year. (*has been / went*)
8. Joe .... his car three times since Christmas. (*has crashed / crashed*)
9. The weather .... terrible last summer. (*has been / was*)
10. This summer .... nice and warm. (*has been / was*)

3 Present Perfect, Simple Past or Simple Present?

1. How long .... here? (*do you live / have you lived / did you live*)
2. I .... Mary since 1980. (*know / have known / knew*)
3. I think I .... her very well. (*know / have known / knew*)
4. How long .... that watch? (*do you have / have you had / did you have*)
5. I .... it last year. (*buy / have bought / bought*)
6. I .... in this school since February. (*am / have been / was*)

4 *Since, for* or *ago*?

1. We've lived in London .... eight years.
2. I've only known her .... yesterday.
3. My grandmother died three years ....
4. I've been working .... four o'clock this morning.
5. She's been a teacher .... eighteen years.
6. It's been raining .... three days.
7. I first went to Africa about seven years ....
8. Mary phoned a few minutes ....
9. I haven't seen her .... weeks.

20C Choose

> A choice of listening, writing, pronunciation and speaking exercises.

Look at the exercises, decide which ones are useful to you, and do two or more.

LISTENING

1 Listen to the sounds. What is happening? Example:

1. 'Somebody is walking.'

2 Listen, and choose the correct one. Example:

1. 'It's smaller than a piano; it's got more strings than a violin.' Answer: 'Guitar.'

1. piano   clarinet   organ   guitar   violin
2. cloud   snow   sun   ice   rain
3. dog   mouse   kangaroo cat   elephant
4. fridge   car   cooker   typewriter bus
5. horse   taxi   bicycle   car   bus
6. Everest   Mont Blanc Eiffel Tower   tree
7. Japan   Kenya   France   Germany   Norway
8. champagne whisky   Coca-Cola milk
9. sofa   chair   table   wardrobe   TV

Now make your own questions about these.

10. shirt   raincoat   skirt   shoe   belt
11. India   Tibet   Bolivia   Switzerland Canada
12. the USA the USSR   China   Norway   Ghana
13. London   Paris   New York Hong Kong Cairo
14. doctor   teacher   dentist   shop assistant footballer
15. cheese   carrot   potato   ice cream apple

3 Read these questions about Thomas Morley, an English musician. Then listen to the recording and try to answer the questions.

1. When was Morley born?
2. Who was Queen at the time?
3. What was the name of Morley's writer friend?
4. What was the date of Morley's own book?
5. Was Morley's best music dramatic or light?

4 Listen to the song and try to write down the words.

WRITING

1 Copy the text, and put one of these words or expressions into each blank.

after	at midnight	began
finally	as soon as	about
dancing	and then	others
on the night of	some	so
sang	some of them	went

.... December 31st, we invited .... friends to a New Year's Eve party. .... the first guests arrived, we offered them drinks, ... we put on some music. .... half an hour there were .... thirty people in our small flat. .... to dance; .... just went on talking, eating and drinking. .... we all joined hands and .... an old Scottish song called *Auld Lang Syne*; then we went on ....

At seven o'clock in the morning there were still eight people left, ... we had breakfast. .... the last guest went home, and we .... to bed.

2 Write about a party that you have been to, using at least five of the words and expressions from the box in Exercise 1.

PRONUNCIATION

1 Say these words after the recording or after your teacher.

1. hungry   husband   under   much
2. blue   Tuesday   excuse   July
3. purple   burn   surname   Thursday

1, 2 or 3? Decide how to pronounce these words and check with your teacher or the recording.

furniture   lunch   supermarket   supper   true   number   uncle   turn   June   summer   sun

2 Intonation. Look at these two conversations, and listen to the recording.

1. 'Cambridge 31453.'   'Mary?'
   'No, this is Sally.'
2. 'What's your name?'   'Mary.'

In the first conversation, *Mary* is a question. The voice goes up. *Mary?*
In the second conversation, *Mary* is a statement. The voice goes down. *Mary.*

Now copy these words and expressions; then listen to the recording and decide whether they are questions or statements. Write *Q* or *S* after the words.

three o'clock ......Q......
London ......S......
Michael   Tuesday   a girl   at the pub   a cigarette   two pounds   Washington   trinitrotoluene

SPEAKING

1 Who is who?

Jane, Pete, Joe and Alice are from Birmingham, London, New York and Canberra (not in that order).
One is a doctor, one a dentist, one an artist and one a shop assistant.
Their ages are 19, 22, 36 and 47.
Apart from English, one of them speaks French, one German, one Greek and one Chinese.

Only one of them is tall, only one is good-looking, only one is blue-eyed, only one is dark. The tall one is 22.
One of them is a 36-year-old blue-eyed dentist from Canberra who speaks Chinese. What are the others?

Ask your teacher questions. He or she can only answer *Yes* or *No*. Examples:

'Is Jane a dentist?'   'No.'
'Is the artist good-looking?'   'Yes.'
'Does Joe speak Chinese?'   'Yes.'

		ALICE	JOE	PETE	JANE
APPEARANCE	Tall				
	Good-looking				
	Blue-eyed				
	Dark				
AGE	19				
	22				
	36				
	47				
PROFESSION	Doctor				
	Dentist				
	Artist				
	Shop assistant				
HOME	Birmingham				
	London				
	New York				
	Canberra				
LANGUAGES	French				
	German				
	Greek				
	Chinese				

2 Getting to know somebody. Work in groups. Prepare and practise a sketch with several characters. Include some of the following:

getting to know somebody   asking for things   a letter   lending and borrowing   inviting   exchanging opinions   addresses   saying how often you do things   a meal in a restaurant   names   spelling   telephone numbers   telling the time   telephoning   asking the way

20D Test yourself

LISTENING

1 Look at the picture and listen to the description. Can you find five differences?

GRAMMAR

1 Which is correct – *a*, *b*, or both *a* and *b*?

1. .... this film before?
   a. *Have you seen*
   b. *Did you see*
2. .... to Australia?
   a. *Have you ever been*
   b. *Did you ever go*
3. I .... the doctor yesterday.
   a. *have seen*
   b. *saw*
4. I .... a lot of tennis this year.
   a. *have played*
   b. *played*
5. We've lived in this house .... 50 years.
   a. *since*
   b. *for*
6. Could you .... me where the station is?
   a. *tell*
   b. *say*
7. I always .... what I think.
   a. *tell*
   b. *say*
8. .... everything all right?
   a. *Is*
   b. *Are*
9. Could you .... me some sugar?
   a. *borrow*
   b. *lend*
10. Let's .... a drink.
    a. *to have*
    b. *have*
11. Would you like .... dinner with me?
    a. *to have*
    b. *have*
12. He was .... in Saigon.
    a. *a student*
    b. *student*

2 Write the past tense and past participle. Example:

go *went gone (or been)*

bring; buy; catch; come; cost; draw; drink; eat.

3 Put the words in the right order.

1. water me could bring some you ?
2. I little can you more give a coffee ?

4 Write questions to find out:

1. how Louis Blériot travelled from France to England.
2. when the Second World War started.
3. what animals Hannibal took across the Alps.
4. where Napoleon was born.
5. who wrote the James Bond novels.

VOCABULARY

1 Put in suitable words or expressions.

1. Is this seat ....?
2. 'What is your .... colour?' 'Red.'
3. Karl Marx was .... in 1818.
4. I'm very good at ...., but I'm bad at ....
5. 'What would you like?' 'I'll .... roast beef.'
6. Would you like something to ....?
7. I first met Annie seven years ....
8. I'm much .... than my mother.
9. Could you .... water?
10. 'Could you lend me £5?' 'I'm sorry, I'm .... I can't.'
11. Is service ....?
12. 'Can I help you?' '................ looking.'
13. What size ....?
14. Those shoes are nice. Can I ....?

LANGUAGE IN USE

1 Give suitable answers to these sentences.
Example:

I'm tired. <u>So am I.</u>

OR: <u>Are you?</u>

1. John's got a new car.
2. My sister works in New York.
3. My father can speak five languages.
4. Would you like to come to a party?
5. Let's go and have a drink.
6. Do you mind if I smoke?
7. Do you like mountains?
8. I love skiing.
9. I slept very badly last night.
10. Could I borrow your pen for a moment?

PRONUNCIATION

1 Which word is different?

1. dinner   since   fine   build
2. funny   just   once   June
3. south   though   round   out
4. walk   wash   on   not
5. lead   great   seat   east
6. so   show   who   though
7. caught   north   walk   dog
8. twice   piece   fly   mind

2 Which syllable is stressed?

moment; cigarette; idea; century; animal; policeman; radio; disagree; believe; usual; important; famous; wonderful; somewhere; together; finally; already; tonight; occasionally; about; across; everything.

WRITING

1 Write 100–200 words about what you do at weekends. Use some of the following words and expressions:

always; usually; often; quite often; sometimes; hardly ever; never.

SPEAKING

1 Act out this conversation. The teacher will act the other part.

You are sitting next to a stranger on a plane or a train. The two of you start talking. Answer the other person's questions, give some information about yourself, and find out something about him or her. Try to find at least three things that you have in common.

Unit 21 Knowing about the future

21A I'm going to learn Chinese

> Plans for the future; *going to*.

1 What are your plans for this evening? Are you going to do any of these things?

write letters   see a film
play cards   see friends
watch TV   wash your hair
listen to music   study

Examples:

'*I'm going to write letters.*'
'*I'm not going to watch TV.*'

Have you got any plans for the next year or so? Are you going to make any changes in your life? Think of something that you are never going to do again in your life.

2 You are going to hear a man talking about what he is going to do next year. First, look at the pictures and see if you can guess some of the things he is going to do. Example:

'*I think he's going to learn Chinese.*'

3 Now listen to the conversation. Which of these things is the man going to do during his year off work?

take a big rest; listen to the radio; watch videos; study biology; walk right across Ireland; write a novel; play some rugby; travel round the world; learn karate; get married.

Listen again. Can you make a complete list of the things he is going to do?

4 Pronunciation. Say these words and expressions.

1. first   first of all   third
   thirsty   thirty
2. certain   certainly
3. Thursday on Thursday
   burn
4. world   round the world
   word   work
5. learn   early   heard

Can you think of any other words that are pronounced with the vowel /ɜː/?

5 Work in groups. Each group has £100,000; you must use it to do some good to three or more groups of people in your country or somewhere else in the world. What are you going to do with the money? You have fifteen minutes to decide. Useful structures:
Let's . . . ; Why don't we . . . ?
Example:

'*Let's give most of the money to poor people in Africa.*' '*No, why don't we use it to help people in this country?*'

> **Learn:** rest (*noun*); video; use; decide; get married (got, got); right across; do good to somebody (did, done).

21B   This is going to be the kitchen

Planning a house; *going to*; vocabulary study.

1 Look at the plan. The house isn't finished yet. Which room do you think is going to be the bathroom? Work in pairs. Turn to page 133 OR page 134: you will find some more information about the house. Exchange information with your partner until you know what all the rooms are going to be.

2 Vocabulary revision and extension. How many of these words do you know already? Find out what the rest mean. How many of them can you see?

carpet   ceiling   door   floor   garden
lift   light   paint   roof   stairs
steps   switch   wall   wallpaper   window

3 Redesign your school. Decide what the different rooms are going to be. Tell the class. Example:

'Classroom 6 is going to be a games room. This is going to be my bathroom.'
'I'm going to put purple wallpaper in all the rooms.'
'I'm going to move all the furniture out of this room and put cushions on the floor.'

Learn: bedroom; bathroom; kitchen; living room; dining room; information (*uncountable*); find (found, found); put (put, put); move; finished; over; out of.

Learn three or more other words from the lesson.

21C It's going to rain

> Predictions with *going to*.

1 Look at the pictures. What is going to happen? (If you don't know the words, use your dictionary or ask your teacher.)

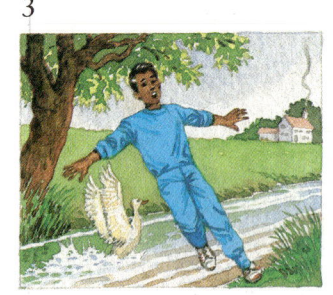

1 2 3 4 5 6 7 8

2 Pronunciation: 'long *o*' (/əʊ/). Can you say these words and expressions?

go so no home don't know coat
Don't go.   I don't know.   I don't think so.
I'm going home.   It's going to rain.

Can you think of any more words that are pronounced with /əʊ/?

3 Other pronunciations of *o*. Can you say these words?

1. holiday Scotland not job stop cost
2. north more born short or organise
3. work world worse
4. some one mother cover tough young country

Which groups do these words go in?

on sport brother got bored come
forty word dog morning clock
love worst

Can you add more words to any of the groups?

4 Read the advertisement. Then make up advertisements yourself (working in groups and using the phrases in the box) to get people to join your holiday trip. Useful words: *spring, summer, autumn, winter*.

HOLIDAY IN SCOTLAND
We are organising a holiday walking tour in the north of Scotland this summer.
We are going to cover 150 miles of mountainous country in ten days.
It's going to be hard work.
It's going to be tough.
You're going to be wet, cold and tired a lot of the time.
But it's going to be fun!
If you're young and fit, and if you like beautiful places – why not join us?
Cost £95 inclusive.
For more details, write Box 1346, *Edinburgh Times*.

We are organising a trip to . . .
We are going to . . .
It's going to be . . .
It's going to be . . .
And/But it's going to be . . .
If you're . . . , and if . . . , why not join us?
Cost: £ . . . inclusive.

Learn: advertisement; fun; spring; summer; autumn; winter; baby; have a baby (had, had); win (won, won); crash; fall (fell, fallen); break (broke, broken).

21D Why? To . . .

> Why we do things: *to* . . . ; joining sentences into paragraphs.

1 Vocabulary study. You go to a supermarket to buy food. Do you know where you go:

to study; to buy books; to borrow books; to post letters; to catch a train; to catch a plane; to get a visa; to have a drink; to have a meal; to meet people; to buy meat; to buy bread; to borrow money; to get an injection; to see interesting animals?

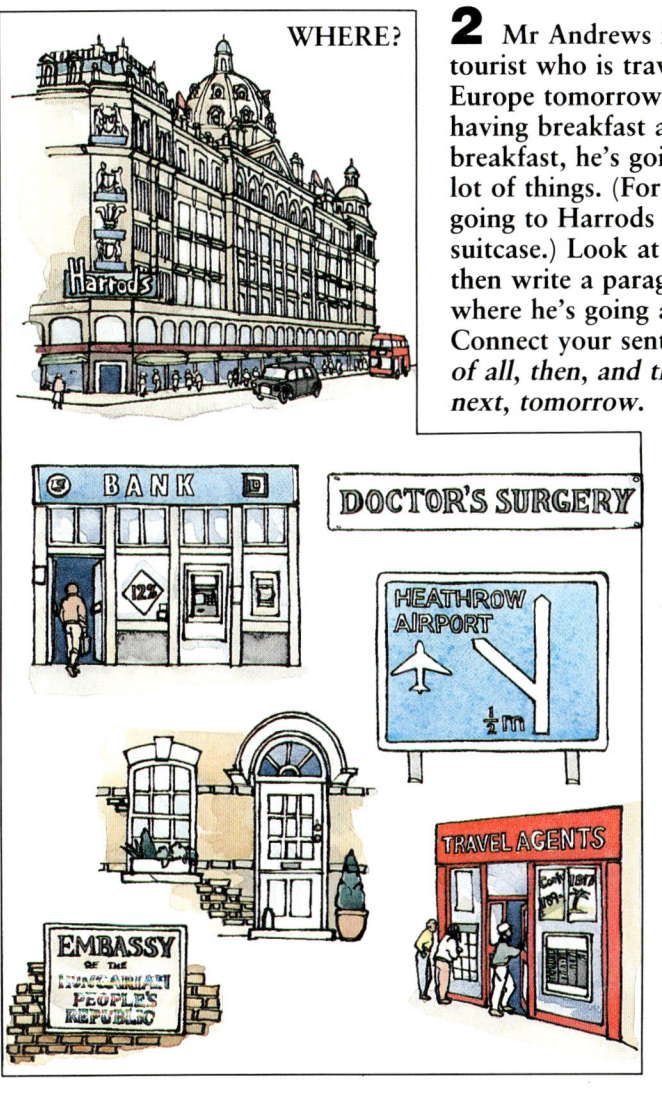

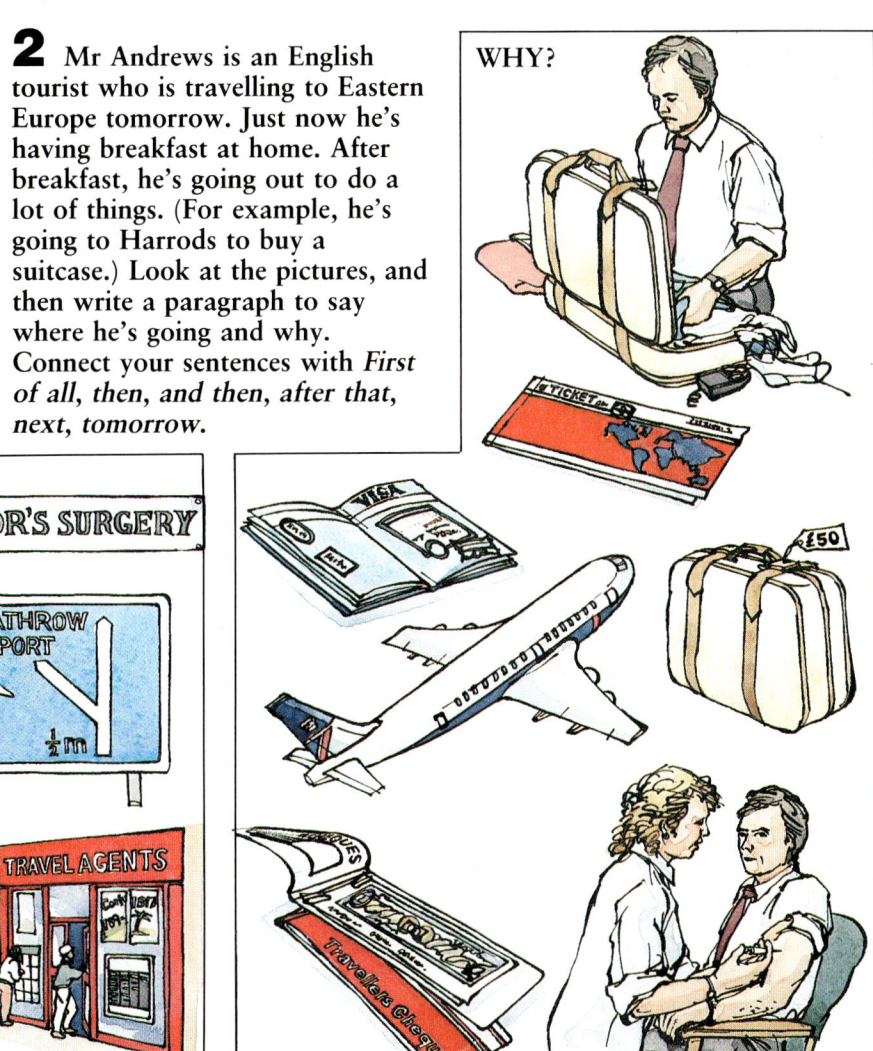

WHERE?

2 Mr Andrews is an English tourist who is travelling to Eastern Europe tomorrow. Just now he's having breakfast at home. After breakfast, he's going out to do a lot of things. (For example, he's going to Harrods to buy a suitcase.) Look at the pictures, and then write a paragraph to say where he's going and why. Connect your sentences with *First of all, then, and then, after that, next, tomorrow.*

WHY?

3 Why are you learning English? People learn English all over the world. Why do you think most of them do it? Put these reasons in order of importance.

- to read English literature
- to travel to English-speaking countries
- to do business in English
- to understand songs and films in English
- to use English for international communication
- just because they like the language
- because they have to learn it at school
- for other reasons (what?)

> **Learn:** meal; meat; bread (*uncountable*); reason; country; song; airport; business; do business (did, done); international.
>
> **Learn these if you want to:** injection; suitcase; embassy; visa; travel agent; literature; communication; pack.

Unit 22 Telling people to do things

22A I feel ill

Illness; sympathy; suggestions.

1 Use your dictionary to match the pictures and the words. Then match the problems and the suggestions.

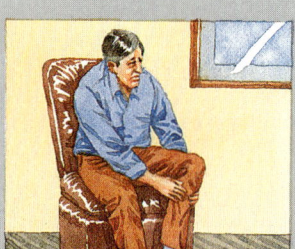

1. I've got a cold.
2. I've got toothache.
3. I've got a temperature.
4. I've got flu.
5. I've got a headache.
6. My leg hurts.

a. Why don't you go home and lie down?
b. Why don't you take an aspirin?
c. Why don't you see the doctor?
d. Why don't you see the dentist?

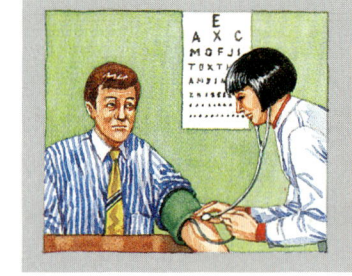

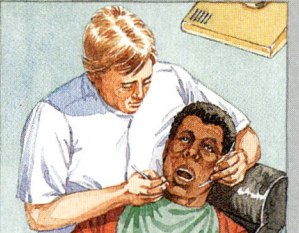

2 What do you think they will say next? Listen to check.

3 Use your dictionary to look up three other words or expressions you can use at the doctor's.

4 At the doctor's. Work in groups to write the other half of this dialogue.

DOCTOR: Good morning. What's the problem?
YOU: Well, ...
DOCTOR: I see. Does it / Do they hurt very badly?
YOU: ....
DOCTOR: How long have you had this?
YOU: ....
DOCTOR: Yes, right. I'd like to examine you, then. Mmm . . . Mmm . . .
YOU: ....?
DOCTOR: No, it doesn't look too bad. Here's a prescription for some medicine. Phone me if you're not better by the day after tomorrow.
YOU: ....
DOCTOR: Goodbye.
YOU: ....

Learn: headache; aspirin; problem; temperature; (a) cold; flu (*uncountable*); toothache (*uncountable*); medicine (*uncountable*); catch (caught, caught) (flu, *etc.*); hurt (hurt, hurt); hope; What's the matter?; take medicine (took, taken).

108

22B Always warm up

> Instructions and advice; imperatives.

1 Here is some advice about running. Some of it is good, and some is not. Which sentences give you good advice?

RUNNING[1] – DOs and DON'Ts

Wear good running shoes.
Run early in the morning – it's better.
Wear comfortable clothing[2].
Always warm up[3] before you run.
Always run with somebody – never run alone.
Rest every ten minutes or so.
Walk for a few minutes after you finish.

Don't run if you feel tired.
Never drink water while you are running.
Don't run until two hours after eating.
Don't run if you have got a cold[4].
Don't run fast downhill[5].
Don't run if you are over 50.
Don't run on roads in fog[6].

2 Listen to two English people doing Exercise 1. Are all their answers right? Words to listen for:

a good/bad idea   not true
a good piece of advice
you should/shouldn't
I don't think it matters
it's up to you   your own choice

3 Say these words after the recording or your teacher.

1. fog   hot   long   doctor
   dollar   office
2. comfortable   front
   another   brother

Find some more words that go in group 1.
Can you find any more that go in group 2?

4 Make sure you know what the words in the box mean. Then listen, and try to draw the picture.

| cat   chair   fork   knife |
| spoon   table   window |
| child/children   man/men |
| woman/women   in   on |
| under   to the right of |

5 Work in groups. Think of some advice (good or bad) for somebody who:

– is a tourist in your country
– is learning to drive
– is learning your language
– is learning English
– wants to get rich
– wants more friends

Make a list of three (or more) DOs and three (or more) DON'Ts.

Learn: advice (*uncountable*); shoe; picture; fork; knife; spoon; rest (*verb*); right; wrong; alone; before (*conjunction*); after (*conjunction*); while; mistake; make a mistake (made, made).

22C Look out!

> Imperatives; requests, instructions, warnings.

1 Put the following expressions into the pictures.

Please hurry, darling.
Take your time, darling.   Don't worry.
Look.   Please come in.   Wait here, please.
Be careful, dear.   Follow me, please.   Look out!

1
2 
3 
4 
5 
6 
7 
8 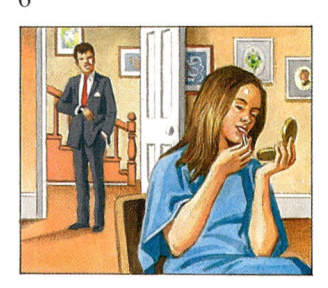
9 

2 Listen to the recording. Write ✓ every time you hear an imperative (like *Walk, Come in, Be careful*), and ✗ every time you hear a negative imperative (like *Don't run, Don't worry*). Listen again, and then try to remember some of the imperatives and negative imperatives.

3 Work in groups. Prepare and practise a very short sketch using one or more of the expressions from Exercise 1.

> **Learn:** be; darling; dear; hurry; Look out!; (Don't) worry; follow; Follow me; (Be) careful; Take your time.

110

22D Please speak more slowly

Adverbs; instructions.

1 🔊 How are the people speaking? Listen to the recording, and choose one adverb for each sentence.

| angrily | coldly | happily | kindly |
| loudly | sleepily | | |

2 Now listen to the next five sentences, and find more adverbs to say how the people are speaking.

3 Spelling. Look carefully at these adverbs.

| badly | quietly | nicely | completely |
| carefully | angrily | happily | comfortably |

Now make adverbs from these adjectives.

| warm | great | extreme | sincere |
| hungry | lazy | real | terrible |

4 Adjective or adverb?
1. I'm very .... with you. (*angry/angrily*)
2. She spoke to me .... (*angry/angrily*)
3. I don't think your mother drives very .... (*good/well*)
4. You've got a .... face. (*nice/nicely*)
5. I play the guitar very .... (*bad/badly*)
6. It's .... cold. (*terrible/terribly*)
7. Your father's got a very .... voice. (*loud/loudly*)
8. Why are you looking at me ....? (*cold/coldly*)
9. You speak very .... English. (*good/well*)
10. You speak English very .... (*good/well*)

5 Put the adverb in the right place.
1. He read the letter without speaking. (*slowly*)
   He read the letter slowly without speaking.
2. She speaks French. (*badly*)
3. I like dancing. (*very much*)
4. Please write your name. (*clearly*)
5. You should eat your food. (*slowly*)
6. She read his letter. (*carefully*)
7. I said 'Hello' and walked away. (*coldly*)

6 Now work with a partner and make up a short conversation. One partner tells the other to be careful, or to look out, or to wait, etc. Each partner speaks coldly, or angrily, or fast, etc.; the other students must say how you are speaking.

Learn: lazy; angry; clear; complete; loud; sleepy.

Unit 23 Predictions

23A Are you sure you'll be all right?

Talking about the future with will.

1 Read the dialogue and then practise it in pairs.

A: I'm going to hitchhike round the world.
B: Oh, that's very dangerous.
A: No, it isn't. I'll be all right.
B: Where will you sleep?
A: Oh, I don't know. In youth hostels. Cheap hotels.
B: You'll get lost.
A: No, I won't.
B: You won't get lifts.
A: Yes, I will.
B: What will you do for money?
A: I'll take money with me.
B: You haven't got enough.
A: If I need money I'll find jobs.
B: Well . . . are you sure you'll be all right?
A: Of course I'll be all right.

2 Write and practise the contractions.

I will *I'll*	we will	I will not *I won't*
you will	they will	you will not
he will		it will not
she will		
it will		

3 Listen. Which sentence do you hear?

1. I stop work at six.
   I'll stop work at six.
2. You know the answer.
   You'll know the answer.
3. I have coffee for breakfast.
   I'll have coffee for breakfast.
4. You have to change at Coventry.
   You'll have to change at Coventry.
5. I drive carefully.
   I'll drive carefully.
6. I know you like my brother.
   I know you'll like my brother.

4 Work in pairs. Complete one of these dialogues and practise it.

A: I'm going to be a racing driver.
B: dangerous
A: isn't | all right
B: crash | get killed
A: won't
B: find a job
A: will | good driver
B: sure | all right
A: course

A: I'm going to be a doctor.
B: have to study | seven years
A: know | I don't mind
B: finish your studies
A: will
B: have | really hard life
A: interesting
B: have to work very long hours
A: know | don't mind
B: OK — if that's what you want.
A: is

5 Make up and practise a short conversation beginning:

A: 'I'm going to get married.'
or A: 'I'm going to work in a circus.'
or A: 'I'm going to be a teacher.'
or A: 'I'm going to ski down Everest.'
or A: 'I'm going to be a pilot.'

Will

I will go (I will to go) (I'll go)
you will go (you'll go)
he/she/it will go (he wills go) (he'll/she'll/it'll go)
we will go (we'll go)
you will go (you'll go)
they will go (they'll go)

will I go? (do I will go?)

I will not (won't) go

Learn: finish; get lost (got, got); get killed; have to do something (had, had); dangerous; all right; if; I don't mind.

Learn some other words and expressions from the lesson if you want to.

23B If you push lever B, ...

If and will; meanings of get.

1 How does the machine work? Write sentences.

| If you | press / pull / push / turn | button / lever / handle | A, B, C, D, E, F, | I think you'll get ... |

Check with the teacher. Example:

'If you push lever B, what will you get?'

2 Put in the correct verb forms.

1. If you .... that button, you .... a cup of coffee. (*press*; *get*)
2. If I .... time, I .... and see you. (*have*; *come*)
3. If it ...., we .... the party inside. (*rain*; *have*)
4. I .... you if I .... help. (*tell*; *need*)
5. I hope you .... and see us if you .... in Chicago again. (*come*; *be*)
6. If you .... that door, you .... something strange. (*open*; *see*)
7. I .... surprised if she .... before 7 o'clock. (*be*; *arrive*)
8. If you .... fast, we .... time to play a game of tennis. (*eat*; *have*)
9. If you .... up early tomorrow, I .... you swimming. (*get*; *take*)
10. I .... my car if I .... to live in London. (*sell*; *go*)

3 Pronunciation. Say these words and expressions.

1. if   it   is   will   drink   him   his   swimming   without   English   women   minute
2. eat   east   feel   see   need   tea   meat   free   week   please
3. evening   seeing   feeling   eating   needing   extremely
4. I think it is.   I think I agree.
   if you eat too much   if you see him
   if you meet him   if you feel ill

4 Do you know the right adjectives to complete these sentences?

1. If you don't eat, you'll get ....
2. If you eat too much, you'll get ....
3. If you don't drink, you'll get ....
4. If you drink too much alcohol, you'll get ....
5. If you run a long way, you'll get ....
6. If you go out in the rain without an umbrella, you'll get ....
7. If you go out in the snow without a coat, you'll get ....
8. In the evening, when the sun goes down, it gets ....
9. We are all getting ....

5 *Get* has several different meanings. Put these sentences in four groups, according to the meaning of *get*.

What time do you usually get up?
It's getting late.
My English is getting better.
Where can I get some stamps?
John got into his car and drove away.
It takes me an hour to get to work.
I get a letter from my mother every week.
Get on the bus outside the station, and get off at Park Street.
The housing problem is getting worse.
If you go to the shops, can you get me some bread, please?
Get out! I don't want to see you any more. Get out of my life!
You've got beautiful eyes.

Learn: press; push; pull; turn; get on (got, got); get off; get in(to); get out (of); sell (sold, sold).

Learn four or more other words from the lesson.

23C What do the stars say?

Predictions: people's futures.

AQUARIUS (Jan 21 – Feb 18)
An old friend will come back into your life, bringing new problems. Don't make any quick decisions.

PISCES (Feb 19 – Mar 20)
In three days you will receive an exciting offer. But your family will make difficulties.

ARIES (Mar 21 – Apr 20)
Money will come to you at the end of the week. If you're not careful it will go away again very fast.

TAURUS (Apr 21 – May 21)
You will have trouble with a child. Try to be patient. You will have a small accident on Sunday – nothing serious.

GEMINI (May 22 – June 21)
This will be a good time for love, but there will be a serious misunderstanding with somebody close to you. Try to tell the truth if you can.

CANCER (June 22 – July 22)
You will meet somebody who could change your life. Don't be too cautious – if you lose the opportunity, it won't come again.

LEO (July 23 – Aug 23)
Something very strange will happen next Thursday. Try to laugh about it.

VIRGO (Aug 24 – Sept 23)
This will be a terrible week. The weekend will be the worst time. Stay in bed on Sunday. Don't open the door. Don't answer the phone.

LIBRA (Sept 24 – Oct 23)
There will be bad news the day after tomorrow; but the bad news will turn to good.

SCORPIO (Oct 24 – Nov 22)
You will make an unexpected journey, and you will find something very good at the end of it.

SAGITTARIUS (Nov 23 – Dec 21)
You will have trouble from a person who loves you; and you will have help from a person who doesn't.

CAPRICORN (Dec 22 – Jan 20)
A letter will bring a very great surprise. If there are problems, a good friend will make things better.

1 Read your horoscope with a dictionary. Memorise it – and see if it comes true! Read some of the others too.

2 *There* or *it*?

1. *There* will be bad news the day after tomorrow.
2. *It* will be cold and wet tomorrow.
3. .... will be rain at the weekend.
4. .... will be warm and sunny next week.
5. .... will be problems with somebody you love.
6. .... will probably be difficult to finish the work in time.
7. .... will be a meeting at 8.00 this evening.
8. .... will be a public holiday next Tuesday.
9. Do you think .... will be enough food for everybody?
10. 'We're going to Japan for our holiday.' 'That's nice, but .... will be expensive.'
11. We're late – .... will be after ten o'clock when we arrive.
12. .... won't be many cars on the road this evening.

3 If possible, work with somebody else who has the same sign as you. Write a new horoscope for your sign, and a new one for a different sign.

Learn: decision; make a decision (made, made); trouble; truth; tell the truth (told, told); surprise; strange; bad news.

Learn some more words from the lesson if you want to.

23D What will happen next?

> Predicting the end of a story.

1 Find out what these words mean. Ask your teacher or use a dictionary.

dead   prison   revolution   employer
royal   procession   duke   palace
mistress   famous   successful   heart
refuse   cousin

2 Read the opera synopsis. Then close your book and see how much you can remember.

3 What do you think will happen in the third act? Work in groups and finish the synopsis.

> **Learn:** heart; cousin; dream (dreamt, dreamt); pass; become (became, become); dead; away.
>
> **Learn three or more of these:** lover; prison; revolution; employer; mistress; refuse; join; unkind.

DEATH IN PARIS

An Opera in Three Acts by Zoltan Grmljavina

SYNOPSIS

ACT ONE

Anna, a beautiful 18-year-old girl, works in a shop in the old town of Goroda, in Central Moldenia. Her parents are dead; her lover, Boris, is in prison for revolutionary activities; her employer is very unkind to her. She dreams of a happier life. One day a royal procession passes in the street. The Grand Duke sees Anna and falls in love with her. He sends for her; when she goes to the palace he tells her that she must become his mistress. If not, Boris will die. Anna agrees. Boris is released from prison; in a letter Anna tells him that she can never see him again. Boris leaves Moldenia.

ACT TWO

Three years have passed. Anna and the Duke are in Paris. The Duke is dying – he has only six months to live – but the doctors have not told him. Only Anna knows the truth.

One day, Anna is walking in the Tuileries when a man stops her. It is Boris. He tells her that he is now a famous artist, rich and successful. He is married to a Frenchwoman, Yvette; but in his heart he still loves Anna. 'Come away with me', he says. Anna refuses, and Boris says that he will do something terrible. At this moment, Yvette joins them. Boris tells Yvette that Anna is his cousin from Moldenia, but Yvette does not believe him.

ACT THREE

Anna and...

Unit 24 Consolidation

24A Things to remember: Units 21, 22 and 23

Going to
I'm **going to learn** Chinese.
What **are** you **going to do** next year?
It'**s going to rain**.
She'**s going to have** a baby.

Will

I will go (~~I will to go~~) (I'll go) you will go (you'll go) he/she/it will go (~~he wills go~~) (he'll/she'll/it'll go) we will go (we'll go) you will go (you'll go) they will go (they'll go)
will I go? (~~do I will go?~~)
I will not (won't) go

Examples:
Are you sure **you'll be** all right?
Manchester **will beat** Liverpool 2–0.
If you press button F, **you'll get** a cup of coffee.
This **will be** a terrible week.
There **will be** bad news the day after tomorrow.

If ... will ...
If you **press** button F, **you'll get** a cup of coffee.
   (~~If you will press ...~~)
If I **have** time, **I'll come** and see you.
   (~~If I will have time ...~~)
I'll be surprised if she **writes** to you.

There will be + noun; it will be + adjective
There will be rain at the weekend.
It will be warm next week.

Infinitive of purpose
You go to a supermarket **to buy** food.
He's going to Harrods **to buy** a suitcase.

Adjectives and adverbs
– Adjectives with nouns
   You've got a **nice** face.
   She speaks **good** English.
– Adjectives after *be*
   I am **angry** with you.
– Adverbs after other verbs
   She spoke **angrily**.
   She speaks English **well**.
– Adverbs with adjectives
   It's **terribly** cold.

Adverbs after objects
She speaks **English well**. (~~She speaks well English.~~)
I like **skiing very much**. (~~I like very much skiing.~~)

Adverbs of manner: spelling
slow ⟶ slowly
quiet ⟶ quietly
kind ⟶ kindly
bad ⟶ badly
careful ⟶ carefully (~~carefuly~~)
extreme ⟶ extremely (~~extremly~~)
happy ⟶ happily
angry ⟶ angrily
comfortable ⟶ comfortably

Articles with words for illnesses
I've got **a** cold.
       a headache.   } COUNTABLE
       a temperature.

I've got toothache. } UNCOUNTABLE
       flu.

The meanings of *get*
– *Get* + direct object (= 'receive', 'obtain')
   Where can I **get** some stamps?
   I **get** a letter from my mother every week.
   Can you **get** me some bread, please?

– *Get* + adverb particle / preposition (= 'move')
   What time do you usually **get up**?
   It takes me an hour to **get to** work.
   Get on the bus outside the station, and **get off** at Park Street.
   Get out!!

– *Get* + adjective / past participle (= 'become')
   It's **getting** late.
   If you work too hard you'll **get** tired.
   get married/lost/killed

– *Have got* (= 'possess')
   You've **got** beautiful eyes.

Sentences with *before* and *after*
Always warm up **before** you run.
Walk for a few minutes **after** you finish.

Joining sentences into paragraphs
First of all he's going to buy a suitcase. **Then** he's going to go to the embassy, **and then** he's going to get his traveller's cheques from the bank. **After that** he's going to the doctor for a vaccination. **Next**, he's going to the travel agent's to get his tickets.

Telling stories with present tenses
One day, Anna **is walking** in the Tuileries when a man **stops** her. It **is** Boris. He **tells** her . . .

Feelings
I feel ill.
What's the matter?
My eyes hurt. My arm hurts.
Do they / Does it hurt very badly?
I've got a (bad) cold / a (bad) headache /
 (bad) toothache / flu / a temperature.
Why don't you see the doctor/dentist?

Giving advice and instructions
Run early in the morning – it's better.
Always wear comfortable clothing.
 (~~Wear always comfortable clothing.~~)
Never run in fog. (~~Run never in fog.~~)
Don't run if you have got a cold.

Please hurry!	Wait here, please.
Take your time.	Be careful.
Don't worry.	Follow me, please.
Look.	Look out!
Come in.	

Words and expressions

Nouns
rest	summer	business	picture
video	autumn	headache	fork
bedroom	winter	aspirin	knife (knives)
bathroom	baby	problem	spoon
kitchen	meal	temperature	mistake
living room	meat	flu (*uncountable*)	decision
dining room	bread (*uncountable*)	toothache (*uncountable*)	trouble
information (*uncountable*)	reason	medicine (*uncountable*)	truth
advertisement	country	advice (*uncountable*)	surprise
fun	song	shoe	heart
spring	airport	cold	cousin

Verbs
use	fall (fell, fallen)	worry	turn
decide	break (broke, broken)	follow	sell (sold, sold)
find (found, found)	catch (caught, caught)	hurry	dream (dreamt, dreamt)
put (put, put)	hurt (hurt, hurt)	finish	pass
move	hope	press	become (became, become)
win (won, won)	rest	push	
crash	be (was/were, been)	pull	

Adjectives
international
right
wrong
alone
lazy
angry
clear
complete
loud
sleepy
dangerous
strange
dead

Prepositions
right across
over
out of
into

Other words and expressions to learn
get married (got, got)	have to do something
do good to somebody (did, done)	darling
have a baby (had, had)	dear
do business	before (*conjunction*)
take medicine (took, taken)	after (*conjunction*)
make a mistake (made, made)	while
make a decision	if
get lost	finished
get killed	all right
get on	away
get off	bad news
get in(to)	What's the matter?
get out (of)	I don't mind
tell the truth (told, told)	

Optional words and expressions to learn
injection; suitcase; embassy; visa; travel agent; literature; communication; pack; lover; prison; revolution; employer; mistress; refuse; join; unkind.

24B Choose

> A choice of listening, pronunciation and speaking exercises.

Look at the exercises, decide which ones are useful to you, and do two or more.

LISTENING

1 Listen to the recording. When each sentence stops, say what you think the next word will be. Example:

1. 'What's the time?' 'Three . . .'
'I think the next word will be "o'clock".'

2 Listen to the recording of a man dictating a telegram over the telephone, and correct the following text.

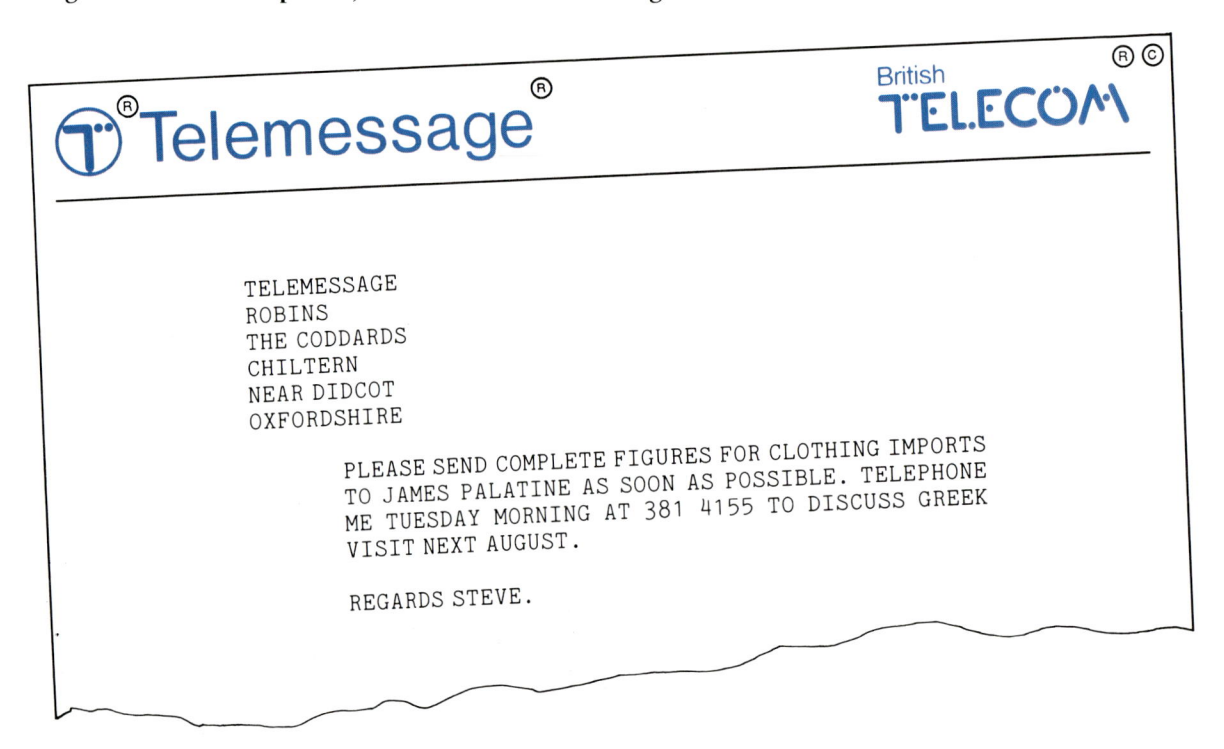

Telemessage British TELECOM

```
TELEMESSAGE
ROBINS
THE CODDARDS
CHILTERN
NEAR DIDCOT
OXFORDSHIRE

PLEASE SEND COMPLETE FIGURES FOR CLOTHING IMPORTS
TO JAMES PALATINE AS SOON AS POSSIBLE. TELEPHONE
ME TUESDAY MORNING AT 381 4155 TO DISCUSS GREEK
VISIT NEXT AUGUST.

REGARDS STEVE.
```

3 Listen to the song. Can you sing along?

Hush, little baby, don't say a word.
Mama's gonna buy you a mocking bird.

If that mocking bird don't sing,
Mama's gonna buy you a diamond ring.

If that diamond ring is brass,
Mama's gonna buy you a looking glass.

If that looking glass gets broke,
Mama's gonna buy you a billy goat.

If that billy goat don't pull,
Mama's gonna buy you a cart and bull.

If that cart and bull turn over,
Mama's gonna buy you a dog named Rover.

If that dog named Rover won't bark,
Mama's gonna buy you a horse and cart.

If that horse and cart fall down,
You'll still be the sweetest little baby in town.

PRONUNCIATION

1 How does -*e* change the pronunciation?

WITHOUT -*e*:	fat	cat	am	plan	hat	NOW PRONOUNCE:	man same take that
WITH -*e*:	gate	late	name	plane	hate		lemonade bale safe tap tape
WITHOUT -*e*:	sit	in	begin	if	swim	NOW PRONOUNCE:	fit inside still mile
WITH -*e*:	invite	fine	wine	wife	time		hid ride tide like pipe strip
WITHOUT -*e*:	stop	top	not	hot	clock	NOW PRONOUNCE:	job stone rose God
WITH -*e*:	hope	home	note	nose	smoke		joke dome bone on spot coke
WITHOUT -*e*:	bus	run	pub	sun	just	NOW PRONOUNCE:	much fuse cube cub
WITH -*e*:	excuse	June	tube	rude	use		fuss tune gun fun duke luck
	EXCEPTIONS:	some	come	one	have	give	live love

SPEAKING

1 Mime a person who is going to do something. The other students will say what you are going to do.

You're going to swim.

2 Look at the pictures and listen to the recording. Prepare a story about the pictures and the sounds. When you are ready, tell the other students.

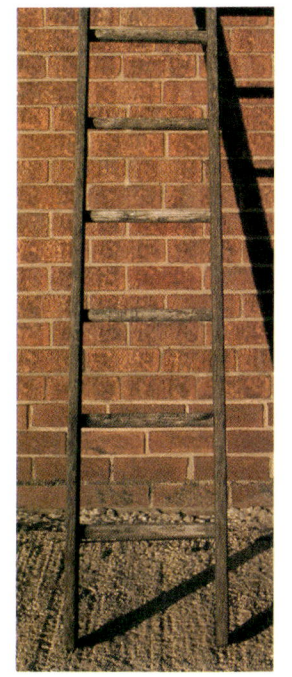

24C When you grow up

> Revision of tenses.

1 Listen to the recording. Which of these do you hear?

I'm not going to do anything at all.
I really am going to stop smoking now.
I'm never going to see you again.
I'm going to have the steak.
I'm going to have a bath.
I'm going to write a letter to the Prime Minister.

2 Choose the correct verb forms to complete the sentences.

1. 'Can you help me?' 'Sorry, not just now. I ....' (*work*)
2. 'What does she do?' 'I'm not sure. I think she .... in a bank.' (*work*)
3. We .... to Canada on holiday nearly every summer. (*go*)
4. But next summer we .... to Scotland. (*go*)
5. I .... Matthew yesterday. He sends you his love. (*see*)
6. I .... three good films this week. (*see*)
7. Alice .... her boyfriend for three weeks, and they're already talking about getting married. (*know*)
8. .... you ever .... to change your job? (*want*)
9. If you .... help I .... what I can. (*need; do*)
10. Look at those black clouds. I'm sure it .... (*rain*)
11. Your horoscope says that this .... a difficult week for you. You .... a tall dark stranger; he .... all your money. (*be; meet; take*)

3 📼 Read the poems. Do you like them or not? Can you say why?

WHEN YOU GROW UP

If you are beautiful
when you grow up
we will be pleased.
And if you look like your father
we will still be quite pleased.

If you are angry at the world
we will understand.

If you fight us
we will try
not to fight back.

If you grow up
to be an artist
an airline pilot
or an import-export-expert
that will be fine.
Shop assistant
sheep farmer
professor of palaeontology
will be great.
Anything you want to be
will be fine
(except advertising
religion
or the military).

If you become rich and famous
don't worry.
We will not be too proud
to live on your money.

If you marry
marry anybody you want to
we will not mind
it will be your decision
you will be absolutely free.
Nobody will be good enough for you anyway.
(Only
don't marry somebody we don't like.)

If you realise
one day
that your parents are idiots
we hope you will tell us
in the nicest possible way.

Have a good life.

WEATHER FORECAST

Tomorrow
if it rains
I will dance in the rain with you.

If it snows
we will make snow pancakes
and eat them together.

If it is cold
I will warm myself
with your smile.

If it is hot
I will cool myself
with your slow clear voice.

If there is fog
I will be happy
to lose myself for a time.
(But please
come and find me
won't you?)

4 Complete some of these sentences; make some more of your own if you want to. And if you like, put them together to make a poem.

Tomorrow, if I am happy, . . .
If I am unhappy, . . .
If life is difficult, . . .
If I see you, . . .
If I have no money, . . .
If I am tired, . . .
If I want to sing, . . .
If I break a cup, . . .
If the weather is bad, . . .
If I get bills in the post, . . .
If I am bored, . . .

5 Match the captions with the cartoons (there is one caption too many), and choose the right verb forms.

1. Yes, Ron's in. Who shall I say (*calls* / *is calling*)?
2. I'm not worried. You (*always think* / *'re always thinking*) of something.
3. The milk (*boils* / *'s boiling*) over.
4. Nobody (*knows* / *is knowing*) what Ann (*does* / *'ll do*) next.
5. Hello, police! It's my husband's hang-glider. It (*came* / *'s come*) back without him.
6. We (*are* / *were* / *'ve been*) married for twenty-five years, Helen. You could at least give me a chance to run.

24D Test yourself

LISTENING

1 Copy the table. Then listen to the recording and fill in the information.

	DEPARTURE TIME	GOING TO	ARRIVAL TIME	CHANGE?
1				no
2		?		
3				
4				
5				

GRAMMAR

1 Write the adverbs. Example:

slow *slowly*

certain; cheap; complete; dangerous; easy; economical; expensive; free; happy; lazy; nice; possible; probable; terrible; usual; wonderful.

2 Put the adverb in the right place. Example:

I agree with you. (*certainly*)

I certainly agree with you.

1. She speaks English. (*well*)
2. I like skiing. (*very much*)
3. We go on holiday together. (*often*)
4. She is late for work. (*usually*)

3 Put in *a*, *an*, *the* or – (= no article). Examples:

What's *the* time?

She comes from *–* London.

I live in *a* small flat.

1. My brother's .... doctor.
2. Do you like .... music?
3. 'What are you eating?' '......... orange.'
4. Where's .... nearest toilet?
5. It's over there by .... stairs, on .... right.
6. Do you know, ... tomatoes are £3.50 a kilo?

4 Write the past tense and past participle. Example:

go *went gone*

become; fall; find; have; hear; hurt; know; make; put; read; see; sell; write.

5 Write out the letter with the correct forms of the words in brackets.

Agios Demetrios
Monday

Dear Jan and Phil,

Just a note to let you know that we (*have*) a wonderful holiday. This really is a great place – I (*never be*) anywhere like it before. The people are friendly, the food's great, and the weather's a lot better (*as/than*) at home. We (*be*) here (*for/since*) ten days now, and we (*have*) sun every day. Can you (*believe*) it?

Most days are pretty (*lazy/lazily*). I (*swim*) two or three times a day, but Bill just (*spend*) all his time lying on the beach with his eyes closed. Sometimes he (*write*) a postcard, but then he (*forget*) to post it.

Last Saturday I (*get*) on the bus and (*go*) to the north end of the island. It's much (*quiet*) there than here – very beautiful, but no tourists. Tomorrow we (*go*) across to the east coast (*see*) some of the old villages, if Bill (*wake*) up in time. And next week, if the weather (*be*) still nice, I (*think*) I (*do*) some walking in the mountains.

I (*learn*) Greek – I still can't (*say*) much, but it's fun to try. Bill actually (*speak*) it quite well, but he's afraid to open his mouth, so I'm the one who talks to people.

Love to Joe and the family. See you soon, I (*hope*).

Alex

VOCABULARY

1 Give the opposites of these words. Example:

white black

big; cheap; dark; easy; fat; happy; hot; long; noisy; slow; tall; well; young.

2 Add some more words to these lists.

1. uncle, sister, . . .
2. arm, nose, . . .
3. bathroom, . . .
4. spring, . . .
5. north, . . .
6. breakfast, . . .
7. spoon, . . .

3 Answer these questions.

1. Where do you go to buy a book?
2. Where do you go to read or borrow a book?
3. Where do you go to catch a plane?
4. Your aunt's daughter is your ....
5. What do you wear if you have bad eyes?
6. What is a window made of?
7. Give examples of: a noun, a verb, an adjective.

LANGUAGE IN USE

1 Write a typical sentence or expression for each of these situations:

1. in a restaurant
2. in a shop
3. on the telephone
4. at the doctor's
5. giving advice or instructions
6. inviting

PRONUNCIATION

1 Which word is different?

1. meal   meat   bread   reason
2. country   fun   summer   truth
3. trouble   flu   tooth   shoe
4. heart   turn   early   third
5. song   one   long   gone
6. fork   fall   wrong   caught
7. pull   push   but   put
8. worry   hurry   sorry

2 Which syllable is stressed?

advertisement; advice; airport; alone; autumn; bathroom; become; business; complete; dangerous; decision; headache; information; international; medicine; mistake; picture; problem; surprise; temperature; video.

WRITING

1 Write 100–200 words about what you are going to do *either* next weekend, *or* for your next holidays, *or* next year, *or* when you leave school, *or* when you stop work.

SPEAKING

1 Look at the pictures and tell the teacher the story.

2 Find out as much as you can about *either* the teacher's family, *or* the teacher's childhood, *or* the teacher's last holiday, *or* the teacher's plans for the next few years.

Vocabulary index

Dieses Wörterverzeichnis enthält in alphabetischer Reihenfolge das Wortgut aus den Units 1 bis 24.

In der äußeren linken Spalte finden Sie das englische Stichwort mit der Ausspracheerklärung und in verschiedenen Fällen einen englischen Kontext. Die für den Kontext gewählten Beispiele sind unitbezogen; nur in wenigen Ausnahmefällen sind die Beispiele frei gewählt.

Bei Doppel- bzw. Mehrfachnennungen von Einträgen steht der Kontext jeweils nur bei dem bedeutungstragenden Wort. Bei dem Eintrag *for a moment* finden Sie demzufolge den Kontext unter *moment* – als dem sogenannten Schlüsselbegriff – und nicht unter *for*.

Die mittlere Spalte gibt die Fundstellen zu den jeweiligen Stichwörtern an, z.B. 6D = Unit 6, Teil/Block D.

Angemessene Übersetzungen zu allen englischen Stichwörtern inkl. Kontextübersetzungen finden sich in der äußeren rechten Spalte.

a /ə/	2A	ein(e)
a bit /ə 'bɪt/	9C	ein bißchen
a little /ə 'lɪtl/	1D	ein wenig, etwas
a little more /mɔː(r)/	17A	noch etwas
a lot of /ə 'lɒt əv/	7D	viel(e), eine Menge
a.m. /'eɪ 'em/	9D	vormittags
a moment /ə 'məʊmənt/	3D	ein(en) Augenblick, Moment
a quarter /ə 'kwɔːtə(r)/	6B	ein Viertel
a ... one /ə...wʌn/	10B	ein(e) ... (-e, -er, -es)
ABCDEFG etc.	1B	
about /ə'baʊt/	17C	über
Let's think about this.		*Laß(t) uns darüber nachdenken.*
about: What about ...?	15C	Wie wär's mit ...?
about	2D	ungefähr
about 50		*ungefähr 50*
across /ə'krɒs/	18A	über
across: right across /raɪt/	21A	(quer) durch
actor /'æktə(r)/	13C	Schauspieler
actress /'æktrɪs/	2C	Schauspielerin
actually /'æktʃəli/	11D	tatsächlich, eigentlich (nicht: aktuell)
address /ə'dres/	2C	Adresse
advertisement /əd'vɜːtɪsmənt/	21C	Anzeige, Annonce
advice /əd'vaɪs/	22B	Rat(schlag)
afraid /ə'freɪd/	10B	
I'm afraid I haven't got them.		*Leider habe ich sie nicht.*
after /'ɑːftə(r)/	22B	nachdem
... after you finish.		*... nachdem Sie fertig sind.*
after	14C	nach (Reihenfolge)
afternoon /ɑːftə'nuːn/	2B	Nachmittag, am Nachmittag, nachmittags
in the afternoon	6B	
again /ə'gen/	11D	wieder
age /eɪdʒ/	3D	Alter
... ago /ə'gəʊ/	11C	vor ...
... forty years ago		*... vor 40 Jahren*
agree /ə'griː/	14B	zustimmen
ahead: go ahead /'gəʊ ə'hed/	19A	Nur zu! (Erlaubnis geben)
airport /'eəpɔːt/	21D	Flughafen
all /ɔːl/	9C	alle
all my life	19D	mein ganzes Leben (lang)
all right /'ɔːl 'raɪt/	17C	in Ordnung, okay
All right. I'll get the paper.		*Okay, ich hole die Zeitung.*
I'll be all right.	23A	*Ich komme zurecht.*
Is everything all right?	17A	*Ist alles in Ordnung?*
alone /ə'ləʊn/	22B	allein
already /ɔːl'redi/	19D	schon
always /'ɔːlweɪz/	6D	immer, ständig
am /əm, æm/	1C	bin
America /ə'merɪkə/	11C	Amerika
American /ə'merɪkn/	1D	amerikanisch; Amerikaner(in)
She's American.		*Sie ist Amerikanerin.*
an /ən/	2A	ein(e)
and /ənd, ən, ænd/	1C	und
and so on	19D	usw.
angry /'æŋgri/	22D	ärgerlich, böse
animal /'ænɪml/	18C	Tier (aber nicht Vogel oder Fisch)
another /ə'nʌðə(r)/	10B	noch ein(e,r)...; ein(e) ander(e,er, es)
answer /'ɑːnsə(r)/	15A	antworten
any /'eni/	3D	(im Fragesatz nicht immer übersetzt) *Haben Sie Kinder?*
Have you got any children?		
There isn't any snow.	7C	*Es gibt keinen Schnee.*
anybody /'enibɒdi/	15A	(irgend) jemand
anything /'eniθɪŋ/	10B	(irgend) etwas
anyway /'eniweɪ/	5C	
Thank you anyway.		*Trotzdem vielen Dank.*
anywhere /'eniweə(r)/	19C	irgendwo
anywhere else /els/	19C	sonst irgendwo, irgendwo anders
apple /'æpl/	7C	Apfel
April /'eɪprl/	14C	April
are /ə(r), ɑː(r)/	1C	bist, seid, sind
aren't /ɑːnt/	3B	bist, seid, sind nicht (Kurzform)
arm /ɑːm/	9A	Arm
armchair /'ɑːmtʃeə(r)/	5A	Sessel
arrive /ə'raɪv/	9D	ankommen
arrive at /ə'raɪv ət/	9D	ankommen an
I am arriving at the station at 11.40 a.m.		*Ich komme um 11.40 Uhr am Bahnhof an.*

English		German
artist /'ɑːtɪst/	2A	Künstler(in)
as … as /əz, æz/	13D	so … wie
ask /ɑːsk/	11D	fragen
aspirin /'æsprɪn/	22A	Aspirin, (Kopf)schmerztablette
at /ət, æt/	5B	
at 16 Norris Road		in der Norris Road 16 (Ort)
at seven o'clock	6C	um sieben Uhr (Zeit)
at a university /juːnəˈvɜːsəti/	18A	an einer Universität
at home /həʊm/	6B	zu Hause
at school /skuːl/	6B	in der Schule
at the weekend /wiːkˈend/	6C	am Wochenende
at work /wɜːk/	6B	bei der Arbeit
at: arrive at /əˈraɪv/	9D	ankommen an
Atlantic /ətˈlæntɪk/	18A	Atlantik
August /'ɔːɡəst/	14C	August
aunt /ɑːnt/	9C	Tante
Australia /ɒsˈtreɪliə/	1D	Australien
Australian /ɒsˈtreɪliən/	1D	australisch; Australier(in)
He's Australian.		Er ist Australier.
autumn /'ɔːtəm/	21C	Herbst
away /əˈweɪ/	23D	weg, fort
baby /'beɪbi/	21C	Baby
back /bæk/	15D	zurück
I won't be back before six.		Ich werde nicht vor sechs zurück sein.
bad /bæd/ (Eigenschaftswort)	9D	schlecht
bad news /njuːz/	23C	schlechte Nachricht(en)
bad: not bad	2B	nicht schlecht
bad-tempered /ˈbædˈtempəd/	14B	schlecht gelaunt
badly /'bædli/ (Umstandswort)	19B	schlecht
I slept badly last night.		Ich habe letzte Nacht schlecht geschlafen.
bag /bæɡ/	3A	Tasche
banana /bəˈnɑːnə/	7A	Banane
bank /bæŋk/	5C	Bank
bath /bɑːθ/	10A	Bad
bathroom /'bɑːθruːm/	21B	Bad (Badezimmer)
be /biː/	22C	sein
be careful /ˈbiː ˈkeəfl/	22C	Sei vorsichtig!
beautiful /'bjuːtɪfl/	13C	schön
because /bɪˈkɒz/	18A	weil
become /bɪˈkʌm/	23D	werden
bed /bed/	6B	Bett
bedroom /'bedruːm/	21B	Schlafzimmer
beef /biːf/	17A	Rindfleisch
beer /bɪə(r)/	6D	Bier
before /bɪˈfɔː(r)/	22B	bevor
Always warm up before you run.		Wärm Dich immer auf, bevor du läufst.
before	11A	vor
She never studied except before exams.		Sie hat nur vor Prüfungen gelernt.
behind /bɪˈhaɪnd/	10C	hinter
The clock is behind the chair.		Die Uhr ist hinter dem Stuhl.
believe /bɪˈliːv/	19D	glauben
best /best/	13C	der (die, das) beste …
better /'betə(r)/ (Eigenschaftswort)	13C	besser
better (Umstandswort)	13B	besser
She can swim better than her brother.		Sie kann besser schwimmen als ihr Bruder.
between /bɪˈtwiːn/	10C	zwischen
between jobs /dʒɒbz/	2A	zur Zeit gerade arbeitslos
big /bɪɡ/	5B	groß
bill /bɪl/	17A	Rechnung
birthday /'bɜːθdeɪ/	14C	Geburtstag
bit: a bit /ə ˈbɪt/	9C	ein bißchen
black /blæk/	9B	schwarz
blouse /blaʊz/	9B	Bluse
blue /bluː/	9A	blau
book /bʊk/	3A	Buch
bookshop /'bʊkʃɒp/	5D	Buchhandlung
boots /buːts/	9B	Stiefel
bored; be bored /bɔːd/	10A	sich langweilen
When Fred's bored he goes to the cinema.		Wenn Fred sich langweilt, geht er ins Kino.
boring /'bɔːrɪŋ/	13C	langweilig
This is the most boring book I know.		Dies ist das langweiligste Buch, das ich kenne.
born: was born /wəz ˈbɔːn/	11B	bin (ist) geboren
I was born in Africa.		Ich bin in Afrika geboren.
borrow /'bɒrəʊ/	17B	sich etw. (aus)leihen
Could I borrow your umbrella?		Könnte ich mir Ihren Schirm leihen?
boss /bɒs/	14D	Chef
both /bəʊθ/	6D	beide
We both like the sea.		Wir mögen beide das Meer.
boy /bɔɪ/	3C	Junge
boyfriend /'bɔɪfrend/	3B	(fester) Freund
bra /brɑː/	9B	BH (Büstenhalter)
bread /bred/	7A	Brot
break /breɪk/	21C	(zer)brechen
breakfast /'brekfəst/	6C	Frühstück
bring /brɪŋ/	14D	(mit)bringen
Can I bring something?		Kann ich etw. mitbringen?
Britain /'brɪtn/	1D	(Groß)Britannien
British /'brɪtɪʃ/	1D	britisch
She's British.		Sie ist Britin.
brother /'brʌðə(r)/	3C	Bruder
brown /braʊn/	9A	braun
build /bɪld/	18C	bauen
bus /bʌs/	6C	Bus
bus stop /'bʌs stɒp/	5C	Bushaltestelle
business /'bɪznɪs/	21D	Geschäfte, Geschäftsbeziehungen
business: do business	21D	Geschäfte machen
We do business in English.		Wir benutzen Englisch für unsere Geschäfte.
but /bət, bʌt/	6B	aber
buy /baɪ/	10C	kaufen
by /baɪ/	5C	bei, an, neben
…by the reception desk		hier: … bei der Rezeption
by bus /baɪ ˈbʌs/	6C	mit dem Bus
by car /baɪ ˈkɑː(r)/	6C	mit dem Auto
Bye /baɪ/	1C	Wiedersehen! Tschüß!
cake /keɪk/	13A	Kuchen
(pocket)calculator /'kælkjəleɪtə(r)/	11C	(Taschen)rechner
call: What's this called? /kɔːld/	9B	Wie heißt das (hier)? / Wie nennt man das (hier)?

calm /kɑːm/	14B	ruhig
can /kn, kæn/	13A	kann, kannst, können
Can I …? /kn aɪ/	10B	Kann ich…? Darf ich...?
Can I look round? /raʊnd/	10C	Kann ich mich umschauen? (z.B. in einem Geschäft)
Can I take a message? /ˈmesɪdʒ/	14D	Kann ich etwas ausrichten?
can't /kɑːnt/	13A	kann, kannst, können nicht
car /kɑː(r)/	6C	Auto
car park /ˈkɑː pɑːk/	5C	Parkplatz
car: by car	6C	mit dem Auto
careful /ˈkeəfl/	22C	vorsichtig
carry /ˈkæri/	18D	tragen
Both of them carried guns.		*Beide trugen Waffen.*
cat /kæt/	7D	Katze
catch /kætʃ/	17D	(z.B. ein Flugzeug) nehmen
catch	22A	(z.B. die Grippe) bekommen
century /ˈsentʃəri/	18A	Jahrhundert
certainly /ˈsɜːtənli/	17A	selbstverständlich, sicher(lich)
chair /tʃeə(r)/	3A	Stuhl
change /tʃeɪndʒ/	11A	wechseln
She changed schools three times.		*Sie hat dreimal die Schule gewechselt.*
cheap /tʃiːp/	5D	billig, preiswert
cheese /tʃiːz/	7A	Käse
chemist's /ˈkemɪsts/	5D	Apotheke, Drogerie
Is there a chemist's near here?		*Gibt es hier in der Nähe eine Apotheke/Drogerie?*
chess /tʃes/	13A	Schach(spiel)
chicken /ˈtʃɪkɪn/	17A	Hähnchen
child (children) /tʃaɪld, ˈtʃɪldrən/	3C	Kind (Kinder)
China /ˈtʃaɪnə/	1D	China
Chinese /tʃaɪˈniːz/	1D	chinesisch; Chinese, Chinesin
She's Chinese.		*Sie ist Chinesin.*
chips /tʃɪps/	7D	Pommes frites
church /tʃɜːtʃ/	5D	Kirche
cigarette /ˌsɪgəˈret/	17B	Zigarette
cinema /ˈsɪnəmə/	19B	Kino
city /ˈsɪti/	15B	Stadt, Großstadt
clear /klɪə(r)/	22D	deutlich, klar
Please write your name clearly.		*Bitte schreiben Sie Ihren Namen deutlich.*
clothes /kləʊðz/	10B	Kleidung, Bekleidung
coat /kəʊt/	3A	Mantel
coffee /ˈkɒfi/	7A	Kaffee
cold (a cold) /kəʊld/	22B	eine Erkältung
Don't run if you have a cold.		*Laufe nicht, wenn du eine Erkältung hast/wenn du erkältet bist.*
cold	10A	kalt
I'm cold.		*Mir ist kalt.*
colour /ˈkʌlə(r)/	9B	Farbe
colour: What colour is/ are …?	9C	Welche Farbe hat/haben …?
come /kʌm/	11D	kommen
comfortable /ˈkʌmftəbl/	13D	bequem
communication /kəˌmjuːnɪˈkeɪʃn/	21D	Verständigung, Kommunikation
complete /kəmˈpliːt/ (Eigenschaftswort)	22D	vollständig
completely /kəmˈpliːtli/ (Umstandswort)	22D	vollständig
I've completely forgotten it.		*Ich habe es völlig vergessen.*
concert /ˈkɒnsət/	15C	Konzert
cook /kʊk/	13A	kochen
cooker /ˈkʊkə(r)/	5A	Herd
cost /kɒst/	7B	kosten
could /kəd, kʊd/	17B	könnte
Could I speak to …? /kʊd aɪ ˈspiːk tə/	14D	Könnte ich … sprechen?
Could you possibly …? /ˈpɒsəbli/	17B	Könntest du/Könnten Sie vielleicht … ?
Could you speak more slowly, please? /ˈsləʊli/	10D	Könnten Sie bitte langsamer sprechen?
count /kaʊnt/	13B	zählen
country /ˈkʌntri/	21D	Land
English-speaking countries		*Länder mit Englisch als Muttersprache*
cousin /ˈkʌzn/	23D	Cousin, Cousine
crash /kræʃ/	21C	abstürzen, zusammenstoßen
cup /kʌp/	7C	Tasse
cupboard /ˈkʌbəd/	5A	Schrank
dance /dɑːns/	13A	tanzen
dangerous /ˈdeɪndʒərəs/	23A	gefährlich
dark /dɑːk/	9B	dunkel- (z.B. dunkelgrün)
dark	3B	dunkelhaarig
darling /ˈdɑːlɪŋ/	22C	Liebling
date /deɪt/	14C	Datum
daughter /ˈdɔːtə(r)/	3C	Tochter
day /deɪ/	11A	Tag
day: the day after tomorrow /təˈmɒrəʊ/	14C	übermorgen
day: the day before yesterday /ˈjestədi/	14C	vorgestern
dead /ded/	23D	tot
dear /dɪə(r)/	22C	Schätzchen
Dear	9D	Lieber …, Liebe …
December /dɪˈsembə(r)/	14C	Dezember
decide /dɪˈsaɪd/	21A	entscheiden
decision /dɪˈsɪʒn/	23C	Entscheidung
dentist /ˈdentɪst/	2A	Zahnarzt (-ärztin)
depend: It depends /ɪt dɪˈpendz/	6A	Je nachdem; es kommt darauf an
Do you like cooking? – It depends.		*Kochst du gern? – Je nachdem; es kommt darauf an.*
dictionary /ˈdɪkʃənri/	17B	Lexikon, Wörterbuch
did /dɪd/	11C	Hilfsverb
didn't /ˈdɪdnt/	11C	Hilfsverb (Kurzform, vgl. doesn't etc.)
die /daɪ/	11B	sterben
different /ˈdɪfrənt/	11A	verschieden, unterschiedlich
She played in four different rock groups.		*Sie spielte in vier verschiedenen Rockgruppen.*
difficult /ˈdɪfɪkəlt/	13C	schwierig
dining room /ˈdaɪnɪŋ ruːm/	21B	Eßzimmer
dinner /ˈdɪnə(r)/	17D	Abendessen (Hauptmahlzeit des Tages)
dirty /ˈdɜːti/	10A	schmutzig
disagree /ˌdɪsəˈgriː/	18C	nicht übereinstimmen, anderer Meinung sein
He disagreed with her.		*Er war anderer Meinung als sie.*

dislike /dɪsˈlaɪk/	6A	nicht mögen	
He dislikes opera.		*Er mag keine Opern.*	
divorced /dɪˈvɔːst/	2D	geschieden	
do /də, dʊ, duː/	2A	tun, machen	
do business /ˈbɪznɪs/	21D	Geschäfte machen	
do good to somebody	21A	jdm. etw. Gutes tun	
Do you know? /də ju ˈnəʊ/	7B	Weißt du/Wissen Sie…?	
Do you mind if … ? /maɪnd/	19A	Hast du/Haben Sie etwas dagegen, wenn … ?	
doctor /ˈdɒktə(r)/	2A	Arzt, Ärztin	
does /dəz, dʌz/	6A	Hilfsverb	
doesn't /ˈdʌznt/	6A	Hilfsverb (Kurzform)	
dog /dɒg/	18D	Hund	
don't /dəʊnt/	1B	Hilfsverb (Kurzform)	
Don't worry /ˈdəʊnt ˈwʌri/	22C	Mach' dir/Machen Sie sich keine Sorgen.	
door /dɔːr/	5A	Tür	
double (letters) /ˈdʌbl/	1B	doppelt; Doppelbuchstaben	
downstairs /ˈdaʊnˈsteəz/	5C	unten (im Haus)	
Dr /ˈdɒktə(r)/	2B	Dr.	
draw /drɔː/	13B	zeichnen	
dream /driːm/	23D	träumen	
dress /dres/	9B	Kleid	
drink /drɪŋk/	15A	trinken	
drive /draɪv/	13A	fahren	
He can drive.		*Er kann autofahren; er hat den Führerschein.*	
each other /ˈiːtʃ ˈʌðə(r)/	19D	sich, einander	
We've known each other for only 24 hours.		*Wir kennen uns erst seit 24 Stunden.*	
ear /ɪə(r)/	9A	Ohr	
ear-rings /ˈɪərɪŋz/	9B	Ohrringe	
early /ˈɜːli/	18D	früh	
They went to bed early.		*Sie gingen früh zu Bett.*	
earn /ɜːn/	11A	verdienen	
She earns a lot of money.		*Sie verdient viel Geld.*	
east /iːst/	18B	Osten	
easy /ˈiːzi/	13C	leicht	
eat /iːt/	14D	essen	
economical /ekəˈnɒmɪkl/	13D	sparsam (im Verbrauch), wirtschaftlich	
A Volkswagen is more economical than a Rolls Royce.		*Ein Volkswagen ist wirtschaftlicher als ein Rolls-Royce.*	
egg /eg/	7A	Ei	
Egypt /ˈiːdʒɪpt/	1D	Ägypten	
Egyptian /iːˈdʒɪpʃən/	1D	ägyptisch; Ägypter(in)	
She's Egyptian.		*Sie ist Ägypterin.*	
eight /eɪt/	2C	acht	
eighteen /ˈeɪˈtiːn/	2C	achtzehn	
eighteenth /ˈeɪˈtiːnθ/	14C	(der, die, das) achtzehnte	
eighth /eɪtθ/	5B	(der, die, das) achte	
eightieth /ˈeɪtɪəθ/	14C	(der, die, das) achtzigste	
eighty /ˈeɪti/	2D	achtzig	
electrician /ɪlekˈtrɪʃn/	2A	Elektriker(in)	
eleven /ɪˈlevn/	2C	elf	
eleventh /ɪˈlevnθ/	14C	(der, die, das) elfte	
else: anywhere else /ˈeniweər ˈels/	19C	sonst irgendwo, irgendwo anders	
I've never wanted to live anywhere else.		*Ich wollte noch nie irgendwo anders wohnen/leben.*	

embassy /ˈembəsi/	21D	Botschaft (Gebäude)	
employer /ɪmˈplɔɪə(r)/	23D	Arbeitgeber(in)	
engineer /endʒəˈnɪə(r)/	2A	Ingenieur(in)	
England /ˈɪŋglənd/	1D	England	
English /ˈɪŋglɪʃ/	1D	englisch	
She's English.		*Sie ist Engländerin.*	
enough /ɪˈnʌf/	7D	genug	
Europe /ˈjʊərəp/	11C	Europa	
evening /ˈiːvnɪŋ/	2B	Abend	
evening: in the evening	6B	am Abend, abends	
ever /ˈevə(r)/	19C	jemals	
Have you ever been to America?		*Warst Du schon mal in Amerika?*	
ever: hardly ever /ˈhɑːdli/	19B	selten	
I hardly ever drink coffee.		*Ich trinke selten Kaffee.*	
every /ˈevri/	11A	jede(r, s)	
every day	19B	jeden Tag	
every three days *etc.*	19B	alle drei Tage, jeden dritten Tag	
everybody /ˈevribɒdi/	6A	jeder, alle	
everything /ˈevriθɪŋ/	17A	alles	
excellent /ˈeksələnt/	17A	ausgezeichnet	
except /ɪkˈsept/	9C	außer	
Excuse me /ɪksˈkjuːz miː/	1C	Entschuldigung, entschuldigen Sie	
Excuse me. Are you Fred Andrews?		*Entschuldigen Sie, sind Sie Fred Andrews?*	
expensive /ɪksˈpensɪv/	7B	teuer	
extremely /ɪksˈtriːmli/	14B	äußerst	
eye /aɪ/	9A	Auge	
face /feɪs/	9A	Gesicht	
fair /feə(r)/	3B	hell, blond	
She is tall and fair.		*Sie ist groß und blond.*	
fall /fɔːl/	21C	fallen	
family /ˈfæmli/	3C	Familie	
famous /ˈfeɪməs/	18C	berühmt	
far /fɑː(r)/	5D	weit (weg)	
fast /fɑːst/ (Eigenschaftswort)	13D	schnell	
He has a fast car.		*Er hat ein schnelles Auto.*	
fast (Umstandswort)	13B	schnell	
He can run fast.		*Er kann schnell laufen.*	
faster /ˈfɑːstə(r)/ (Umstandswort)	13B	schneller	
She can run faster.		*Sie kann schneller laufen.*	
fat /fæt/	3B	dick	
He's quite fat.		*Er ist ziemlich dick.*	
father /ˈfɑːðə(r)/	3C	Vater	
favourite /ˈfeɪvrɪt/	11C	Lieblings-	
What is your favourite sport?		*Was ist Dein Lieblingssport?*	
February /ˈfebruəri/	14C	Februar	
feel /fiːl/	19D	fühlen	
fifteen /ˈfɪfˈtiːn/	2C	fünfzehn	
fifteenth /ˈfɪfˈtiːnθ/	14C	(der, die, das) fünfzehnte	
fifth /fɪfθ/	5B	(der, die, das) fünfte	
fiftieth /ˈfɪftɪəθ/	14C	(der, die, das) fünfzigste	
fifty /ˈfɪfti/	2D	fünfzig	
film /fɪlm/	18C	Film	
film star /ˈfɪlm stɑː(r)/	13D	Filmstar	
finally /ˈfaɪnəli/	18B	schließlich, endlich	
Finally, they left Whitehaven.		*Schließlich verließen sie Whitehaven.*	

English			German
find /faɪnd/		21B	finden
find out /'faɪnd 'aʊt/		17C	herausfinden, herausbekommen
fine /faɪn/		17C	In Ordnung, gut
Fine, thanks		1C	Danke, gut.
finish /'fɪnɪʃ/		23A	beenden
finished /'fɪnɪʃt/		21B	fertig, beendet
The house isn't finished yet.			*Das Haus ist noch nicht fertig.*
first /fɜːst/		5B	(der, die, das) erste
first name /neɪm/		1B	Vorname
first of all /əv 'ɔːl/		18B	zuerst, zunächst
first: the first person to		18A	der erste Mensch, der …
She was the first woman to fly a plane across the Atlantic.			*Sie war die erste Frau, die ein Flugzeug über den Atlantik flog.*
fish /fɪʃ/		6D	Fisch
five /faɪv/		1B	fünf
flat /flæt/		5B	Wohnung
floor /flɔː(r)/		5B	Stockwerk, Etage
flower /'flaʊə(r)/		18D	Blume
flu /fluː/		22A	Grippe
fly /flaɪ/		18A	fliegen
follow /'fɒləʊ/		22C	folgen
Follow me		22C	Folgen Sie mir.
food /fuːd/		7D	Lebensmittel, Essen, Nahrung
foot /fʊt/ (feet /fiːt/)		9A	Fuß
football /'fʊtbɔːl/		6D	Fußball
football match /'fʊtbɔːl 'mætʃ/		15C	Fußballspiel
for /fə(r), fɔː(r)/		17A	für (z.B. für dich)
for		5D	(Entfernung)
Walk for 300 m.			*Gehen Sie 300 m.*
for		19D	seit (Zeitraum)
for 24 hours			*seit 24 Stunden*
for a moment /'məʊmənt/		19A	für einen Augenblick, Moment
foreign /'fɒrən/		13B	ausländisch
forget /fə'get/		15D	vergessen
fork /fɔːk/		22B	Gabel
fortieth /'fɔːtɪəθ/		14C	(der, die, das) vierzigste
forty /'fɔːti/		2D	vierzig
four /fɔː(r)/		1B	vier
fourteen /'fɔː'tiːn/		2C	vierzehn
fourteenth /'fɔː'tiːnθ/		14C	(der, die, das) vierzehnte
fourth /fɔːθ/		5B	(der, die, das) vierte
France /frɑːns/		1D	Frankreich
free /friː/		15C	frei
Are you free?			*Hast Du Zeit?*
free time /'friː 'taɪm/		18A	Freizeit
French /frentʃ/		1D	französisch
She's French.			*Sie ist Französin.*
Friday /'fraɪdi/		6C	Freitag
fridge /frɪdʒ/		5A	Kühlschrank
friend /frend/		3B	Freund(in)
friendly /'frendli/ (Eigenschaftswort)		14B	freundlich
She looks quite friendly.			*Sie sieht ganz freundlich aus.*
from /frəm, frɒm/		6C	von (Zeit)
from twelve o'clock until five o'clock			*von zwölf bis siebzehn Uhr*
from		1D	woher (z.B. Woher kommst du/kommen Sie?)
front: in front of /ɪn 'frʌnt əv/		10C	vor
in front of the shop			*vor dem Laden, Geschäft*
fun /fʌn/		21C	Spaß
It's going to be fun!			*Es wird Spaß machen!*
funny /'fʌni/		13C	lustig, witzig
funny		19D	merkwürdig, seltsam
furniture /'fɜːnɪtʃə(r)/		5A	Möbel
garage /'gærɑːʒ/		5A	Garage
German /'dʒɜːmən/		1D	deutsch; Deutsche(r)
I'm German.			*Ich bin Deutsche(r).*
Germany /'dʒɜːməni/		1D	Deutschland
get /get/		11D	ankommen
get		15D	bekommen
get home /həʊm/		11D	nach Hause kommen
get in /ɪn/		23B	hinein-/hereinkommen, hinein-/hereinsteigen
get into /'ɪntə, 'ɪntʊ/		23B	in etw. hinein-/hereinkommen, in etw. hinein-/hereinsteigen
get killed /kɪld/		23A	getötet werden
get lost /lɒst/		23A	sich verirren
He won't get lost.			*Er wird sich nicht verirren.*
get married /'mærɪd/		21A	heiraten
She's not going to get married.			*Sie hat nicht die Absicht zu heiraten.*
get off /ɒf/		23B	aussteigen (Bus)
get on /ɒn/		23B	einsteigen (Bus)
get out /aʊt/		23B	herauskommen, -steigen; als Befehl: Verschwinde!
get out of /'aʊt əv/		23B	aus etw. herauskommen, -steigen; verschwinden aus …
Get out of my car!			*Steig aus meinem Auto aus!*
get up /ʌp/		6C	aufstehen (morgens)
What time does she get up?			*Wann steht sie morgens auf?*
girl /gɜːl/		3C	Mädchen
girlfriend /'gɜːlfrend/		3B	(feste) Freundin
give /gɪv/		15D	geben
glass /glɑːs/		7C	Glas
a glass of milk			*ein Glas Milch*
There is some glass on the floor.			*Da liegt Glas auf dem Boden.*
glasses /'glɑːsɪz/		9B	Brille
*Where **are** my glasses?*			*Wo **ist** meine Brille?*
go /gəʊ/		6C	gehen
go ahead /ə'hed/		19A	Nur zu! (Erlaubnis geben)
go for a walk /wɔːk/		19B	spazierengehen
go shopping /'ʃɒpɪŋ/		10A	einkaufen (gehen, fahren)
go to the cinema /'sɪnəmə/		19B	ins Kino gehen
good /gʊd/ (Eigenschaftswort)		5D	gut
Good afternoon /'gʊd ɑːftə'nuːn/		2B	Guten Tag (nur nachmittags anzuwenden)
good at …ing /'gʊd ət/		13B	etw. gut können
She is good at playing tennis.			*Sie kann gut Tennis spielen.*
good: do good to somebody		21A	jdm. etw. Gutes tun
Good evening /'iːvnɪŋ/		2B	Guten Abend
good-looking /'lʊkɪŋ/		3B	gutaussehend
Good morning /'mɔːnɪŋ/		2B	Guten Morgen
Good night /naɪt/		2B	Gute Nacht

English	Ref	German
good time /taɪm/: have a good time!	15A	Viel Spaß!
Goodbye /ˈgʊd ˈbaɪ/	1C	Auf Wiedersehen!
gram /græm/	7A	Gramm
great /greɪt/	19C	fantastisch, super
Greece /griːs/	1D	Griechenland
Greek /griːk/	1D	griechisch; Grieche(in)
She's Greek.		Sie ist Griechin.
green /griːn/	9A	grün
grey /greɪ/	9A	grau
ground floor /ˈgraʊnd ˈflɔː(r)/	5B	Erdgeschoß
gun /gʌn/	18D	Pistole, Gewehr
hair /heə(r)/	7D	Haar, Haare
He has very short hair.		Er hat sehr kurze Haare.
half /hɑːf/	6B	halb
at half past **nine**		um halb **zehn**
half a...of... /ˈhɑːf ə...əv/	7A	ein(e) halb(e, er, es)
half a litre of milk		ein halber Liter Milch
half an hour /ˈhɑːf ən ˈaʊə(r)/	15D	eine halbe Stunde
hand /hænd/	9A	Hand
handsome /ˈhændsəm/	13D	gutaussehend
happen /ˈhæpn/	15A	geschehen, sich ereignen; (los sein)
What's happening?		Was ist los?
happy /ˈhæpi/	10A	glücklich
Happy Birthday /ˈhæpi ˈbɜːθdeɪ/	14C	Herzlichen Glückwunsch zum Geburtstag!
hard /hɑːd/	11B	schwer, schwierig, hart
Life was very hard.		Es war ein schweres Leben.
hardly ever /ˈhɑːdli ˈevə(r)/	19B	selten
has /həz, hæz/	6C	(er, sie, es) hat
hasn't /ˈhæznt/	9C	(er, sie, es) hat nicht (Kurzform)
hat /hæt/	3A	Hut
hate /heɪt/	6A	hassen
I hate the picture.		Ich hasse das Bild.
have /həv, hæv/	6C	haben
have a baby /ˈbeɪbi/	21C	ein Baby, Kind bekommen
have a bath /bɑːθ/	10A	ein Bad nehmen (in der Badewanne)
have a good time /ˈgʊd ˈtaɪm/	15A	Viel Saß!
have a shower /ˈʃaʊə(r)/	10A	duschen
have to do something /ˈhæf tə ˈduː ˈsʌmθɪŋ/	23A	etw. tun müssen
Have you got a light? /laɪt/	17B	Hast du/Haben Sie Feuer? (für Zigarette)
have: I'll have	17A	ich nehme (bei einer Auswahl), bekomme
haven't /ˈhævnt/	7D	nicht haben (Kurzform)
he /hiː/	1D	er
he's /hiːz/	1D	er ist
he's = he has	3C	er hat
head /hed/	15A	Kopf
headache /ˈhedeɪk/	22A	Kopfschmerzen
I've got a headache.		Ich habe Kopfschmerzen.
hear /hɪə(r)/	11D	hören
heart /hɑːt/	23D	Herz
heavy /ˈhevi/	13D	schwer (Gewicht)
A cat is not as heavy as an elephant.		Eine Katze ist nicht so schwer wie ein Elefant.
height /haɪt/	14A	Höhe, Größe
Hello! /heˈləʊ/	1A	Hallo!
help /help/	10B	helfen
her /(h)ə(r), hɜː(r)/	1B	ihr(e)
Her surname is Quinton.		Ihr Nachname ist Quinton.
her	6A	sie (Fürwort als Ergänzung)
I like her very much.		Ich mag sie sehr gern.
here /hɪə(r)/	5D	hier
here's /hɪəz/	1C	hier ist
Here you are /ˈhɪə juː ˈɑː/	17B	Bitteschön (wenn man etw. übergibt)
Could I have my watch back? – Yes, of course. Here you are.		Könnte ich meine Uhr zurückhaben? – Ja, natürlich. Bitteschön.
Hi /haɪ/	1C	Hallo!
high /haɪ/	14A	hoch
him /(h)ɪm/	6A	ihn
his /(h)ɪz/	1B	sein(e)
holiday /ˈhɒlədi/	6D	Urlaub, Ferien
I often go on holiday.		Ich fahre oft in Urlaub.
home /həʊm/	6B	Heim, Zuhause
hope /həʊp/	22A	hoffen
horse /hɔːs/	7C	Pferd
hot /hɒt/	10A	heiß
He's hot.		Ihm ist heiß.
hotel /həʊˈtel/	5D	Hotel
hour /aʊə(r)/	15D	Stunde (Zeit)
house /haʊs/	5A	Haus
housewife /ˈhaʊswaɪf/	2A	Hausfrau
how /haʊ/	17A	wie
How's the chicken?		Wie schmeckt das Hähnchen?
How are you? /haʊ ə ˈjuː/	1C	Wie geht es dir/Ihnen?
How do you do? /haʊ də juː ˈduː/	1C	(bei Vorstellung mit Handschlag) Guten Tag/Abend, angenehm (formell)
How do you pronounce ...? /prəˈnaʊns/	9B	Wie spricht man ... aus?
How do you say ...? /seɪ/	9B	Wie sagt man ...?
How do you spell it? /spel/	2D	Wie schreibt man das?
How far ... ? /fɑː(r)/	5D	Wie weit ...?
How many ... ? /ˈmeni/	7D	Wie viele ...?
How much ... ? /mʌtʃ/	7D	Wieviel ...?
How much is/are ... ?	10C	Was kostet/kosten ...?
How often ... ? /ˈɒfn/	19B	Wie oft ...?
How old are you? /əʊld/	2D	Wie alt bist du/sind Sie?
hundred: a hundred /ə ˈhʌndrəd/	2D	(ein)hundert
hundredth /ˈhʌndrədθ/	14C	(der, die, das) (ein)hundertste
hungry /ˈhʌŋgri/	10A	hungrig
I'm hungry.		Ich habe Hunger.
hurry /ˈhʌri/	22C	sich beeilen
Please hurry!		Beeile dich bitte!
hurt /hɜːt/	22A	weh tun
My leg hurts.		Mein Bein tut weh.
husband /ˈhʌzbənd/	3C	(Ehe)mann
I /aɪ/	1B	ich
I can't remember /rɪˈmembə(r)/	9B	Ich kann mich nicht erinnern.
I'd (= I would) /aɪd/	10C	ich würde
I'd like /aɪd ˈlaɪk/	10C	ich möchte

I'd like to	10C	ich möchte (etw. tun); (Kurzantwort) Ja, gern!
I'd love to /lʌv/	15C	ich würde sehr gern (etw. tun); (Kurzantwort) Ja, sehr gern!
I'd rather you didn't /'rɑːðə/	9A	Lieber nicht!
I don't know /nəʊ/	1B	Ich weiß (es) nicht.
I don't mind /maɪnd/	23A	Ich habe nichts dagegen; Es macht mir nichts aus.
I don't understand /ʌndə'stænd/	7C	Ich verstehe nicht.
I know	7B	Ich weiß (es).
I'll /aɪl/	7A	ich werde (Kurzform)
I'll have	17A	ich nehme (bei einer Auswahl), bekomme
I'll have a rump steak.		*Ich bekomme ein Rumpsteak.*
I'm /aɪm/	1C	ich bin (Kurzform)
I'm afraid /ə'freɪd/	10B	leider
I'm sorry /'sɒri/	1C	Es tut mir leid, Entschuldigung
I'm sorry to trouble you /'trʌbl/	17B	Entschuldigen Sie die Störung …
I'm very well	2B	Mir geht es sehr gut.
I've /aɪv/	3C	ich habe (Kurzform)
I think /θɪŋk/	2D	ich glaube, denke
ice /aɪs/	7C	Eis
ice cream /aɪs 'kriːm/	7A	(Speise)eis
idea /aɪ'dɪə/	17C	Idee
if /ɪf/	23A	wenn, falls
If I need money, I'll find a job.		*Wenn ich Geld brauche, suche ich mir Arbeit.*
ill /ɪl/	10A	krank
impatient /ɪm'peɪʃənt/	14B	ungeduldig
important /ɪm'pɔːtənt/	17D	wichtig
in	3A	in (Ort)
The pen is in the bag.		*Der Füller ist in der Tasche.*
in /ɪn/	14D	da (z.B. Er ist nicht da.)
in front of /ɪn 'frʌnt əv/	10C	vor
in love /ɪn 'lʌv/	19D	verliebt
in the afternoon /ɑːftə'nuːn/	6B	am Nachmittag, nachmittags
in the evening /'iːvnɪŋ/	6B	am Abend, abends
in the morning /'mɔːnɪŋ/	6B	am Morgen, morgens
included: Is service included? /ɪz 'sɜːvɪs ɪŋ'kluːdɪd/	17A	Inklusive Bedienung?
income /'ɪŋkʌm/	11A	Einkommen
India /'ɪndɪə/	1D	Indien
Indian /'ɪndɪən/		indisch; Inder(in)
He's Indian.		*Er ist Inder.*
information /ɪnfə'meɪʃn/	21B	Information(en)
injection /ɪn'dʒekʃən/	21D	Spritze (Impfung)
instrument /'ɪnstrəmənt/	6D	Instrument
intelligent /ɪn'telɪdʒənt/	3B	intelligent
interested in /'ɪntrəstɪd ɪn/	6D	an (etw.) interessiert
Are you interested in politics?		*Sind Sie an Politik interessiert?*
interesting /'ɪntrəstɪŋ/	2C	interessant
That's an interesting book.		*Das ist ein interessantes Buch.*
international /ɪntə'næʃnl/	21D	international
is /ɪz/	1A	ist
Is service included? /ɪz 'sɜːvɪs ɪŋ'kluːdɪd/	17A	Inklusive Bedienung?
Is that …?	14D	Bist du /Sind Sie …? (Telefon)
isn't /'ɪznt/	1A	ist nicht (Kurzform)
It depends /dɪ'pendz/	6A	Je nachdem; es kommt darauf an
It doesn't matter /'mætə(r)/	14D	Es macht nichts, das macht nichts.
it /ɪt/	1A	es
it's /ɪts/	1A	es ist (Kurzform)
Italian /ɪ'tælɪən/	1D	italienisch; Italiener(in)
He's Italian.		*Er ist Italiener.*
Italy /'ɪtəli/	1D	Italien
jacket /'dʒækɪt/	9B	Jacke
January /'dʒænjəri/	14C	Januar
Japan /dʒə'pæn/	1D	Japan
Japanese /dʒæpə'niːz/	1D	japanisch; Japaner(in)
He's Japanese.		*Er ist Japaner.*
jeans /dʒiːnz/	9B	Jeans
job /dʒɒb/	3D	Job, Arbeit(sstelle)
job: between jobs /bɪ'twiːn/	2A	zur Zeit gerade arbeitslos
join /dʒɔɪn/		hier: dazukommen
At this moment, Yvette joins them.	23D	*In diesem Augenblick kommt Yvette dazu.*
journey /'dʒɜːni/	9D	Reise
juice /dʒuːs/	7A	Saft
July /dʒə'laɪ/	14C	Juli
June /dʒuːn/	14C	Juni
just /dʒəst, dʒʌst/	17A	nur
Just some water, please.		*Nur etwas Wasser, bitte.*
just a minute /'mɪnɪt/	17B	einen Augenblick, Moment
just a moment /'məʊmənt/	17B	einen Augenblick, Moment
key /kiː/	17B	Schlüssel
killed: get killed /kɪld/	23A	getötet werden
kilo /'kiːləʊ/	7B	Kilo(gramm)
kind /kaɪnd/	11B	lieb, freundlich
kind to /'kaɪnd tə/	1B	lieb, freundlich zu
kiss /kɪs/	11D	küssen
kitchen /'kɪtʃɪn/	5A	Küche
knife /naɪf/ (knives /naɪvz/)	22B	Messer
know about /'nəʊ ə'baʊt/	11C	von, über (etw./jdm.) wissen
They didn't know about America five hundred years ago.		*Vor fünfhundert Jahren wußte man nichts über Amerika.*
know: Do you know?	7B	Weißt du/ Wissen Sie …?
know: I know	7B	Ich weiß (es).
know: I don't know	1B	Ich weiß (es) nicht.
lager /'lɑːgə(r)/	17A	helles, leichtes Bier
lamp /læmp/	7C	Lampe
language /'læŋgwɪdʒ/	6D	Sprache
large /lɑːdʒ/	10B	groß
last night /'lɑːst 'naɪt/	11D	gestern abend, letzte Nacht
late /leɪt/	11D	spät
lazy /'leɪzi/	22D	faul
lead /liːd/	18C	(an)führen
learn /lɜːn/	18A	lernen
leave /liːv/	15D	wegfahren, weggehen
left /left/	5C	links
leg /leg/	9A	Bein
lend /lend/	17B	etw. (ver)leihen
Could you lend me a dictionary?		*Könntest du /Könnten Sie mir ein Wörterbuch leihen?*

Let's /lets/	17C	Laß(t) uns …
Let's go	9D	Gehen wir!
letter /'letə(r)/	9D	Brief
letter	2C	Buchstabe
lie /laɪ/	15A	liegen
He is lying on the floor.		*Er liegt auf dem Boden.*
life /laɪf/ (lives /laɪvz/)	11B	Leben
life: all my life	19D	mein ganzes Leben (lang)
light /laɪt/	9B	hell- (z.B. hellgrün)
light	7C	Licht
light: Have you got a light?	17B	Hast du/Haben Sie Feuer? (für Zigarette)
like /laɪk/	9C	wie (z.B. aussehen wie)
She looks like her sister.		*Sie sieht wie ihre Schwester aus.*
like	6A	mögen, gern haben
like: I'd like	10C	ich möchte
like: I'd like to	10C	ich möchte (etw. tun); (Kurzantwort) Ja, gern!
I'd like to look at some watches.		*Ich möchte mir einige Uhren anschauen.*
like: Would you like…?	10B	Möchtest du/Möchten Sie …?
listen to /'lɪsn tə/	7A	zu-, anhören
listen to the radio /'reɪdɪəʊ/	18D	Radio hören
literature /'lɪtrətʃə(r)/	21D	Literatur
litre /'liːtə(r)/	7A	Liter
little: a little /ə 'lɪtl/	1D	ein wenig, etwas
little: a little more /mɔː(r)/	17A	noch etwas
… a little more tea?		*… noch etwas Tee?*
live /lɪv/	5B	wohnen, leben
living room /'lɪvɪŋ ruːm/	5A	Wohnzimmer
long /lɒŋ/	9A	lang
long	15D	lange (Zeit)
look /lʊk/	9D	sehen, schauen
look	14B	aussehen
He looks quite friendly.		*Er sieht ganz freundlich aus.*
look at /ət/	9D	(etw./jdn.) ansehen,-schauen
look for /fə(r)/	10B	suchen
look like /laɪk/	9C	aussehen wie
look out /aʊt/	22C	Vorsicht! (Ausruf)
look: Can I look round? /raʊnd/	10C	Kann ich mich umschauen? (z.B. in einem Geschäft)
lost: get lost /lɒst/	23A	sich verirren
lot: a lot of /ə 'lɒt əv/	7D	viel(e), eine Menge
lots of /'lɒts əv/	9C	viel(e)
loud /laʊd/	22D	laut
love /lʌv/	6A	lieben, sehr gern mögen
I love dogs.		*Ich mag Hunde sehr gern.*
love: I'd love to	15C	Ich würde sehr gern (etw. tun); (Kurzantwort) Ja, sehr gern!
Love	15B	Herzliche Grüße, liebe Grüße (informeller Briefschluß)
love: in love /ɪn 'lʌv/	19D	verliebt
I'm in love.		*Ich bin verliebt.*
lover /'lʌvə(r)/	23D	Liebhaber
lunch /lʌntʃ/	6C	das (kleine) Mittagessen
make /meɪk/	13A	machen
He can make cakes.		*Er kann Kuchen backen.*
make a decision /dɪ'sɪʒn/	23C	eine Entscheidung treffen, fällen
make a mistake /mɪs'teɪk/	22B	einen Fehler machen
man /mæn/ (men /men/)	2B	Mann (nicht Ehemann)
many /'meni/	7D	viele
many: How many …?	7D	Wie viele …?
How many houses …?		*Wie viele Häuser …?*
many: too many	7D	zu viele
too many cars		*zu viele Autos*
March /mɑːtʃ/	14C	März
married /'mærɪd/	2C	verheiratet
married: get married	21A	heiraten
match /mætʃ/	15C	(Fußball)spiel
maths /mæθs/	6D	Mathematik
matter: It doesn't matter /'mætə(r)/	14D	Es macht nichts, das macht nichts.
matter: What's the matter?	22A	Was fehlt dir/Ihnen?
May /meɪ/	14C	Mai
me /miː/	1C	mich
meal /miːl/	21D	Essen, Mahlzeit
mean: What does … mean? /miːn/	3D	Was bedeutet …?
meat /miːt/	21D	Fleisch
medical student /'medɪkl 'stjuːdənt/	2A	Medizinstudent(in)
medicine /'medsən/	22A	Medizin
medicine: take medicine	22A	Medizin (ein)nehmen
meet /miːt/	9D	(sich) treffen
Can you meet me there?		*Kannst du/Können Sie mich dort treffen?*
metre /'miːtə(r)/	14A	Meter
milk /mɪlk/	7A	Milch
million /'mɪljən/	11A	Million
mind /maɪnd/	19A	etw. dagegen haben
mind: Do you mind if …?	19A	Hast du/Haben Sie etw. dagegen, wenn …?
Do you mind if I sit here?		*Stört es dich/Sie, wenn ich mich hierhin setze?*
mind: I don't mind	23A	Ich habe nichts dagegen; Es macht mir nichts aus.
minute /'mɪnɪt/	15D	Minute
minute: just a minute	17B	einen Augenblick, Moment
minute: wait a minute	17C	Warte/Warten Sie einen Augenblick, Moment
Miss /mɪs/	2D	Fräulein
mistake /mɪs'teɪk/	22B	Fehler
mistress /'mɪstrɪs/	23D	Geliebte
moment /'məʊmənt/	3D	Augenblick, Moment
moment: for a moment	19A	für einen Augenblick, Moment
Could I borrow your keys for a moment?		*Könnte ich mir für einen Augenblick deine/Ihre Schlüssel leihen?*
moment: just a moment	17B	einen Augenblick, Moment
Monday /'mʌndi/	6C	Montag
money /'mʌni/	7A	Geld
month /mʌnθ/	14A	Monat
more /mɔː(r)/	13C	(zwei- und dreisilbige Eigenschaftswörter werden durch vorangestelltes *more* – 1. Steigerungsform – gesteigert)
more interesting		*interessanter als*
more	9C	(Vergleich)
more like Mum		*mehr wie Mutter*

more: a little more	17A	noch etwas	
more: no more	17A	kein ... mehr	
There's no more roast beef.		*Es ist kein Roastbeef mehr da.*	
morning /ˈmɔːnɪŋ/	2B	Morgen	
morning: in the morning	6B	am Morgen, morgens	
morning: this morning	11D	heute morgen	
most /məʊst/	11C	(der, die, das) meiste	
most	13C	(zwei- und dreisilbige Eigenschaftswörter werden durch vorangestelltes *most* – 2. Steigerungsform – gesteigert)	
most beautiful		*(der, die, das) schönste*	
mother /ˈmʌðə(r)/	3C	Mutter	
mountain /ˈmaʊntɪn/	15B	Berg	
mouth /maʊθ/	9A	Mund	
move /muːv/	21B	(sich) bewegen	
I'm going to move all the furniture.		*Ich werde alle Möbel umstellen.*	
Mr /ˈmɪstə(r)/	2B	Herr	
Mrs /ˈmɪsɪz/	2D	Frau	
Ms /mɪz, məz/	2D	Frau (auch Unverheiratete)	
much /mʌtʃ/	7D	viel	
much: How much ...?	7D	Wieviel ...?	
How much butter?		*Wieviel Butter?*	
much: How much is/are ...?	10C	Was kostet/kosten ...?	
much: not much	6A	nicht viel	
much: too much	7D	zu viel	
much: very much	6A	sehr (viel)	
He likes her very much.		*Er mag sie sehr.*	
mushroom /ˈmʌʃrʊm/	17A	Pilz	
music /ˈmjuːzɪk/	6D	Musik	
my /maɪ/	1A	mein(e)	
myself /maɪˈself/	19A	(ich) selbst	
I'm reading it myself.		*Ich lese es (sie, ihn) selbst.*	
name /neɪm/	1A	Name (Vor- oder Familienname)	
name: first name /fɜːst/	1B	Vorname	
near /nɪə(r)/	3A	in der Nähe von	
Where's your pen? – It's on the table near Carla.		*Wo ist dein Füller? – Er ist auf dem Tisch in der Nähe von Carla.*	
nearest /ˈnɪərɪst/	5D	(der, die, das) nächste (am nächsten gelegene)	
Where's the nearest car park?		*Wo ist der nächste Parkplatz?*	
nearly /ˈnɪəli/	11B	fast	
I was nearly always unhappy.		*Ich war fast immer unglücklich.*	
need /niːd/	17B	brauchen	
nervy /ˈnɜːvi/	14B	nervös	
never /ˈnevə(r)/	6D	nie, niemals	
new /njuː/	14C	neu	
news /njuːz/	11A	Nachricht(en), Neuigkeit(en)	
She watched the news on TV.		*Sie sah sich die Nachrichten im Fernsehen an.*	
news: bad news	23C	schlechte Nachricht(en)	
newspaper /ˈnjuːspeɪpə(r)/	6D	Zeitung	
next /nekst/ (Eigenschaftswort)	9D	(der, die, das) nächste	
next Tuesday		*nächsten Dienstag*	
next (Umstandswort)	18B	als nächstes; nächste(r, s)	
Next they started work.		*Als nächstes begannen sie mit der Arbeit.*	
next to /ˈnekst tə/	5D	neben	
nice /naɪs/	9C	nett, lieb, freundlich	
night /naɪt/	2B	Nacht	
night: last night /lɑːst/	11D	gestern abend, letzte Nacht	
nine /naɪn/	2C	neun	
nineteen /naɪnˈtiːn/	2C	neunzehn	
nineteenth /naɪnˈtiːnθ/	14C	(der, die, das) neunzehnte	
ninetieth /ˈnaɪntɪəθ/	14C	(der, die, das) neunzigste	
ninety /ˈnaɪnti/	2D	neunzig	
ninth /naɪnθ/	5B	(der, die, das) neunte	
no /nəʊ/	1A	nein	
no more /mɔː(r)/	17A	kein ... mehr	
nobody /ˈnəʊbədi/	6A	niemand	
noise /nɔɪz/	15A	Geräusch	
noisy /ˈnɔɪzi/	13D	laut	
A piano is not as noisy as rock music.		*Ein Klavier ist nicht so laut wie Rockmusik.*	
north /nɔːθ/	18B	Norden	
nose /nəʊz/	9A	Nase	
not /nɒt/	1A	nicht	
not at all /nɒt ət ˈɔːl/	5C	(Antwort) *hier:* schon gut, keine Ursache	
not at all	6A	überhaupt nicht	
I don't like it at all.		*Es gefällt mir überhaupt nicht.*	
not at all (bei Eigenschaftswörtern)	10A	überhaupt nicht	
not at all hungry		*überhaupt nicht hungrig*	
not bad /bæd/	2B	nicht schlecht	
not much /mʌtʃ/	6A	nicht viel	
not too bad /nɒt tuː ˈbæd/	17A	nicht schlecht, ganz passabel	
not very /ˈveri/	3B	nicht sehr	
not well /wel/	2B	nicht gut (nicht gesund)	
She's not well today.		*Es geht ihr heute nicht gut.*	
nothing /ˈnʌθɪŋ/	10C	nichts	
November /nəʊˈvembə(r)/	14C	November	
now /naʊ/	11C	jetzt	
number /ˈnʌmbə(r)/	2C	Zahl; Hausnummer	
number: phone number /fəʊn/	5B	Telefonnummer	
Numbers		*Zahlen*	
one – three	1A	eins bis drei	
four – six	1B	vier bis sechs	
seven – twenty	2C	sieben bis zwanzig	
twenty-one – a hundred	2D	einundzwanzig bis einhundert	
first – ninth	5B	erste bis neunte	
tenth – hundredth	14C	zehnte bis (ein)hundertste	
o'clock /əˈklɒk/	6B	... Uhr	
It's three o'clock.		*Es ist drei Uhr.*	
occasionally /əˈkeɪʒənli/	19B	gelegentlich, hin und wieder	
I occasionally write letters.		*Ich schreibe gelegentlich Briefe.*	
October /ɒkˈtəʊbə(r)/	14C	Oktober	
of /əv, ɒv/	7A	von	
half a pound of butter		*ein halbes Pfund Butter*	
of course /əv ˈkɔːs/	3D	natürlich, selbstverständlich	
often /ˈɒfn/	6D	oft	
often: How often ... ?	19B	Wie oft ...?	

Oh /əʊ/	1C	Oh
Oh dear /'əʊ 'dɪə(r)/	7B	Oh je
OK /'əʊ 'keɪ/	2D	in Ordnung, okay
old /əʊld/	3B	alt
old: How old …?	2D	Wie alt …?
on /ɒn/	3A	auf
on holiday /'hɒlədi/	6D	im Urlaub, in den Ferien
on the left /left/	5C	links
the first door on the left		die erste Tür links
on the right /raɪt/	5C	rechts
It's over there on the right.		Es ist drüben rechts.
once /wʌns/	19B	einmal
once a week	19B	einmal pro Woche
one /wʌn/	1A	eins
one: a … one /ə… wʌn/	10B	ein (e)…(-e, -er, -es)
I'm looking for a sweater. – Here's a lovely one.		Ich suche einen Pullover. – Hier ist ein schöner.
only /'əʊnli/	6A	nur
open /'əʊpn/	19A	öffnen
opposite /'ɒpəzɪt/	5D	gegenüber
optimistic /ɒptɪ'mɪstɪk/	14B	optimistisch
or /ɔː(r)/	2B	oder
orange /'ɒrɪndʒ/	9B	orange
orange	7A	Orange, Apfelsine
other /'ʌðə(r)/	10B	andere
other: each other	19D	sich, einander
our /aʊə(r)/	3C	unser(e)
out /aʊt/	6B	nicht da
He's at home but she's out.		Er ist zu Hause, aber sie ist nicht da.
out of	21B	aus … (heraus)
… move the furniture out of the room.		… die Möbel aus dem Zimmer tragen.
outside /aʊt'saɪd/	7C	draußen
over /'əʊvə(r)/	14A	über, mehr als (Alter)
over	21B	über (Ort)
over here /'əʊvə hɪə/	17A	hier, hierher
over there /'əʊvə ðeə(r)/	5C	da, dort, dorthin
p (=pence) /piː/	7B	engl. Währung
pack /pæk/	21D	packen
pants /pænts/	9B	Unterhose, Slip
paper /'peɪpə(r)/	11C	Papier
paper	17C	Zeitung
Pardon? /'pɑːdn/	3D	Wie bitte?
parent /'peərənt/	3C	Elternteil (parents = Eltern)
party /'pɑːti/	14D	Party
pass /pɑːs/	23D	vorüberziehen, vorbeigehen
passport /'pɑːspɔːt/	11C	(Reise)paß
past /pɑːst/	6B	nach
It's ten past three.		Es ist zehn nach drei.
patient /'peɪʃnt/	14B	geduldig
pay /peɪ/	18A	zahlen, bezahlen
pay for /'peɪ fə/	18A	zahlen für
She paid for her flying lessons.		Sie zahlte für ihre Flugstunden.
pen /pen/	3A	Füller
pence /pens/	7B	engl. Währung
pencil /'pensl/	13D	Bleistift
people /'piːpl/	7C	Leute, Menschen
perfume /'pɜːfjuːm/	7D	Parfüm
perhaps /pə'hæps/	15C	vielleicht
person /'pɜːsn/	7D	Person
pessimistic /pesɪ'mɪstɪk/	14B	pessimistisch
phone /fəʊn/	14D	telefonieren
phone box /'fəʊn bɒks/	5C	Telefonzelle
phone number /'nʌmbə(r)/	5B	Telefonnummer
photographer /fə'tɒgrəfə(r)/	2A	Fotograf
piano /pi'ænəʊ/	13A	Klavier
picture /'pɪktʃə(r)/	22B	Bild
piece /piːs/	18B	Stück
pink /pɪŋk/	9B	rosa, pink
place /pleɪs/	13C	Ort, Platz
plane /pleɪn/	17D	Flugzeug
play /pleɪ/	6D	spielen
please /pliːz/	3D	bitte
Please do	19A	Bitte, gern!
Do you mind if I sit here? – No, please do.		Darf ich mich zu Ihnen setzen? – Ja bitte, gern.
plenty of /'plenti əv/	18A	sehr viel(e)
There was plenty of free time.		Es gab viel Freizeit.
p.m. /'piː 'em/	9D	nachmittags und abends (von 12 Uhr bis 24 Uhr)
pocket /'pɒkɪt/	11C	Tasche (in einem Kleidungsstück)
police /pə'liːs/	5C	Polizei
police station /'steɪʃn/	5C	Polizeiwache
policeman /pə'liːsmən/	18D	Polizist
politician /pɒlə'tɪʃn/	13C	Politiker(in)
politics /'pɒlətɪks/	6D	Politik
pool: swimming pool /'swɪmɪŋ puːl/	5D	Schwimmbecken, Swimmingpool
poor /pɔː(r)/	11B	arm
possibly /'pɒsəbli:/	17B	vielleicht
Could you possibly …?		Könntest du/Könnten Sie vielleicht …?
postcard /'pəʊstkɑːd/	15B	Postkarte, Ansichtskarte
potato /pə'teɪtəʊ/	7A	Kartoffel
pound /paʊnd/	7B	engl. Währung (Pfund)
pound	14A	Pfund
president /'prezɪdənt/	13D	Präsident
press /pres/	23B	drücken
pretty /'prɪti/	3B	hübsch
price /praɪs/	7B	Preis (wieviel etw. kostet)
prison /'prɪzn/	23D	Gefängnis
probably /'prɒbəbli/	15A	wahrscheinlich
problem /'prɒbləm/	22A	Problem
pronounce /prə'naʊns/: How do you pronounce … ?	9B	aussprechen Wie spricht man … aus?
pub /pʌb/	13D	Gaststätte
public /'pʌblɪk/	5D	öffentlich
pull /pʊl/	23B	ziehen
purple /'pɜːpl/	9B	violett, lila
push /pʊʃ/	23B	schieben, drücken
put /pʊt/	21B	stellen, setzen
I'm going to put purple wallpaper in all the rooms.		Ich werde alle Zimmer violett tapezieren.
quarter: a quarter /'kwɔːtə(r)/	6B	ein Viertel
question /'kwestʃən/	3D	Frage

quiet /ˈkwaɪət/	13D	leise, still	
quite /kwaɪt/	3B	ziemlich, ganz	
He's quite good-looking.		*Er sieht ganz gut aus.*	
radio /ˈreɪdɪəʊ/	18D	Radio	
railway station /ˈreɪlweɪ/	5D	Bahnhof	
rain /reɪn/	7C	Regen	
rare /reə(r)/	17A	*hier:* nicht durchgebraten	
How would you like your steak? – Rare, please.		*Wie möchten Sie gern Ihr Steak? - Nicht durchgebraten, bitte.*	
rather: I'd rather you didn't /ˈrɑːðə/	19A	Lieber nicht!	
read /riːd/	6D	lesen	
really /ˈrɪəli/	10B	wirklich, eigentlich	
Yellow doesn't really suit me.		*Gelb steht mir eigentlich nicht.*	
reason /ˈriːzn/	21D	Grund	
red /red/	9B	rot	
refuse /rɪˈfjuːz/	23D	ablehnen	
remember /rɪˈmembə(r)/	9B	sich erinnern	
I can't remember the colour of his shoes.		*Ich kann mich nicht an die Farbe seiner Schuhe erinnern.*	
republic /rɪˈpʌblɪk/	18A	Republik	
rest /rest/	21A	(Ruhe)pause	
He's going to take a big rest.		*Er wird sich eine lange Pause gönnen.*	
rest	22B	(sich) ausruhen	
Rest every ten minutes.		*Ruhe dich alle zehn Minuten aus.*	
restaurant /ˈrestərɒnt/	5D	Restaurant	
revolution /revəˈluːʃn/	23D	Revolution	
rich /rɪtʃ/	11B	reich	
right /raɪt/	5C	rechts	
right	22B	richtig	
right across /əˈkrɒs/	21A	von einer Seite (einem Ende) zur/zum anderen	
right: all right	17A, 17C, 23A	in Ordnung, okay	
right: That's right	1B	Das ist richtig; das stimmt.	
road /rəʊd/	5B	Straße	
rock (music) /rɒk/	6D	Rockmusik	
room /ruːm/	5A	Zimmer, Raum	
round /raʊnd/	18A	um … herum	
round the world /wɜːld/	18A	um die Welt	
round: Can I look round?	10C	Kann ich mich umschauen? (z.B. in einem Geschäft)	
run /rʌn/	13A	laufen, rennen	
Russia /ˈrʌʃə/	1D	Rußland	
Russia(n) /ˈrʌʃə(n)/	1D	russisch; Russe/Russin	
She's Russian.		*Sie ist Russin.*	
salad /ˈsæləd/	17A	Salat (nicht Kopfsalat)	
same: the same /ðə ˈseɪm/	11A	der-, die-, dasselbe	
Saturday /ˈsætədi/	6C	Sonnabend, Samstag	
say /seɪ/	11D	sagen	
say: How do you say…?	9B	Wie sagt man …?	
school /skuːl/	6B	Schule	
science fiction /ˈsaɪəns ˈfɪkʃən/	6D	Science-fiction	
Scotland /ˈskɒtlənd/	1D	Schottland	
Scottish /ˈskɒtɪʃ/	1D	schottisch	
He's Scottish.		*Er ist Schotte.*	
sea /siː/	15B	Meer	
seat /siːt/	19A	(Sitz)platz	
second /ˈsekənd/	5B	(der, die, das) zweite	
see /siː/	13A	sehen	
See you	1C	Bis bald!	
self-confident /selfˈkɒnfɪdənt/	14B	selbstbewußt	
sell /sel/	23B	verkaufen	
send /send/	15B	schicken	
sensitive /ˈsensətɪv/	14B	empfindlich, einfühlsam	
separated /ˈsepəreɪtɪd/	2D	getrennt	
September /sepˈtembə(r)/	14C	September	
service: Is service included? /ɪz ˈsɜːvɪs ɪŋˈkluːdɪd/	17A	Inklusive Bedienung?	
seven /ˈsevən/	2C	sieben	
seventeen /ˈsevənˈtiːn/	2C	siebzehn	
seventeenth /ˈsevənˈtiːnθ/	14C	(der, die, das) siebzehnte	
seventh /ˈsevənθ/	5B	(der, die, das) siebte	
seventieth /ˈsevəntɪəθ/	14C	(der, die, das) siebzigste	
seventy /ˈsevənti/	2D	siebzig	
Shall we … ? /ʃæl/	17D	Sollen wir …?	
shave /ʃeɪv/	15A	(sich) rasieren	
shaving cream /ˈʃeɪvɪŋ kriːm/	7D	Rasierschaum	
she /ʃiː/	1D	sie	
she's /ʃiːz/	1D	sie ist (Kurzform)	
she's = she has	3C	sie hat (Kurzform)	
shirt /ʃɜːt/	9B	Hemd	
shoe /ʃuː/	9B	Schuh	
shop /ʃɒp/	10B	Geschäft, Laden	
shop	15A	einkaufen	
She's shopping.		*Sie kauft (gerade) ein; sie ist einkaufen (gegangen).*	
shop assistant /ˈʃɒp əˈsɪstənt/	2A	Verkäufer(in)	
shopping: go shopping	10A	einkaufen (gehen, fahren)	
short /ʃɔːt/	9A	kurz (z.B. Haare)	
short	9D	klein	
He's quite short.		*Er ist ziemlich klein.*	
show /ʃəʊ/	17B	zeigen	
shower /ˈʃaʊə(r)/	10A	Dusche	
shy /ʃaɪ/	14B	schüchtern	
since /sɪns/	19D	seit (Zeitpunkt)	
since yesterday		*seit gestern*	
sincerely: Yours sincerely /ˈjɔːz sɪnˈsɪəli/	9D	Mit freundlichen Grüßen (Briefschluß)	
sing /sɪŋ/	13B	singen	
singer /ˈsɪŋə(r)/	13C	Sänger(in)	
single /ˈsɪŋgl/	2C	alleinstehend, unverheiratet	
sister /ˈsɪstə(r)/	3C	Schwester	
sit /sɪt/	15A	sitzen	
sit down /daʊn/	3D	(sich) (hin)setzen	
six /sɪks/	1B	sechs	
sixteen /ˈsɪksˈtiːn/	2C	sechzehn	
sixteenth /ˈsɪksˈtiːnθ/	14C	(der, die, das) sechzehnte	
sixth /sɪksθ/	5B	(der, die, das) sechste	
sixtieth /ˈsɪkstɪəθ/	14C	(der, die, das) sechzigste	
sixty /ˈsɪksti/	2D	sechzig	
size /saɪz/	10B	Größe	
ski /skiː/	13B	skifahren, skilaufen	
Michael can ski better now.		*Michael kann jetzt besser skilaufen.*	
skiing /ˈskiːɪŋ/	6D	Skilaufen, Skifahren	
Do you like skiing?		*Läufst du /Laufen Sie gerne Ski?*	

English	Ref	German
skirt /skɜːt/	9B	Rock
sleep /sliːp/	13A	Schlaf; schlafen
Can you go without sleep? Can you sleep in the daytime?		*Kannst du /Können Sie ohne Schlaf auskommen? Kannst du /Können Sie am Tag schlafen?*
sleepy /ˈsliːpi/	22D	schläfrig
slim /slɪm/	3B	schlank
slow /sləʊ/	13C	langsam
slowly /ˈsləʊli/:	10D	
Could you speak more slowly, please?		*Könnten Sie bitte langsamer sprechen?*
small /smɔːl/	5B	klein
smile /smaɪl/	19D	Lächeln
smoke /sməʊk/	15A	rauchen
snow /snəʊ/	7C	Schnee
so /səʊ/		(übereinstimmender Kommentar)
I always come here on Sunday mornings. – So do I.	19B	*Ich komme immer Sonntag morgens hierher. – Ich auch.*
so	18B	daher, deshalb
so on	19D	usw.
sock /sɒk/	9B	Socke
sofa /ˈsəʊfə/	5A	Sofa, Couch
some /sʌm/	7C	einige, etwas
There are some books on the table. There is some snow outside.		*Da liegen einige Bücher auf dem Tisch. Draußen liegt etwas Schnee.*
somebody /ˈsʌmbədi/	15A	jemand
something /ˈsʌmθɪŋ/	9B	etwas
sometimes /ˈsʌmtaɪmz/	6D	manchmal
somewhere /ˈsʌmweə(r)/	17C	irgendwo
son /sʌn/	3C	Sohn
song /sɒŋ/	21D	Lied
sorry: I'm sorry /ˈsɒri/	1C	Es tut mir leid, Entschuldigung
sorry: I'm sorry to trouble you	17B	Entschuldigen Sie die Störung …
Sorry to trouble you /ˈtrʌbl/	17B	Entschuldigen Sie die Störung … (etw. umgangssprachlicher)
sort: What sort of … ? /sɔːt/	6D	Was für …?
What sort of books do you like?		*Was für Bücher magst du/ mögen Sie?*
soup /suːp/	17A	Suppe
south /saʊθ/	18B	Süden
Soviet /ˈsəʊviˈet/	1D	sowjetisch; Sowjet
Spain /speɪn/	1D	Spanien
Spanish /ˈspænɪʃ/	1D	spanisch
She's Spanish.		*Sie ist Spanierin.*
speak /spiːk/	1D	sprechen
speak: Could I speak to…?	14D	Könnte ich … sprechen?
speak: Could you speak more slowly, please? /ˈsləʊli/	10D	Könnten Sie bitte langsamer sprechen?
spell: How do you spell it? /spel/	2D	Wie schreibt man das?
spend /spend/	17C	verbringen
spoon /spuːn/	22B	Löffel
sport /spɔːt/	11A	Sport
spring /sprɪŋ/	21C	Frühling, Frühjahr
stairs /steəz/	5A	Treppe (im Haus)
stand /stænd/	15A	stehen
start /stɑːt/	6C	anfangen, beginnen
station /ˈsteɪʃn/	5C	Bahnhof
stay /steɪ/	15D	bleiben
steak /steɪk/	7A	Steak
still /stɪl/	6B	(immer) noch
He's still in bed.		*Er ist (immer) noch im Bett.*
stop /stɒp/	6C	aufhören
straight on /streɪt/	5D	geradeaus
strange /streɪndʒ/	23C	seltsam, merkwürdig
street /striːt/	5B	Straße
strong /strɒŋ/	3B	stark, kräftig
student /ˈstjuːdənt/	2A	Student(in)
study /ˈstʌdi/	11A	studieren, lernen
She never studied except before exams.		*Sie hat nur vor Prüfungen gelernt.*
stupid /ˈstjuːpɪd/	14B	dumm
sugar /ˈʃʊgə(r)/	17B	Zucker
suitcase /ˈsuːtkeɪs/	21D	Koffer
summer /ˈsʌmə(r)/	21C	Sommer
sun /sʌn/	15B	Sonne
Sunday /ˈsʌndi/	6C	Sonntag
supermarket /ˈsuːpəmɑːkɪt/	5C	Supermarkt
supper /ˈsʌpə(r)/	6C	Abendessen; (später) Imbiß
sure /ˈʃɔː(r)/	15B	sicher
surname /ˈsɜːneɪm/	1B	Nachname
surprise /səˈpraɪz/	23C	Überraschung
sweater /ˈswetə(r)/	9B	Pullover
swim /swɪm/	13A	schwimmen
swimming pool /ˈswɪmɪŋ puːl/	5D	Schwimmbecken, Swimmingpool
Swiss /swɪs/	1D	schweizerisch; Schweizer(in)
He is Swiss.		*Er ist Schweizer.*
Switzerland /ˈswɪtsələnd/	1D	die Schweiz
table /ˈteɪbl/	3A	Tisch
take /teɪk/	10B	nehmen (z.B. Ich nehme es/ ihn/sie.)
take	22A	(ein)nehmen (Medizin)
take	5D	gehen, fahren (z.B. Gehen Sie die erste Straße links.)
Take your time	22A	Laß dir/Lassen Sie sich Zeit.
talk /tɔːk/	11D	sprechen
talkative /ˈtɔːkətɪv/	14B	gesprächig
tall /tɔːl/	3B	groß
tea /tiː/	11C	Tee
teacher /ˈtiːtʃə(r)/	3D	Lehrer(in)
telephone /ˈtelɪfəʊn/	14D	telefonieren
television /teliˈvɪʒn/	5A	Fernsehen
tell /tel/	11D	sagen, erzählen
She told her father (that) she went to Alice's place.		*Sie sagte ihrem Vater, daß sie zu Alice gegangen sei.*
tell the truth /truːθ/	23C	die Wahrheit sagen
temperature /ˈtemprɪtʃə(r)/	22A	
I've got a temperature.		*Ich habe Fieber.*
ten /ten/	2C	zehn
tennis /ˈtenɪs/	6D	Tennis
tenth /tenθ/	14C	(der, die, das) zehnte
terrible /ˈterəbl/ (Eigenschaftswort)	7B	schrecklich
than /ðən, ðæn/	13B	… als …
She can spell better than all the others.		*Sie ist in Rechtschreibung besser als alle anderen.*

English	Lesson	German
Thank you /ˈθæŋk ju:/	1A	Danke
Thank you anyway /ˈeniweɪ/	5C	Trotzdem vielen Dank.
thanks: Fine thanks /faɪn/	1C	Danke, gut.
that /ðət, ðæt/	14B	daß
We both think that he looks like a scientist.		*Wir denken beide, daß er wie ein Wissenschaftler aussieht.*
that /ðæt/	9B	das (da)
That's interesting /ˈɪntrəstɪŋ/	2C	Das ist ja interessant.
That's right /raɪt/	1B	Das ist richtig; das stimmt.
the /ðə, ði:/	3A	der, die, das
the day after tomorrow	14C	übermorgen
the day before yesterday	14C	vorgestern
the first person to	18A	der erste Mensch, der …
the person who	18A	der Mann, der …/die Frau, die …
the same /seɪm/	11A	der-, die-, dasselbe
the United States /ðə juˈnaɪtɪd ˈsteɪts/	1D	die Vereinigten Staaten (von Amerika)
their /ðeə(r)/	3C	ihr(e) (Plural)
them /ðm, ðem/	6A	sie (Fürwort als Ergänzung)
then /ðen/	5D	dann, danach
then	11C	da, damals
There weren't any pocket calculators then, but now there are millions of them.		*Damals gab es keine Taschenrechner, aber heute gibt es Millionen.*
then	17A	dann
There's no more roast beef. – All right, then. I'll have a rump steak.		*Es gibt kein Roastbeef mehr. – Also gut, dann nehme ich Rumpsteak.*
There is/are /ðər ɪz, ðər ə(r)/	5A	Es gibt …; da ist/sind
there /ðeə(r)/	5C	da, dort
there's /ðəs/	5A	es gibt
these /ði:s/	9A	diese (hier)
they /ðeɪ/	3B	sie (Plural)
they're /ðeə(r)/	7B	sie sind (Kurzform)
they've /ðeɪv/	3D	sie haben (Kurzform)
thing /θɪŋ/	10C	Ding, Sache, Gegenstand
think: I think /θɪŋk/	2D	Ich glaube, denke
I think she's about 50.		*Ich glaube, sie ist ungefähr 50 (Jahre alt).*
third /θɜ:d/	5B	(der, die, das) dritte
thirsty /ˈθɜ:sti/	10A	durstig
thirteen /ˈθɜ:ˈti:n/	2C	dreizehn
thirteenth /ˈθɜ:ˈti:nθ/	14C	(der, die, das) dreizehnte
thirtieth /ˈθɜ:tɪəθ/	14C	(der, die, das) dreißigste
thirty /ˈθɜ:ti/	2D	dreißig
this /ˈðɪs/	3B	dies(es) (hier)
This is …	14D	Hier spricht …; Hier ist … (Telefon)
this morning /ˈmɔ:nɪŋ/	11D	heute morgen
this: What's this?	9A	Was ist das (hier)?
those /ðəʊz/	10C	die, diese (da)
though /ðəʊ/	17A	jedoch
The steak's a bit tough. The vegetables are nice, though.		*Das Steak ist etwas zäh. Das Gemüse ist jedoch gut.*
thousand /ˈθaʊzənd/	11A	(ein) tausend
three /θri:/	1A	drei
three times	19B	dreimal
Thursday /ˈθɜ:zdi/	6C	Donnerstag
ticket /ˈtɪkɪt/	15D	Fahrkarte, (Flug)ticket
tie /taɪ/	9B	Krawatte, Schlips
tights /taɪts/	9B	Strumpfhose
time /taɪm/	6B	Zeit
time: have a good time	15A	Viel Spaß!
time: Take your time	22C	Laß dir/Lassen Sie sich Zeit.
times: three times	19B	dreimal
tired /taɪəd/	10A	müde
to /tə, tu:/	6B	nach, zu (Ort)
on his way to work		*auf seinem Weg zur Arbeit*
to	6B	vor (Zeit)
It's ten to four.		*Es ist zehn vor vier.*
today /təˈdeɪ/	14C	heute
together /təˈgeðə(r)/	18A	zusammen
toilet /ˈtɔɪlɪt/	5A	Toilette
tomato /təˈmɑ:təʊ/	7A	Tomate
tomorrow /təˈmɒrəʊ/	14C	morgen
tomorrow: the day after tomorrow	14C	übermorgen
tonight /təˈnaɪt/	19B	heute abend
too /tu:/	3D	auch (nachgestellt)
He's British, and she's British, too.		*Er ist Brite, und sie ist auch Britin.*
too many	7D	zu viele
too much	7D	zu viel
toothache /ˈtu:θeɪk/	22A	Zahnschmerz(en)
toothpaste /ˈtu:θpeɪst/	7D	Zahnpasta
tough /tʌf/	17A	zäh
town /taʊn/	15B	Stadt
train /treɪn/	9D	Zug
travel /ˈtrævl/	6D	reisen
travel agent /ˈtrævl ˈeɪdʒənt/	21D	Reisebürokaufmann, -kauffrau
trouble /ˈtrʌbl/	23C	Ärger
trouble: Sorry to trouble you /ˈsɒri/	17B	Entschuldigen Sie die Störung …
trousers /ˈtraʊzəz/	9B	Hose(n)
true /tru:/	18D	wahr
truth /tru:θ/	23C	Wahrheit
try /traɪ/	7A	versuchen
try /ˈtraɪ ˈɒn/	10B	anprobieren
Can I try them on?		*Kann ich sie anprobieren?*
Tuesday /ˈtju:zdi/	6C	Dienstag
turn /tɜ:n/	23B	drehen
TV /ˈti: ˈvi:/	5A	TV, Fernsehen
twelfth /twelfθ/	14C	(der, die, das) zwölfte
twelve /twelv/	2C	zwölf
twentieth /ˈtwentɪəθ/	14C	(der, die, das) zwanzigste
twenty /ˈtwenti/	2C	zwanzig
twice /twaɪs/	19B	zweimal
two /tu:/	1A	zwei
type /taɪp/	13A	Schreibmaschine schreiben, tippen
typewriter /ˈtaɪpraɪtə(r)/	13D	Schreibmaschine
typist /ˈtaɪpɪst/	13D	Schreibkraft, Stenotypist(in)
umbrella /ʌmˈbrelə/	17B	Regenschirm
uncle /ˈʌŋkl/	9C	Onkel
under /ˈʌndə(r)/	14A	unter
She's under 30.		*Sie ist unter 30 (jünger als 30).*
under	3A	unter(halb)
His bag's under the chair.		*Seine Tasche ist unter dem Stuhl.*

English	Ref	German
understand: I don't understand /ˌʌndəˈstænd/	7C	Ich verstehe nicht.
unhappy /ʌnˈhæpi/	10A	unglücklich
United States, the /ðə juˈnaɪtɪd ˈsteɪts/	1D	die Vereinigten Staaten (von Amerika)
university /juːnəˈvɜːsəti/	18A	Universität
unkind /ʌnˈkaɪnd/ (Eigenschaftswort)	23D	unfreundlich
until /ənˈtɪl/	6C	bis
from twelve o'clock until five o'clock		*von zwölf Uhr bis siebzehn Uhr*
upstairs /ˈʌpˈsteəz/	5C	oben (im Haus)
us /əs, ʌs/	10C	uns
use /juːz/	21A	(be)nutzen
USSR /juː es es ˈɑː(r)/	1D	Union der sozialistischen Sowjetrepubliken (UdSSR)
usual /ˈjuːʒʊəl/	17D	normal, üblich
at the usual time		*zur üblichen Zeit*
usually /ˈjuːʒəli/	6D	normalerweise, gewöhnlich
I usually watch the nine o'clock news.		*Ich sehe normalerweise die neun Uhr Nachrichten.*
vegetable /ˈvedʒtəbl/	17A	Gemüse
very /ˈveri/	2B	sehr
very much	6A	sehr (viel)
very: not very	3B	nicht sehr
video /ˈvɪdiːəʊ/	21A	Video
village /ˈvɪlɪdʒ/	11B	Dorf
violin /vaɪəˈlɪn/	13A	Geige, Violine
visa /ˈviːzə/	21D	Visum
wait /weɪt/	17C	warten
wait a minute /ˈmɪnɪt/	17C	Warte/Warten Sie einen Augenblick, Moment
wake up /ˈweɪk ˈʌp/	11D	aufwachen
walk /wɔːk/	18D	Spaziergang
They took the dog for a walk.		*Sie haben den Hund ausgeführt.*
walk	18D	gehen, zu Fuß gehen
They walked to the town centre.		*Sie sind ins (Stadt)zentrum gegangen.*
walk: go for a walk	19B	spazierengehen, einen Spaziergang machen
wall /wɔːl/	5A	Wand; Mauer
want /wɒnt/	11D	wollen
wardrobe /ˈwɔːdrəʊb/	5A	Kleiderschrank
warm /wɔːm/	13D	warm
was /wəz, wɒz/	7B	war
wasn't /ˈwɒznt/	11B	war nicht (Kurzform)
was born /wəz ˈbɔːn/	11B	bin/ist geboren
wash /wɒʃ/	18D	waschen
watch /wɒtʃ/	10C	(Armband)uhr
I'd like to look at some watches.		*Ich möchte mir einige Uhren anschauen.*
watch	6D	beobachten, zusehen
I often watch tennis.		*Ich sehe oft beim Tennis zu.*
watch TV /ˈtiː ˈviː/	18D	fernsehen
water /ˈwɔːtə(r)/	7A	Wasser
we /wiː/	3B	wir
we're /wɪə(r)/	3B	wir sind (Kurzform)
we've /wiːv/	3D	wir haben (Kurzform)
wear /weə(r)/	9B	tragen (Kleidung)
weather /ˈweðə(r)/	15B	Wetter
Wednesday /ˈwenzdi/	6C	Mittwoch
week /wiːk/	14C	Woche
weekend /ˈwiːkˈend/	6C	Wochenende
weigh /weɪ/	14A	wiegen
weight /weɪt/	14A	Gewicht
welcome: You're welcome /ˈwelkəm/	14D	Bitte, gern geschehen!
well /wel/ (Eigenschaftswort)	2B	gut (gesund)
I'm very well, thank you.		*Mir geht es sehr gut, danke.*
well (Umstandswort)	10B	gut
They (the shoes) fit very well.		*Sie (die Schuhe) passen sehr gut.*
well	17C	Nun, …; na gut,…
were /wə, wɜː/	7B	warst, waren, wart
weren't /ˈwɜːnt/	11B	warst nicht, waren nicht, wart nicht (Kurzform)
west /west/	18B	Westen
what /wɒt/	1A	was
What a nice …! /naɪs/	10C	Was für ein(e) nette(r,s)/ (schöne, freundliche …)
What a nice colour!		*Was für eine schöne Farbe!*
What about …? /əˈbaʊt/	15C	Wie wär's mit …?
What are these?	9A	Was sind das?
What are these called? /kɔːld/	9B	Wie heißen die (hier)?
What colour is/are /ˈkʌlər/	9C	Welche Farbe hat/haben …?
What do you do?	2A	Was machst du/machen Sie? (beruflich)
What does … mean? /miːn/	3D	Was bedeutet …?
What sort of … ? /sɔːt/	6D	Was für …?
What's the matter? /ˈmætə/	22A	Was fehlt dir/Ihnen?
What's this?	9A	Was ist das (hier)?
What's this called? /kɔːld/	9B	Wie heißt das (hier)?/Wie nennt man das (hier)?
What time is it? /taɪm/	6B	Wie spät ist es?
when /wən/	10A	wenn
When he's dirty he has a bath.		*Wenn er schmutzig ist, badet er.*
when	18C	wann
When did the Second World War start?		*Wann begann der Zweite Weltkrieg?*
where /weə(r)/	1D	wo
Where is London?		*Wo liegt London?*
where	18B	wo
They sailed to Scotland, where they carried out more attacks.		*Sie segelten nach Scotland, wo sie weitere Überfälle verübten.*
Where are you from?	1D	Woher kommst du/kommen Sie?
which /wɪtʃ/	10D	welche(r,s)
Which platform, please?		*Welcher Bahnsteig, bitte?*
while /waɪl/	22B	während
Don't drink water while you are running.		*Trinke kein Wasser, während du läufst.*
white /waɪt/	9B	weiß
who /huː/	3C	wer
Who is Helen?		*Wer ist Helen?*
who	18A	(bezügliches Fürwort)
Galileo was the man who discovered sunspots.		*Galileo war der Mann, der die Sonnenflecken entdeckte.*

why /waɪ/	11D	warum	
Why don't we … ?	17C	Laß(t) uns doch …	
Why not?	17C	Warum nicht?	
widow /'wɪdəʊ/	2D	Witwe	
widower /'wɪdəʊə(r)/	2D	Witwer	
wife (wives) /waɪf, waɪvz/	3C	(Ehe)frau	
will /wɪl/	23A	werde, wirst, werden	
I'll take money with me.		*Ich werde Geld mitnehmen.*	
win /wɪn/	21C	gewinnen	
window /'wɪndəʊ/	5A	Fenster	
wine /waɪn/	7D	Wein	
winter /'wɪntə(r)/	21C	Winter	
with /wɪð/	17C	mit	
Let's ask her to come with us.		*Fragen wir sie (doch), ob sie mit uns kommen möchte.*	
with	9D	mit	
I'm quite short, with dark hair and a beard.		*Ich bin ziemlich klein, habe dunkle Haare und einen Bart.*	
without /wɪð'aʊt/	13A	ohne	
woman /'wʊmən/ (women /'wɪmɪn/)	2B	Frau	
wonderful /'wʌndəfl/	19D	wunderbar	
won't /wəʊnt/	23A	werde nicht (Kurzform)	
word /wɜːd/	7D	Wort	
work /wɜːk/	6B	Arbeit	
on her way to work		*auf ihrem Weg zur Arbeit*	
work	5B	arbeiten	
Where do you work?		*Wo arbeiten Sie?*	
world /wɜːld/	13C	Welt	
world: round the world /raʊnd/	18A	um die Welt	
worry /'wʌri/	22C	sich Sorgen machen	
worse /wɜːs/	13C	schlechter(e)	
He's worse at English than his sister.		*Er ist schlechter in Englisch als seine Schwester.*	
worst /wɜːst/	13C	schlechtest(e)	
It was the worst holiday I've ever had.		*Es war der schlechteste Urlaub, den ich je gehabt habe.*	
would /wəd, wʊd/	10B	würde	
Would you like …? /'wʊd ju 'laɪk/	10B	Möchtest du/Möchten Sie …?	
write /raɪt/	13A	schreiben	
writer /'raɪtə(r)/	13C	Autor, Schriftsteller	
wrong /rɒŋ/	22B	falsch	
yard /jɑːd/	5D	engl. Längenmaß (0,91m)	
year /jɪə(r)/	11C	Jahr	
yellow /'jeləʊ/	9B	gelb	
yes /jes/	1A	ja	
yesterday /'jestədi/	7B	gestern	
yesterday: the day before yesterday	14C	vorgestern	
you /juː/	1C	du, Sie (Singular), ihr, Sie, (Plural)	
you're /jɔː(r)/	3D	du bist, ihr seid, Sie sind (Kurzform)	
You're welcome /'welkəm/	14D	Bitte, gern geschehen!	
you've /juːv/	3D	du hast, Sie haben, ihr habt (Kurzform)	
young /jʌŋ/	3B	jung	
your /jɔː(r)/	1A	dein, Ihr, euer	
Yours /jɔːz/	17D	Dein(e), Ihr(e)(Briefschluß)	
Yours sincerely /'jɔːz sɪn'sɪəli/	9D	Mit freundlichen Grüßen (Briefschluß)	

Additional material

Lesson 1C, Exercise 6

Mickey Mouse   Minnie Mouse
James Bond   Greta Garbo
William Shakespeare   Marlene Dietrich
Christopher Columbus   Marie Curie
Marco Polo   Maria Callas
Karl Marx   Rosa Luxembourg
Charles de Gaulle   Eleanor Roosevelt
Clark Kent   Lois Lane
Jesse James   Annie Oakley
Wolfgang Mozart   Marilyn Monroe

Lesson 3A, Exercise 3

Lesson 3A, Exercise 4, Student A

Lesson 4C, Exercise 1

A: Hello, Dan. How are you?
D: Oh, hi, Andrew. Not bad, not bad.
A: And how's your mother?
D: Oh, very well now, thanks. And you, Andrew? How are you?
A: Fine, thanks. Yes, very fine: I've got a new girlfriend.
D: Have you? I've got a new girlfriend, too.
A: Oh? Is she pretty?
D: Pretty, *and* intelligent.
A: What does she do?
D: She's a student, a business student.
A: Yeah? My girlfriend's a business student, too. She's very pretty: tall, and fair . . .
D: Er, is she English?
A: English? Oh, no, she's Swedish, in fact.
D: Swedish? From Stockholm?
A: No, from Malmö.
D: Oh. And her name is Kirsten, isn't it?
A: Well, yes, it is. Do you mean . . . ?
D: Yeah, I think Kirsten has got two new boyfriends.

Lesson 10C, Exercise 1

Lesson 11D, Exercise 4, Student A

A: ....
B: I'm really sorry. My car broke down and I couldn't get a taxi, and then I missed the train.
A: ....
B: I did, but your secretary didn't answer.
A: ....
B: The tennis? You know I couldn't get tickets.
A: ....
B: That's funny. People often tell me they know somebody who looks like me. You know, only yesterday . . .

Lesson 12B, Exercise 2

On Saturday I got up at seven and had a big breakfast. I read the newspaper until a quarter past eight, and then went shopping. In front of Anderson's, I met my sister Ruth, and she told me my mother was ill. I went to my mother's house, but she wasn't at home. When I arrived home, my sister phoned and said that my mother was in hospital. I went to the hospital to see her, and the doctor said that she was OK.

   I had lunch with my friend Ann, and watched television until three. Then we played tennis and went to the swimming pool. In the evening we went to the cinema with friends.

Lesson 21B, Exercise 1, Student A

The study is going to be on the ground floor.
The living room is going to be next to the dining room.
The parents' bedroom is going to be over the living room.
The kitchen is going to be under the bathroom.

Ask your partner these questions:
'Where is Alice's bedroom going to be?'
'Where is Mary's bedroom going to be?'
'Where is the playroom going to be?'
'Where is the dining room going to be?'

Lesson 3A, Exercise 4, Student B

Lesson 11D, Exercise 4, Student B

A: Robin! It's two o'clock! Why didn't you come to work this morning?
B: ....
A: Well, why didn't you phone?
B: ....
A: You weren't watching the tennis, were you?
B: ....
A: Oh? Well, I saw the news on television at lunch, and there was a person there who looked a lot like you.
B: ....

Lesson 21B, Exercise 1, Student B

Alice's bedroom is going to be opposite the parents' bedroom.
Mary's bedroom is going to be over the kitchen.
The playroom is going to be on the first floor.
The dining room is going to be opposite the kitchen.

Ask your partner these questions:
'Where is the study going to be?'
'Where is the living room going to be?'
'Where is the parents' bedroom going to be?'
'Where is the kitchen going to be?'

Acknowledgements

The authors and publishers are grateful to the following copyright owners for permission to reproduce photographs, illustrations, texts and music. Every endeavour has been made to contact copyright owners and apologies are expressed for any omissions.

page 28: *cl* Reprinted by permission of Royal Gallery of Paintings, Mauritshuis; *t* The Tate Gallery (The Tate Gallery, London); *cc* The British Museum (Copyright © Trustees of the British Museum); *cr* Ekdotike Athenon S.A. (Reprinted by permission of Ekdotike Athenon, S.A.)   page 54: The Bodleian Library (By permission of the Bodleian Library, Oxford.)   page 67: Reproduced by permission of *Punch*.   page 88: Hulton-Deutsch Collection (Hulton-Deutsch Collection).   page 118: ® British Telecom logo, and 'T' symbol are registered trademarks of British Telecommunications public limited company. ® TELEMESSAGE is a registered trademark of British Telecommunications public limited company in the United Kingdom. © Copyright of British Telecommunications public limited company.   page 120: *tr* Reprinted by permission of *The Daily Mirror*; *cl* and *cr* From *Weekend Book of Jokes 23* courtesy of Weekend; *bl* and *br* Reproduced by permission of *Punch*.

Happy Birthday To You by Mildred and Patti Hill (Lesson 14C, Exercise 4) is courtesy of International Music Publishers and the Mechanical Copyright Protection Society Ltd.   *Anything You Can Do, I Can Do Better* by Irving Berlin (Lesson 16C, Listening Exercise 3) is courtesy of Warner Chappell Music Ltd and the Mechanical Copyright Protection Society Ltd.   *Hello, Goodbye* by Lennon and McCartney (Lesson 20C, Listening Exercise 4), lyrics by permission of SBK Songs, courtesy of SBK Songs and the Mechanical Copyright Protection Society Ltd.   *Hush, Little Baby* (Lesson 24B, Listening Exercise 3) is traditional.

The following songs were specially written by Steve Hall for *The New Cambridge English Course* Book 1: *If You Can Keep A Secret* (Lesson 8C, page 41); *Please Write* (Lesson 12C, page 60).

Artist Partners: Derek Brazell, pages 32 *b*, 55, 61, 81, 101, 110 *r*, 111; Biz Hull, pages 17, 86, 102; Tony Richards, pages 24, 72, 91, 105.   The Inkshed: Andrew Whiteley, pages 45, 66.   B. L. Kearley: Tony Kenyon, pages 15 *b*, 48 *b*, 50 *l*, 57, 65.   Maggie Mundy: Hemesh Alles, pages 8 *c*, 9 *t* and *c*, 15 *t*, 50 *r*, 51, 70, 73, 106, 108, 109, 112, 115; Nick Garner, page 113, 133; Sharon Pallent, pages 26, 107.   Young Artists: Amy Burch, pages 14 *c*, 16, 33, 132, 134; Pat Fogarty, pages 46, 47, 80; Sarah John, pages 8 *b*, 9 *bl*, 10 *b*, 22 *b*, 28 *bl*, 44, 45 *t* and *c*.

Nancy Anderson, pages 100, 104, 114.   John Blackman, pages 90, 123.   Caroline Church, page 89.   Richard Deverell, pages 29, 39.   Joe McEwan, pages 11, 21 *t*, 34, 53, 60, 110 *l*.   Rodney Sutton, pages 14 *t*, 21 *b*, 25, 35, 40, 49.   Tony Watson, pages 64, 68.

Mark Edwards, pages 6, 9 *br*, 10 *tc*, *tr* and *cc*, 30, 31 *cl*.   Darren Marsh, pages 7, 8 *t*, 22 *t*, 48 *top row*, *second row cl* and *cr*, 52 *l*, 59, 69, 71, 84, 85, 92, 93, 94, 119 *l*, *cl*, *bl*, *cr* and *r*.   Ken Weedon, pages 20 and 21, 27, 32 *t*, 87, 95.   The Image Bank, pages 10 *tl*, *cl* and *cr*, 12, 13, 21 *bl*, *br* and *tl*, 31 *bl*, *c*, *t*, *cr* and *tr*, 48 *second row l*, *c* and *r*, 52 *r*, 74, 75, 119 *br*.

(*t* = top   *b* = bottom   *c* = centre   *r* = right   *l* = left)

Phonetic symbols

Vowels

symbol	example
/iː/	eat /iːt/
/i/	happy /ˈhæpi/
/ɪ/	it /ɪt/
/e/	when /wen/
/æ/	cat /kæt/
/ɑː/	hard /hɑːd/
/ɒ/	not /nɒt/
/ɔː/	sort /sɔːt/; all /ɔːl/
/ʊ/	look /lʊk/
/uː/	too /tuː/
/ʌ/	cup /kʌp/
/ɜː/	first /fɜːst/; turn /tɜːn/
/ə/	about /əˈbaʊt/; mother /ˈmʌðə(r)/
/eɪ/	day /deɪ/
/aɪ/	my /maɪ/
/ɔɪ/	boy /bɔɪ/
/aʊ/	now /naʊ/
/əʊ/	go /ɡəʊ/
/ɪə/	here /hɪə(r)/
/eə/	chair /tʃeə(r)/
/ʊə/	tourist /ˈtʊərɪst/

Consonants

symbol	example
/p/	pen /pen/
/b/	big /bɪɡ/
/t/	two /tuː/
/d/	do /duː/
/k/	look /lʊk/; cup /kʌp/
/ɡ/	get /ɡet/
/tʃ/	China /ˈtʃaɪnə/
/dʒ/	Japan /dʒəˈpæn/
/f/	fall /fɔːl/
/v/	very /ˈveri/
/θ/	think /θɪŋk/
/ð/	then /ðen/
/s/	see /siː/
/z/	zoo /zuː/; is /ɪz/
/ʃ/	shoe /ʃuː/
/ʒ/	measure /ˈmeʒə(r)/; decision /dɪˈsɪʒn/
/h/	who /huː/; how /haʊ/
/m/	meet /miːt/
/n/	no /nəʊ/
/ŋ/	sing /sɪŋ/
/l/	long /lɒŋ/
/r/	right /raɪt/
/j/	yes /jes/
/w/	will /wɪl/

Stress

Stress is shown by a mark (ˈ) in front of the stressed syllable.
mother /ˈmʌðə(r)/   China /ˈtʃaɪnə/
about /əˈbaʊt/   Japan /dʒəˈpæn/

Irregular verbs

Infinitive	Simple Past	Participle
be /biː/	was /wəz, wɒz/ were /wə(r), wɜː(r)/	been /bɪn, biːn/
become /bɪˈkʌm/	became /bɪˈkeɪm/	become /bɪˈkʌm/
break /breɪk/	broke /brəʊk/	broken /ˈbrəʊkn/
bring /brɪŋ/	brought /brɔːt/	brought /brɔːt/
build /bɪld/	built /bɪlt/	built /bɪlt/
buy /baɪ/	bought /bɔːt/	bought /bɔːt/
can /k(ə)n, kæn/	could /kʊd/	been able /bɪn ˈeɪbl/
catch /kætʃ/	caught /kɔːt/	caught /kɔːt/
come /kʌm/	came /keɪm/	come /kʌm/
cost /kɒst/	cost /kɒst/	cost /kɒst/
do /dʊ, də, duː/	did /dɪd/	done /dʌn/
draw /drɔː/	drew /druː/	drawn /drɔːn/
dream /driːm/	dreamt /dremt/	dreamt /dremt/
drink /drɪŋk/	drank /dræŋk/	drunk /drʌŋk/
drive /draɪv/	drove /drəʊv/	driven /ˈdrɪvn/
eat /iːt/	ate /et/	eaten /ˈiːtn/
fall /fɔːl/	fell /fel/	fallen /ˈfɔːlən/
feel /fiːl/	felt /felt/	felt /felt/
find /faɪnd/	found /faʊnd/	found /faʊnd/
fly /flaɪ/	flew /fluː/	flown /fləʊn/
forget /fəˈɡet/	forgot /fəˈɡɒt/	forgotten /fəˈɡɒtn/
get /ɡet/	got /ɡɒt/	got /ɡɒt/
give /ɡɪv/	gave /ɡeɪv/	given /ˈɡɪvn/
go /ɡəʊ/	went /went/	gone /ɡɒn/, been /bɪn, biːn/
have /(h)əv, hæv/	had /(h)əd, hæd/	had /hæd/
hear /hɪə(r)/	heard /hɜːd/	heard /hɜːd/
hurt /hɜːt/	hurt /hɜːt/	hurt /hɜːt/
know /nəʊ/	knew /njuː/	known /nəʊn/
lead /liːd/	led /led/	led /led/
learn /lɜːn/	learnt /lɜːnt/	learnt /lɜːnt/
leave /liːv/	left /left/	left /left/
lend /lend/	lent /lent/	lent /lent/
lie /laɪ/	lay /leɪ/	lain /leɪn/
make /meɪk/	made /meɪd/	made /meɪd/
meet /miːt/	met /met/	met /met/
pay /peɪ/	paid /peɪd/	paid /peɪd/
put /pʊt/	put /pʊt/	put /pʊt/
read /riːd/	read /red/	read /red/
run /rʌn/	ran /ræn/	run /rʌn/
say /seɪ/	said /sed/	said /sed/
see /siː/	saw /sɔː/	seen /siːn/
sell /sel/	sold /səʊld/	sold /səʊld/
send /send/	sent /sent/	sent /sent/
show /ʃəʊ/	showed /ʃəʊd/	shown /ʃəʊn/
sing /sɪŋ/	sang /sæŋ/	sung /sʌŋ/
sit /sɪt/	sat /sæt/	sat /sæt/
sleep /sliːp/	slept /slept/	slept /slept/
speak /spiːk/	spoke /spəʊk/	spoken /ˈspəʊkn/
spend /spend/	spent /spent/	spent /spent/
stand /stænd/	stood /stʊd/	stood /stʊd/
swim /swɪm/	swam /swæm/	swum /swʌm/
take /teɪk/	took /tʊk/	taken /ˈteɪkn/
tell /tel/	told /təʊld/	told /təʊld/
think /θɪŋk/	thought /θɔːt/	thought /θɔːt/
wake up /ˈweɪk ˈʌp/	woke up /ˈwəʊk ˈʌp/	woken up /ˈwəʊkn ˈʌp/
wear /weə(r)/	wore /wɔː(r)/	worn /wɔːn/
will /wɪl/	would /wʊd/	—
win /wɪn/	won /wʌn/	won /wʌn/
write /raɪt/	wrote /rəʊt/	written /ˈrɪtn/